Mastering AmigaDOS 2

Volume Two

Revised Edition

Bruce Smith and Mark Smiddy

Bruce Smith Books

Mastering AmigaDOS 2
Volume Two

ISBN: 1-873308-09-4 Revised Edition: May 1992
(previously published under ISBN: 1-873308-01-9)

Editors: Syd Day, Mark Webb
Typesetting: Bruce Smith Books
Cover concept: Ross Alderson

This books was produced using a variety of publishing systems. The authors' original text was prepared using WordPerfect (Mac) and Protext (PC). All programs in this book were developed on an Amiga 3000 and transferred directly into the text files. The text was typeset on a Macintosh SE/30 using Aldus PageMaker 4. Final camera-ready copy was output directly onto film.

Bruce Smith Books is an imprint of Bruce Smith Books Limited.

Published by Bruce Smith Books Limited. Smug Oak Green BC, Lye Lane, Bricket ,Wood, Herts, AL2 3UD.
Telephone: (0923) 894355, Fax: (0923) 894366

Registered in England No. 2695164. Registered Office: 51 Quarry Street, Guildford, Surrey, GU1 3UA.

Printed and bound in the UK by Ashford Colour Press, Gosport.

"Experts are not born.
They are hewn from the bedrock of
endeavour,
and the granite of experience."

The Authors

MARK SMIDDY is a former Editorial Coordinator of *Amiga User International'*, technical consultant to *The Directory!* and is one of the most respected and best known technical journalists on today's Amiga scene. Best known for his cynical wit, Mark has worked with micro computers since 1981 cutting his teeth on the Dragon 32and Acorn BBC – on which he wrote games including: Sea Wolf, Omega Probe and Crazee Caverns. He has worked on the editorial team of *Electron User* and *Atari ST User.* After becoming a freelance consultant in 1987 he quickly moved to the Amiga and regularly contributes to *Amiga Format* and *Computer Trade Weekly.* He is also Consultant Editor to *Amiga Shopper.*

BRUCE SMITH is one of the best known computer journalists in the UK. A former technical editor of *BBC Acorn User* (then *Acorn User*) he has some 40 book titles to his credit. His style is renowned for being easy going and highly readable and led one reviewer to write *"This is the first computer book I have read in bed for pleasure rather than to cure insomnia!"*

In December 1988 he was awarded the accolade of Desktop Publishing Journalist of the Year and contributes columns to a number of national publications.

He is a regular broadcaster and covering Non-League football twice a week for *BBC Radio Bedfordshire.*

In 1990 he founded Bruce Smith Books – a publishing house dedicated to the support of the Amiga.

Acknowledgments

The authors gratefully acknowledge the assistance and cooperation of the following people who have made this book possible.

Syd Day: Who laboured through every inch of text making sure it read clearly and correctly.

Our families: For patience and understanding when the going got tough.

CBL: Ian McLean, Ross Alderson, and Tim Beaumont for their much valued support, advice and help.

Commodore UK:
Barry Thurston, Sharon Rodrigo, David Pocock, Saj and the rest of the technical support team for putting up with the barrage of queries and complaints we fired at them.

Commodore USA:
Gail Wellington and Carolyn Scheppner.

Commodore-Amiga:
For the Amiga. Without this fantastic machine this book would not exist.

Roger Warrington:
His many comments and suggestions which have enhanced this revised edition of the book.

Contents

AmigaDOS Command Reference Section 13

ADDBUFFERS 19
ADDMONITOR 21
ALIAS 23
ASK 25
ASSIGN 27
AUTOPOINT 33
AVAIL 35
BINDDRIVERS 37
BINDMONITOR 38
BLANKER 40
BREAK 42
BRU 44
CD 46
CHANGETASKPRI 48
CLICKTOFRONT 50
CLOCK 52
CMD 54
COLORS 56
CONCLIP 57
COPY 58
CPU 63
DATE 67
DELETE 70
DIR 73
DISKCHANGE 77
DISKCOPY 79
DISKDOCTOR 82
DISPLAY 87
DPAT 89
ECHO 91
ED 96
EDIT 98

ELSE 107
ENDCLI 108
ENDSHELL 109
ENDIF 111
ENDSKIP 112
EVAL 113
EXCHANGE 118
EXECUTE 120
FAILAT 124
FASTMEMFIRST 126
FAULT 127
FF 128
FILENOTE 129
FIXFONTS 131
FKEY 132
FONT 134
FORMAT 136
GET 139
GETENV 140
GRAPHICDUMP 142
ICONTROL 143
ICONX 145
IF 146
IHELP 150
INFO 152
INITPRINTER 154
INPUT 155
INSTALL 157
JOIN 159
LAB 161
LIST 162
LOADWB 170
LOCK 172
MAGTAPE 174
MAKEDIR 175

MAKELINK 177
MEMACS 179
MERGEMEM 181
MORE 182
MOUNT 184
NEWCLI 186
NEWSHELL 188
NOCAPSLOCK 192
NOFASTMEM 194
OVERSCAN 195
PALETTE 197
PARK 199
PATH 201
PCD 205
POINTER 207
PREFERENCES 209
PRINTER 210
PRINTERGFX 212
PRINTFILES 214
PROMPT 215
PROTECT 218
QUIT 221
RELABEL 224
REMRAD 226
RENAME 228
RESIDENT 231
REXXMAST 237
RUN 238
SAY 241
SCREENMODE 242
SEARCH 244
SERIAL 248
SET 250
SETCLOCK 252
SETDATE 254

SETENV 256

SETFONT 258

SETMAP 261

SETPATCH 262

SKIP 264

SORT 266

SPAT 269

STACK 271

STATUS 273

TIME 276

TYPE 277

UNALIAS 280

UNSET 281

UNSETENV 282

VERSION 283

WAIT 287

WBPATTERN 291

WHICH 293

WHY 296

Wildcards 297

; 299

? 300

<, >, >> 301

* 302

"" 303

* 304

' 305

CTRL+\ 306

ALT+' 307

A: AmigaDOS Error Codes 308

B: The Virus Menace 315

Beyond Goldilocks 315

What Is a Virus? 316

When Is a Virus Not a Virus? 316

Who Writes Viruses? 317
Count on Dracula 318
Limpet 318
Doppleganger 318
Trojan Horse 318
Parasite or Linkvirus 319
Signs of Infection 319
Nuisance Effects 319
Nasty Effects 319
Protecting Against Them 320
Virus Mythology 320
Conclusion 321

C: The Interchange File Format 322

Why a Standard? 322
How IFF works 323
How Chunk Data is Arranged 324
The Form Wrapper 326
The Big Squeeze 330
Data Types and Their Meanings 330
Why ACBM for BASIC? 331
Using ChkIFF 331
Caveats 331

D: The Mountlist 332

Baud= 333
Control= 333
BlocksPerTrack= 333
BootPri= 333
Buffers= 333
BufMemType= 333
Device= 333
DosType= 334
Flags= 334
GlobVec= 334
Handler= 334

HighCyl= 334
Interleave= 334
LowCyl= 334
Mask= 334
MaxTransfer= 335
Mount= 335
PreAlloc= 335
Priority= 335
Reserved= 335
Stacksize= 335
Startup= 335
Surfaces= 335
Unit= 335
Examples 336

E: Telling FIBs 339

More Bytes from the Cherry 340
Directories and So On 341
What about FFS 341
The Bitmap 341
Disk Layout – Ready Reckoner 342

F: Mastering Amiga Guides 343

Mastering AmigDOS Volume One 345
Mastering Amiga Beginners 345
Mastering Amiga C 346
Mastering Amiga Printers 346
Mastering Amiga System 347
Mastering Amiga Workbench 347
Ordering Information 348

Index 351

Foreword by Barry Thurston

Technical Director
COMMODORE BUSINESS MACHINES (UK) LTD.

To Boldly Go

Speaking as one who started his career with relays and valves and generally regarding myself as a nuts and bolts man, I was convinced that software people were a strange breed.

This was reinforced with the results of my first attempts to understand the CP/M operating system. Self preservation of my sanity being one of my major priorities, I retreated to the world of hardware vowing never to return.

Graphics User Interfaces (GUI's) such as Xerox's WIMP (Windows, Icons, Mouse, pulldown Menu's) environment changed all that and now at Commodore I'm perfectly at home in my AmigaDOS 2 world.

But open that Shell window and all the old fears come flooding back. Nervously reaching for the reference manual I try to convince myself that I'm Captain Kirk going boldly where no hardware man has gone before. It doesn't work! Nothing makes sense! If only there was a *Hitch Hikers Guide* to Workbench 2.

Well if you're like me, don't panic! You may find, as I have, that this book not only clears away the mystique of the operating system but does it in a way that's intuitive. Taking you from novice through to expert and who knows? Maybe where no user has been before.

Perhaps I'll see you there. I'll be the one with the screwdriver.

Barry Thurston
Technical Director,
COMMODORE BUSINESS MACHINES (UK) LTD.

Preface

L. Ron Hubbard made an interesting observation as part of the introduction to his study of Dianetics. In essence, what Hubbard says is this, readers fail to grasp the meaning of what is written because they failed to understand the meaning of one of the words in the preceding text. However, it seems Hubbard overlooked something, readers also fail to grasp a concept or idea because they failed to comprehend the meaning of the concepts that gave rise to it. Nowhere is this more true than in specialist subjects like computing.

To ensure this situation is not made worse (exacerbated) we as authors have endeavoured to keep this – primarily reference text - as simple as possible. Inevitably, for the sake of brevity we have found it necessary to use some buzz words and phrases. These can usually be found either in the glossary accompanying this work or else one of numerous texts on the subject.

For the same reason we have kept the English as simple as possible without resorting to too many colloquialisms, humm? We are not out to confuse the reader by embroidering this text with flowery language when the subject is complex enough as it is. When explanations seem wordy therefore, consider yourself fortunate that you have already grasped a concept that others will still be struggling with.

This book forms the second part of what we hope will be the most complete work ever produced on the topic of AmigaDOS. Although entitled *Mastering AmigaDOS 2* the two volume set fully encompasses all previous releases of AmigaDOS from 1.2. This includes versions 1.2, 1.3, 1.3.2 and 2.04. Placed on the shelf together Volume One and Volume Two should provide you with all the information you are ever likely to need when using an Amiga, in a simple easy-to-digest form, for many years to come.

Mark Smiddy and Bruce Smith

November 1990. Revised – May 1992.

AmigaDOS Command Reference Section

AmigaDOS is a complex and comprehensive operating system – but it can be a joy to use – as we hope to have demonstrated already in this manual. It has endured a slightly chequered history. From the early days when it was written in BCPL through to the new version (AmigaDOS 2) re-coded entirely in C and assembler. From those first tentative steps with the unforgiving CLI – to the beautifully integrated Shell. From a machine with a woman's name – to a machine whose name reflects a woman's charm. Yet still, 'Hell hath no fury like an Amiga about to go guru!'

Although this is called the Command Reference Section of *Mastering AmigaDOS 2* – beginners should not be put off. In fact, we'd encourage you to work through the examples presented here to help you learn even more about this fascinating machine. Not every command will be of interest at first. Many will look bewilderingly complex. Some will make no sense at all until you have learned about other features of the system.

In this section we have covered every executable (CLI) command supplied by Commodore – not just AmigaDOS. We have found it necessary to give some commands – like ED – sections of their own in Volume One. In order to discriminate between AmigaDOS and others we have shown the path (directory) where the command lives. Most AmigaDOS specific commands live in the C directory – some have been made internal – that is, placed permanently in the Amiga's ROMs – with version 2. However, this should be invisible to most users.

For beginners we have the following message: Rome was not built in a day, neither was the Amiga. There is no need therefore, to feel that you have to absorb this great wealth of knowledge in a few short hours. Take your time: this is the start of a wonderful journey. The road to expertise is a long one, so relax and enjoy the scenery. Before you know it you'll know more about AmigaDOS than you ever thought possible.

For experts and beginners alike, we have this to say: Expertise is relative – experts are not born, they are hewn from the bedrock of effort. You have learnt a lot in coming this far – but there is always room to learn more. As authors, we have learnt a great deal in bringing you this guide and we were all raw recruits once. In designing this section we have gone to great lengths to make each example as simple (and as useful) as possible. However there are places where we have had to make compromises for the sake of clarity and for this we make no excuse nor offers of apology.

The entire section has been written using Commodore's own conventions wherever possible – those familiar with the representation should, however, read this introduction to familiarise themselves with the new features present in AmigaDOS 2.

Each command has been started on a new page to aid readability and organised alphabetically to speed location. All follow a similar layout:

NAME

The name of the command appears in capital letters.

Synopsis

One of two ways of briefly summarising a command's actions and syntax. This is explained in detail below. Three synopses have been supplied for most commands, one each for version 1.2, 1.3 and 2.04 of AmigaDOS. If a command has been changed significantly for release 1.3.2 then this is also included. If the command does not appear in the release this has been noted: na.

Template

Similar to the synopsis, this provides a carbon copy of the template expected by a command. In most cases this can be recalled by supplying ? as a single argument. Three templates have been provided for each command where applicable. Templates are described in more detail below. These commands also support interactive mode.

Path

Where the command lives on the disk relative to SYS: (the boot disk). All AmigaDOS commands live in C: However we have covered commands which, although not strictly AmigaDOS, have command line options or may be of some interest. Where paths point to hard disks, these conform to Commodore conventions.

Use:

Every command has a detailed description of what it does and how and where to use it. This is the area of most interest to beginners and those new to AmigaDOS.

New – AmigaDOS 2

The text is punctuated like this at various points to describe new features or changes in the operating system. These contain valuable information for those upgrading to the new version.

Options

Describe each of the possible arguments, switches or keywords supplied to a command. For most, an example has been given to reinforce the text so these descriptions will be sufficient for many users. On its own this section refers to all versions of AmigaDOS from 1.2 throughto release 2. However, in later versions of AmigaDOS command options have been extended and these are included under suitable headings. For example, the heading:

Options (>AmigaDOS 2)

indicates that the following items are only available in release 2 of AmigaDOS.

See also

Further information can be gained by following the references given here.

Command Templates

In format descriptions the following conventions apply:

< > Required argument. Something must be entered here – this usually applies to file or device names. When referencing a device name a colon (:) has been added. For instance:

```
MOUNT <device>:
```

[ ] Optional argument. This argument may be omitted – this usually applies to command line switches but may also be applied to keywords and others.

{ } Multiple arguments. Indicates a series of arguments to be used one or more times. This new feature was introduced with AmigaDOS 2 and greatly enhances several commands.

... (Ellipses) is used to indicate that a series may be continued. Example:

```
JOIN...
```

| This symbol (logical OR) means that any of the options enclosed may be used separately. Some options may be combined thus:

```
OPT (A|I|AI|D)
```

Where the options A and I may be used together.

In templates (the help string returned by commands) the following rules apply:

,,, Used to indicate multiple arguments sub AmigaDOS 2 the facility is limited. The number of commas used shows the maximum number of arguments. Example: DELETE.

/A ARGUMENT: Something must be entered here for the command to work.

/K KEYWORD: Keywords indicate optional arguments and must be present so AmigaDOS knows where (in the command line) the argument is. For instance, the Shell can be optionally started from a named startup script. In the template for NEWSHELL, "FROM" is defined as a keyword – FROM/K. This gives rise to:

```
NEWSHELL FROM MyStartup
```

/S SWITCH: Switches define the behaviour of some commands. Like light switches they are either ON or OFF. Specifying the name of a switch in a command line turns the switch ON. Some switches have shortened names for convenience. This appears so:

```
SUB=SUBTRACT/S.
```

Here either SUB or SUBTRACT would set the switch on.

? QUERY: The command has no interactive help template but it does require some form of argument. EXECUTE, for instance, requires a filename.

, COMMA: The command takes no arguments and therefore has no template or help string of any kind. BINDDRIVERS is typical – these commands may generate output however.

In addition AmigaDOS 2 supports the following template features:

/F FINAL: This argument *must* be the last one on the command line. Everything beyond this (up to the terminating return) is used as the argument. NB: this includes white space!

/M MULTIPLE: The command takes multiple arguments. Release 2 features a new command parser which can accept any number of command arguments.

/N NUMERIC: A numerical value is expected as an argument. This is as opposed to a string such as a file or device name.

/T TOGGLE: Changes the state of a Boolean value so ON becomes OFF and vice-versa. This switch is supported in the ROM parser but not used by current AmigaDOS commands.

AmigaDOS Commands – A to Z

A full list of AmigaDOS command availability for each release version from 1.2 is given below.

– indicates that the command is not available.

• indicates that the command is implemented

⊕ indicates that this release of AmigaDOS contains enhancements to the command.

Command	*1.2*	*1.3*	*1.3.2*	*2.04*
ADDBUFFERS	•	•	•	⊕
ADDMONITIOR	–	–	–	•
ALIAS	–	•	•	⊕
ASK	•	•	•	•
ASSIGN	•	⊕	•	⊕
AUTOPOINT	–	–	–	•
AVAIL	–	•	•	⊕
BINDDRIVERS	•	•	•	•
BINDMONITOR	–	–	–	•
BLANKER	–	–	–	•
BREAK	•	•	•	•
BRU	–	–	–	•
CD	•	•	•	⊕
CHANGETASKPRI	•	⊕	⊕	•
CLICKTOFRONT	–	–	–	•
CLOCK	•	•	•	•
CMD	–	•	•	•
COLORS	–	•	•	•
CONCLIP	–	–	–	•
COPY	•	⊕	•	⊕
CPU	–	–	–	•
DATE	•	⊕	•	•
DELETE	•	⊕	•	⊕
DIR	•	⊕	•	⊕
DISKCHANGE	•	•	•	•
DISKCOPY	•	•	⊕	•
DISKDOCTOR	•	•	•	•
DISPLAY	–	–	–	•
DPAT	–	•	•	⊕
ECHO	•	⊕	•	⊕
ED	•	•	•	⊕
EDIT	•	•	•	⊕
ELSE	•	•	•	⊕
ENDCLI	•	•	•	•
ENDSHELL	–	•	•	⊕
ENDIF	•	•	•	⊕
ENDSKIP	–	–	–	•
EVAL	–	•	⊕	⊕
EXCHANGE	–	–	–	•
EXECUTE	•	⊕	•	⊕
FAILAT	•	•	•	⊕

Command	*1.2*	*1.3*	*1.3.2*	*2.04*
FASTMEMFIRST	•	•	⊕	–
FAULT	•	•	•	•
FF	–	•	•	–
FILENOTE	•	•	•	⊕
FIXFONTS	–	•	•	•
FKEY	–	–	–	•
FONT	–	–	–	•
FORMAT	•	⊕	•	⊕
GET	–	–	–	•
GETENV	–	•	•	⊕
GRAPHICDUMP	–	•	•	•
ICONTROL	–	–	–	•
ICONX	•	•	•	•
IF	•	⊕	•	⊕
IHELP	–	–	–	•
INFO	•	⊕	•	•
INITPRINTER	–	•	•	•
INPUT	–	–	–	•
INSTALL	•	⊕	•	⊕
JOIN	•	⊕	•	⊕
LAB	•	•	•	⊕
LIST	•	⊕	•	⊕
LOADWB	•	•	•	•
LOCK	–	•	•	⊕
MAGTAPE	–	–	–	•
MAKEDIR	•	•	•	⊕
MAKELINK	–	–	–	•
MEMACS	–	•	•	•
MERGEMEM	•	•	•	–
MORE	–	•	•	•
MOUNT	•	⊕	•	⊕
NEWCLI	•	•	•	⊕
NEWSHELL	–	•	•	⊕
NOCAPSLOCK	–	–	–	•
NOFASTMEM	•	•	⊕	•
OVERSCAN	–	–	–	•
PALETTE	–	–	–	•
PARK	•	•	•	•
PATH	•	⊕	•	⊕
PCD	–	•	•	⊕
POINTER	–	–	–	•

Command	*1.2*	*1.3*	*1.3.2*	*2.04*
PREFERENCES	–	•	•	•
PRINTER	–	–	–	•
PRINTERGFX	–	–	–	•
PRINTFILES	–	•	•	•
PROMPT	•	⊕	•	⊕
PROTECT	•	⊕	•	⊕
QUIT	•	•	•	⊕
RELABEL	•	•	•	•
REMRAD	–	•	•	⊕
RENAME	•	•	•	•
RESIDENT	•	•	•	⊕
REXXMAST	–	–	–	•
RUN	•	•	•	•
SAY	–	•	•	•
SCREENMODE	–	–	–	•
SEARCH	•	⊕	•	⊕
SERIAL	–	–	–	•
SET	–	–	–	•
SETCLOCK	•	•	⊕	•
SETDATE	•	•	•	⊕
SETENV	–	•	•	⊕
SETFONT	–	–	–	•
SETMAP	•	•	⊕	•
SETPATCH	–	•	⊕	⊕
SKIP	•	⊕	•	•
SORT	•	•	•	⊕
SPAT	–	•	•	⊕
STACK	•	•	•	•
STATUS	•	⊕	•	•
TIME	–	–	–	•
TYPE	•	⊕	•	⊕
UNALIAS	–	–	–	•
UNSET	–	–	–	•
UNSETENV	–	–	–	•
VERSION	–	•	•	⊕
WAIT	•	•	•	•
WBPATTERN	–	–	–	•
WHICH	–	•	•	⊕
WHY	•	•	•	•
;	•	•	•	•
~	–	–	–	•
?	•	•	•	•
<	•	•	•	•
>	•	•	•	•
>>	•	•	•	•
*	•	•	•	•
""	•	•	•	•
'	•	•	•	•
CTRL+\	•	•	•	⊕
ALT+'	–	–	–	•

ADDBUFFERS

Synopsis:

2.04: ADDBUFFERS <drive>: [n]

1.3: ADDBUFFERS <drive>: [n]

1.2: ADDBUFFERS <drive>: [n]

Templates:

2.04: DRIVE/A, BUFFERS/N

1.3: DRIVE/A, BUFFERS/A

1.2: DRIVE/A, BUFFERS/A

Path:

C:

Use:

The Amiga's floppy disk drives are not fast at the best of times; though the situation has improved with the advent of FFS (Fast Filing System). ADDBUFFERS allocates a small amount of RAM to act as a sector cache or buffer.

Examples:

```
1>ADDBUFFERS df0: 22 ; One track's worth of buffers
1>ADDBUFFERS df2: 1  ; NOT enough!
```

Notes:

When Kickstart (more correctly, trackdisk.device) attempts to read the disk, the sector cache is checked to see if the requested sectors have already been read. If so, the sectors are retrieved from RAM; which is much faster than accessing the disk. As new sectors are read their contents are placed in the cache, overwriting any previous information.

The question remains: how much memory to allocate to the buffers? Too little and disk access slows to a crawl – but too much is a waste of precious RAM. In practice all that is usually required is enough to store one complete (double-sided) track cylinder's worth of information: 20 – 25 buffers. This is calculated thus:

1	sector	=	512 bytes
1	buffer	=	512 bytes
1	track	=	11 sectors
2	sides	=	2 tracks (or 1 cylinder)
::	2 x 11	=	22 sectors

Since the buffers are one sector long, 22 buffers are enough to store a complete track which should suffice. To gain the greatest benefit from ADDBUFFERS it should be included very early in the Startup-sequence.

New - AmigaDOS 2:

Two more options are available: First, by not supplying an argument for the number of buffers, the command returns the number of cache buffers currently allocated. Second, if a negative argument is supplied, that number is subtracted from the number of buffers currently allocated:

```
1>ADDBUFFERS df0:
25
1>ADDBUFFERS df0: -5
1>ADDBUFFERS df0:
20
```

FFS is now available on floppy disks. However, this requires Kickstart 2 but not the enhanced chip set . FFS was introduced on hard disks with Workbench 1.3. Even with the FFS in operation the usefulness of ADDBUFFERS should not be overlooked – no matter how fast a physical storage media becomes, it will never be able to exceed the speed of a pure RAM based setup.

Options:

DRIVE/A	This required argument defines the drive number to add the buffers to – DFx: where x=0 to 3.
BUFFERS/A	The number of 512 byte sector buffers to allocate.

See also: COPY, Startup-Sequences (*Mastering AmigaDOS 2 Volume One*).

ADDMONITOR

Synopsis:

2.04: ADDMONITOR <number> <name> [HBSTRT=] [HBSTOP=] [HSSTRT=] [HSSTOP=] [VBSTRT=] [VBSTOP=] [VSSTRT=] [VSSTOP=] [MINROW=] [MINCOL=] [TOTROWS=] [TOTCLKS=] [BEAMCON0=]

1.3: na

1.2: na

Templates:

2.04: NUM/A/N, NAME/A, HBSTRT/K, HBSTOP/K, HSSTRT/K, HSSTOP/K, VBSTRT/K, VBSTOP/K, VSSTRT/K, VSSTOP/K, MINROW/K, MINCOL/K, TOTROWS/K, TOTCLKS/K, BEAMCON0/K

1.3: na

1.2: na

Path:

SYS:System

Use:

This command is used to connect non-standard displays to the Amiga system and to alter the private hardware register settings for special displays. New monitors can be added during boot by dragging their icons into the Monitors drawer; alternatively, you can use this command directly to make the change. Once done, you must use the ScreenMode (Preferences) tool to change to the appropriate display. Under normal circumstances, only the first two parameters are used, the others are reserved for tricky hardware such as video effects units.

Options:

BEAMCON0 Beam sync. Note this argument ends in the number 0 (Zero) *not* the letter O.

HBSTRT Horizontal blanking starts.

HBSTOP Horizontal blanking stops.

HSSTRT Horizontal scan starts.

HSSTOP Horizontal scan stops.

MINCOL Minimum number of screen columns.

MINROW Minimum number of screen rows.

NAME	The name assigned to that monitor: NTSC, PAL, Multiscan, A2024. Example: `AddMonitor NUM=2 NAME=Pal`
NUM	The number assigned to the monitor type from 1 to 4. Example: `AddMonitor NUM=3 NAME=Multiscan`
TOTCLKS	Total clock cycles.
TOTROWS	Total number of screen rows.
VBSTRT	Vertical blanking starts.
VBSTOP	Vertical blanking stops.
VSSTRT	Vertical scan starts.
VSSTOP	Vertical scan stops.

ALIAS

Synopsis:

2.04: ALIAS [<name>] [<string>]

1.3: ALIAS [<name>] [<string>]

1.2: na

Templates:

2.04: NAME, STRING/F

1.3: NAME, STRING

1.2: na

Path:

Internal

Use:

As its name implies, ALIAS produces pseudonyms for commonly used expressions or commands. Although this is essentially a simple command it allows you to tailor AmigaDOS to your own needs. At the very least it can save an awful lot of typing!

Examples:

```
1>ALIAS del DELETE   ; Delete a la MS-DOS!
1>ALIAS a   CD df0: ; If you prefer drives A, B etc
1>ALIAS d1  DIR df1:; Well...
```

ALIAS supports a simple string substitution system which can be used to enhance some aliases. This takes the form of square brackets [ ], placed, at the position where the substring is to be inserted. How about a shortened version of the FORMAT command?

```
1>ALIAS destroy FORMAT DRIVE [] NAME YourName NOICONS
```

Usage:

```
destroy dfx:
```

Perhaps the most important thing to note with ALIAS is its position in the internal search path: aliases are searched first even before the Resident list. This provides a very useful way to prevent access to certain commands. For instance – you might want to stop someone on a remote terminal using FORMAT just in case... Here's how:

```
1>ALIAS FORMAT <space><return>
```

Using at least one space after the alias, makes the Shell attempt to execute a null string – which disables access to the command. A similar effect could be gained by this:

```
1>ALIAS FORMAT ECHO "Access denied"
```

It doesn't work as well however. Needless to say of course, the ALIAS command can still cancel the effects of this. But with a little thought it can be effectively removed from the system. See the RemAlias example listed in *Mastering AmigaDOS 2 Volume One.*

Options:

NAME — The "alias" to give to the following string. If the alias is already defined it takes on the new STRING argument. A NULL string causes the alias to be removed.

STRING — A simple command line to execute when the alias is specified. A single argument may be passed using [&] where the argument will appear. See above.

Note: in AmigaDOS 2 and higher, the string argument must be the *last* argument on the line.

See also: ASSIGN, UNALIAS, plus the following chapters from *Mastering AmigaDOS 2 Volume One:* The Shell, Scripts, Multi-User Machine.

ASK

Synopsis:

2.04: ASK <prompt>

1.3: ASK <prompt>

1.2: ASK <prompt>

Templates:

2.04: PROMPT/A

1.3: PROMPT/A

1.2: ?

Path:

Internal

C: <2.04

Use:

When executing a script file it is frequently necessary to get some information from the user – often some form of confirmation. For instance: if a script needs to delete some files, it should ask if the user wants to continue. ASK is just such a command – it acts on a simple Y or N choice which can be tested with IF. A positive (Y) response at the prompt results in the WARN condition being set. The default (just pressing the Return key) is the same as pressing the N key.

Examples:

```
; Example 1
ASK "Press Y or N"
IF  WARN
ECHO "You pressed Y"
ELSE
ECHO "You pressed N"
ENDIF
```

```
; Example 2
ECHO "This will destroy ALL info on the hard disk!"
ASK "Are you sure you want to do this?"

IF  NOT WARN    ; Check for no!
SKIP fail       ; Jump out if they said no
.
.               ; The formatting stuff would go in
here
.
ENDIF           ; End conditional
QUIT 0          ; Exit the script (neatly)

LAB fail        ; If user pressed "N" they get here
ECHO "Phew, that was a close one!"
```

Options:

PROMPT/A The new prompt string. The argument is required from 1.3 onwards.

See also: Mastering AmigaDOS 2 Volume One.

ASSIGN

Synopsis:

2.04:	ASSIGN [<name>:] {dir} [LIST] [EXISTS] [REMOVE] [DISMOUNT] [DEFER] [PATH] [ADD] [VOLS] [DIRS] [DEVICES]
1.3:	ASSIGN [[<name>:] <dir>] [LIST] [EXISTS] [REMOVE]
1.2:	ASSIGN [[<name>:] <dir>] [LIST] [REMOVE]

Templates:

2.04:	NAME, TARGET/M, LIST/S, EXISTS/S, REMOVE/S, DISMOUNT/S, DEFER/S,PATH/S, ADD/S, VOLS/S, DIRS/S, DEVICES/S
1.3:	NAME, DIR, LIST/S, EXISTS/S, REMOVE/S
1.2:	NAME, DIR, LIST/S

Path:

C:

Use:

ASSIGN is one of the grand manipulators of AmigaDOS and one of the most powerful commands at your disposal. Its primary use is to assign logical directories to the system; and under AmigaDOS any directory or path can be made equivalent to a logical device. The implications of this can only be made apparent with a few examples. Real and logical devices are explained more fully in *Mastering AmigaDOS 2 Volume One* beginners should familiarise themselves with the concepts involved before continuing.

There are many variations of syntax possible with ASSIGN – the default is to display the current assignments. That is, those made by the system, either at power-up or during the Startup-sequence.

Example:

```
1>ASSIGN

Volumes:
WorkBench1.3 [Mounted]
FastBench
RAM Disk [Mounted]
System2.0 [Mounted]
Work [Mounted]

Directories:
CLIPS                   Ram Disk:clipboards
T                       Ram Disk:t
ENV                     Ram Disk:env
ENVARC                  System2.0:prefs/env-
archive
SYS                     System2.0:
C                       System2.0:c
S                       System2.0:s
LIBS                    System2.0:libs
DEVS                    System2.0:devs
FONTS                   System2.0:fonts
+ RAM:MoreFonts
L                       System2.0:l
TOOLS                   [Utils:]
SOURCE                  <Work:Devpac/source>

Devices:
PIPE AUX SPEAK RAM CON
RAW SER PAR PRT DF0
DF2 Work
```

At first this all seems more complex than it really is. Users on Workbench 1.2 and Workbench 1.3 machines may have to expand their CLI/Shell window to the full height of the screen and re-issue the command to see the full effect. The command breaks down system assignments into three sections as you can see: Volumes, Directories and Devices.

Volumes:

These, as you might expect, are the names (labels) of the disks that the machine knows about. They can be on hard or floppy disk since this makes no difference to AmigaDOS – those above are a mixture. Notice in the example, "Fastbench" is the only volume to lack the message "[Mounted]". This is a special case. The "mounted" disks are physically inserted in the machine – either hard disks or floppies.

Disks not marked as mounted are available to AmigaDOS but not currently inserted. This has several causes – the most usual is AmigaDOS has launched a program which has yet to exit and holds a "lock" on something on the disk. It could also be that something is assigned to that disk – say the C: directory. See below.

Directories:

This is the most interesting part of the ASSIGN list. It shows where all the system and user directories reside. ASSIGN gives a directory or path a logical name. The complete directory can then be found by accessing just that logical name. Example:

```
1>MAKEDIR RAM:temp          ; make a directory
1>MAKEDIR RAM:temp/clips ; add another lower down
1>ASSIGN MINE: RAM:temp/clips; give a logical name
1>ECHO >MINE:eg "Hello!"     ; add a file
1>TYPE MINE:eg               ; Type it back. . .
1>TYPE RAM:temp/clips/eg     ; the long way around!
```

Devices:

The device list is simply a list of the current physical devices, – that is, as opposed to directories. For many purposes device, logical directory and volume names are completely interchangeable. Some of the devices listed here must be specifically mounted.

New – AmigaDOS 2:

ASSIGN now takes multiple arguments so it is possible to assign more than one directory or path to the same logical name. Directories will be searched top-down in the order they appear in the assignments list (indicated by a + sign). The following example assigns the FONTS: to three different directories. Note: It is not possible to use the DEFER and PATH switches with the multiple options. Also the meaning of REMOVE has been altered.

```
1>ASSIGN FONTS: SYS:fonts RAM:MoreFonts DF1:fonts
1>ASSIGN
.
.
FONTS   SYS:fonts
+ RAM:MoreFonts
+ Workbench1.3:Fonts
```

Options:

DIR The directory to assign to the logical assignment. This *must* be the complete device and path so the assignment can be reached from anywhere in the directory hierarchy. Wildcards cannot be used but a colon may be used to indicate the root directory of the *current* disk. Example:

```
1>ASSIGN FONTS :fonts
```

LIST/S This is the default switch *unless* you want to examine an individual assignment. In such a case the EXISTS switch must be specified or the assignment itself will be lost. This example clears the FONTS: assignment *then* lists the rest of the assignments:

```
1>ASSIGN FONTS: LIST
```

NAME The logical name to supply to the assignment. Logical directory assignments are treated very much like volumes or devices so the name *must* be followed by a colon (:). Example:

```
1>ASSIGN SOURCE: df1:devpac/source/sleep
```

REMOVE/S Is used to remove a system directory assignment. Provided for development only, it does not free memory and should never be required in normal circumstances. This option is sure to cause GURUs – be warned!

Options (>AmigaDOS 1.3):

EXISTS/S Is an easy way to discover if a particular assignment has been made. For instance to find out where the FONTS: directory is:

```
1>ASSIGN FONTS: EXISTS
Workbench1.3:Fonts
```

If the assignment has not been made ASSIGN will return an error level 5 (WARN) – this is useful in script files for instance. Example:

```
ASSIGN >NIL: FONTS: EXISTS
IF WARN                    ; Check return
ECHO "Can't find the FONTS!"
ENDIF
```

Options (>AmigaDOS 2):

ADD/S Used to add several device assignments to the existing list. Example:

```
1>ASSIGN FONTS: RAM:MoreFonts ADD
```

DEFER/S The first of two powerful switches, this represents the "late binding" assignment. Assignments made with this switch will not be tested until something attempts to reference them. This is useful for users with a floppy based system because it allows assignment to a disk which does not yet exist – as far as AmigaDOS is concerned. Say you have a utilities disk named 'Utils" which you want to assign to the logical name tools:

```
ASSIGN TOOLS: Utils:
```

Should do the trick – but AmigaDOS would immediately scream "Please insert volume Utils in any drive." This is inconvenient at every boot time. Adding thc DEFER switch prevents these mishaps:

```
ASSIGN TOOLS: Utils: DEFER
```

This causes AmigaDOS to keep quiet *until* you specifically reference TOOLS:. Assigns made in this way appear in the list like this enclosed in angle brackets <>. See SOURCE: in the example above.

Note: Once a *late-binding* assignment is made, it remains locked to the volume – like a normal assignment. In some circumstances the PATH switch (below) may be preferable. It does not bind (lock) onto any specific volume.

DISMOUNT/S This switch works in a similar fashion to REMOVE 1.3. It quite literally makes AmigaDOS dismount any mounted device or volume. You could use this to disconnect the external drive on an A500 thus:

```
1>ASSIGN DF1: DISMOUNT
```

Which causes DF1: to be removed. However, disks can still be read by the device and accessed by their VOLUME name. If a volume is dismounted, it can be remounted by DISKCHANGE or reinsertion into the drive:

```
1>ASSIGN Workbench2.0: DISMOUNT
1>DISKCHANGE DFO:
```

• This switch should only be used with great care – the only way of remounting a HD partition is to reboot the machine!

PATH/S This second powerful switch works just like DEFER but creates a "non-binding" assignment. Like DEFER, the assignment does not exist, as far as AmigaDOS is concerned, until something tries to reference it. Unlike DEFER, the assignment is only temporary – any path fitting the bill will do.

```
1>ASSIGN C: Utils: PATH
```

Like DEFER, all references to C: are passed straight to a volume called Utils. The important difference is that *any* disk called Utils will do – provided AmigaDOS can find what it wants. Assigns made in this way appear in the list like this enclosed in square brackets – [ ]. See TOOLS: in the example above

REMOVE/S Used to remove named (multiple) device assignments from an assign list. Example:

```
1>ASSIGN FONTS: LIST
System2.0:fonts
+ RAM:MoreFonts
1>ASSIGN FONTS: RAM:MoreFonts REMOVE
```

DEVICES/S Yep! Just the device list...

DIR/S Adding this switch to the command line causes just the directory assignments to be listed.

VOL/S This switch causes the command to list the available volumes.

See also: PATH, MOUNT, and the following two chapters from *Mastering AmigaDOS 2 Volume One:* Introducing Directories and Devices.

AUTOPOINT

Synopsis:

2.04: AUTOPOINT [CX_Priority=<n>]

1.3: na

1.2: na

Templates:

2.04: CX_Priority=/K/N

1.3: na

1.2: na

Path:

Extras2:Tools/Commodities

Use:

AUTOPOINT is one of those tools you will either love or hate. The idea was borrowed from another windowing system on the Sun Workstations and basically forces a window to become active when the pointer passes over it. This can be irritating when you're working with Shells because the pointer and other windows can get in the way. Basic usage is as follows:

```
1>AUTOPOINT
```

This activates AutoPoint from the current Shell and locks you out; this is not very useful, but you can close the program by entering CTRL-E. A better method is to use RUN:

```
1>RUN AUTOPOINT
```

An even better method, and one you must use if executing AUTOPOINT from a Startup-sequence or User-startup is to re-direct output to NIL: viz:

```
1>RUN >NIL: AUTOPOINT
```

For general Shell use, an ALIAS is useful – add this to Shell-startup:

```
ALIAS AP RUN >NIL: AUTOPOINT
```

If you run AUTOPOINT a second time, the first invocation disappears.

Options:

CX_Priority= The priority passed to the program on startup. This is its priority over other CX programs, not the process priority shown by STATUS. By default all CX programs have a CX_PRIORITY of 0. AUTOPOINT's process priority is very processor greedy at 19.

General Note – Commodities Exchange

The Commodities Exchange (CX) programs are normally stored on the Extras disk. However, to keep the examples simple, we'll assume you have already changed to the correct directory or set the correct path.

Important: Be aware that the CX programs *do not* return error conditions when an incorrect command line is entered. You can check they have launched correctly in scripts using STATUS.

See also: BLANKER, EXCHANGE, CLICKTOFRONT, FKEY, IHELP, NOCAPSLOCK

AVAIL

Synopsis:

2.04: AVAIL [CHIP] [FAST] [TOTAL] [FLUSH]

1.3: AVAIL [CHIP] [FAST] [TOTAL]

1.2: na

Templates:

2.04: CHIP/S, FAST/S, TOTAL/S, FLUSH/S

1.3: CHIP/S, FAST/S, TOTAL/S

1.2: na

Path:

C:

Use:

Memory on every Amiga is split into two distinct types CHIP and FAST. CHIP memory is shared by the custom chips which are affectionally called Paula, Agnes, and Denise. FAST memory is only accessed by the CPU. On early systems CHIP memory is limited to the first 512K. The chips have since been enhanced to allow access to 1Mb and 2Mb respectively depending on the model in use.

The importance of this is twofold: first, CHIP memory is used to store information like graphics, sound samples, disk buffers etc. Second, the processor can lose access to this RAM while the custom chips are busy using it. AVAIL is used to determine how much memory is available, of what type and how fragmented it is. Fragmentation is important - if available memory becomes too broken up into small chunks, large programs will not run. The only remedy for this, albeit rare complication, is to reboot the system.

```
1>AVAIL
Type    Available   InUse    Maximum   Largest
chip     942688     104864   1047552   942560
fast     249952     798624   1048576   246336
total   1192640     903488   2096128   942560
```

Explanation:

Available The total amount of memory of type X that is free.

InUse How much memory of type X is being used.

Maximum The maximum amount of memory type X available to EXEC.

Largest The biggest unfragmented chunk of memory available.

Options:

CHIP/S	Returns the amount of free CHIP RAM.
FAST/S	Returns the amount of free FAST RAM.
TOTAL/S	Returns the total amount available.
FLUSH/S	Flush libraries and devices marked for expurgation, ie, remove unused resources from system.

Note: Due to the Amiga's multi-tasking, the accuracy of the figures returned should only be used as a guide. They only reflect a snapshot of the memory map taken at the instant the program was run.

BINDDRIVERS

Synopsis:

2.04: BINDDRIVERS

1.3: BINDDRIVERS

1.2: BINDDRIVERS

Templates:

2.04: ,

1.3: ,

1.2: ,

Path:

C:

Use:

BINDDRIVERS is used only once in the Startup-sequence to join any additional hardware to the system. This may include software configuring RAM expansions, hard disks and so on. Relevant files will have been supplied by the hardware manufacturer and should be copied to the expansion directory of any system (boot) disks. In all cases follow the instructions supplied.

On unexpanded Amigas (or ones fitted with self-configuring expansion hardware) BINDDRIVERS is not required. This includes the vast majority of machines and, since the command takes up several seconds of the boot sequence, it can safely be removed. If in doubt open the Expansion drawer of the Workbench. An empty drawer means BINDDRIVERS is redundant.

Important:

BINDDRIVERS makes extensive use of the icon.library. Therefore you *must not* remove either the icon.library or any icons supplied with expansion software. This temptation *must* be resisted by CLI buffs when making stripped-down Workbench disks.

See also: *Mastering AmigaDOS Volume One* – Startup-Sequences.

BINDMONITOR

Synopsis:

2.04:	BINDMONITOR <Mode ID> <Mode Name>
1.3:	na
1.2:	na

Templates:

2.04:	MONITORID/A, MONITORNAME/A
1.3:	na
1.2:	na

Path:

SYS:System

Use:

This command is used mainly by the system to attach extra screenmodes and give them meaningful names. It can be accessed from AmigaDOS if you wish like this:

```
1>BINDMONITOR 0x29000 PAL:Normal
```

Standard GFX Modes

0x08000	HiRes
0x08004	HiRes Interlaced
0x08020	SuperHires
0x19000	NTSC:Hires
0x19020	NTSC:SuperHires
0x29000	PAL:Hires
0x29020	PAL:SuperHires
0x39004	VGA-Lores
0x39024	Productivity
0x41000	A2024_10Hz
0x49000	A2024_15Hz
0x08024	SuperHires Interlaced
0x19004	NTSC:Hires Interlaced
0x19024	NTSC:SuperHires Interlaced

0x29004	PAL:Hires Interlaced
0x29024	PAL:SuperHires Interlaced
0x39005	VGA-Lores Interlaced
0x39025	Productivity Interlaced
0x41000	A2024_10Hz
0x49000	A2024_15Hz

Options:

MONITORID — A code understood by the graphics.library relating to a particular screen display mode. This is a hexadecimal number and must be prefixed with "0X" and contain the correct number of digits.

MONITORNAME — The name of the specified mode. (You can invent your own names if you wish.)

BLANKER

Synopsis:

2.04: BLANKER [seconds=<n>] [Hotkey="hotkey(s)"] [display=<no>] [priority=<n>]

1.3: na

1.2: na

Templates:

2.04: SECONDS/K/N, CX_POPKEY/K, CX_POPUP/K, CX_PRIORITY/K/N

1.3: na

1.2: na

Path:

Extras:Tools/Commodities

Use:

BLANKER can be considered an essential accessory if you leave the machine idle for more than a few minutes at a time. The idea is to prevent character *burn-in* on the monitor display. Although this mainly affects monochrome screens (including the A2024) it can affect colour monitors too. Either way, it is a useful precaution to have Blanker running in the background and is, for the most part, totally transparent. Basic use is as follows:

```
1>RUN Blanker
```

This activates BLANKER from the current Shell and brings up its opening screen, showing a 60 second delay to screen blank. (If Blanker is already running, the current setting is displayed.) You can activate the program and leave it running by clicking the HIDE gadget. If RUN is not used the program can be closed by sending it CTRL-E.

If you want to include BLANKER in the User-startup you should redirect output to NIL: and tell it not to display a startup message like this:

```
1>RUN >NIL: BLANKER CX_POPUP=NO
```

For general Shell use, an ALIAS is useful – add this to Shell-startup:

```
ALIAS HIDEME RUN >NIL: BLANKER
```

Options:

SECONDS The number of seconds to wait before the screen is blanked out. This argument must be supplied as a keyword on the command line. Example in a startup script:

```
RUN >NIL: BLANKER seconds=90 CX_POPUP=NO
```

CX_POPKEY The *hotkey* used to awaken BLANKER and open its configuration screen. By default this is Shift-F1.

```
RUN >NIL: BLANKER seconds=90 "CX_POPKEY=Alt F1"
```

POPKEY extensions are as follows:

Shift	–	Either Shift key
Control	–	The Ctrl key
Alt	–	Either Alt key
F<n>	–	Function key N: F1, F2

CX_POPUP This keyword takes a yes or no argument and tells Blanker whether or not to display its startup screen. If this option is not supplied, YES is assumed – strictly, this option should be a switch. Example:

```
RUN BLANKER seconds=60 CX_POPUP=YES
```

CX_PRIORITY The priority passed to the program on startup. This is its priority over other CX programs – not the process priority shown by STATUS. By default all CX programs have a CX_PRIORITY of 0. Higher priority programs have the first grab at incoming messages – key presses and such like. It is possible therefore, that Blanker's default hotkey (Shift-F1) will override FKey.

```
RUN BLANKER CX_POPUP=NO CX_PRIORITY=2
```

General Note – Commodities Exchange

The Commodities Exchange (CX) programs are normally stored on the Extras disk. However, to keep the examples simple, we'll assume you have already changed to the correct directory or set the correct path.

Important: Note that the CX programs *do not* return error conditions when an incorrect command line is entered. You can check they have launched correctly in scripts using STATUS.

See also: AUTOPOINT, EXCHANGE, CLICKTOFRONT, FKEY, IHELP, NOCAPSLOCK

BREAK

Synopsis:

2.04: BREAK <process> [ALL|C|D|E|F]

1.3: BREAK <process> [ALL|C|D|E|F]

1.2: BREAK <process> [ALL|C|D|E|F]

Templates:

2.04: PROCESS/A, ALL/S, C/S, D/S, E/S, F/S

1.3: PROCESS/A, ALL/S, C/S, D/S, E/S, F/S

1.2: TASK/A, ALL/S, C/S, D/S, E/S, F/S

Path:

C:

Use:

Many AmigaDOS commands react to the break sequence CTRL-C. In order for this to work, however, the command must be running from an interactive window, that is, a CON: or NEWCON:. Commands launched using RUN will not respond to break because they will not (normally) have their own console. BREAK offers the solution – it sends the the equivalent of a break code (or sequence of codes) as if they had come from the console.

```
1>DIR
Trashcan (dir)
System (dir)                <CTRL-C pressed here>
*** Break ***

RUN DIR
[CLI 3]
Trashcan (dir)
System (dir)                <CTRL-C pressed here>
C
S
L                           <and here>
Libs
Devs
Fonts                       <and here ...>
```

The command cannot be stopped. However, if you open another CLI and issue the command BREAK 3 (the actual number may be different) – the listing would stop as before with the *** Break message. This is not a very useful example but it shows the effect clearly. It should be noted that BREAK needs to know the process number to be stopped; this value can be gleaned from the STATUS command.

The introduction of AmigaDOS 1.3 saw the STATUS command enhanced to allow named processes to be sought. This is directly relevant because it allows users to automate the use of BREAK, in scripts for instance:

```
STATUS >RAM:qwe COM=DIR      ; find the DIR command
BREAK >NIL: <RAM:qwe ALL ?   ; and send it a break
```

This may look a little odd, but it works. BREAK sees the "?" and puts up its command line options which are then redirected to the NIL: device. This puts the command in interactive mode and input is drawn from the file. QED!

Options:

PROCESS/A This argument must be supplied to BREAK and tells the command which process *number* to signal. This was incorrectly called "task" in the 1.2 release.

C/S Send a CTRL-C break – this is default. The options:
D/S, E/S, F/S
all work in exactly the same way.

ALL/S Send all four break codes.

The BREAK technique can be applied to scripts, as Commodore demonstrated in Workbench 1.3 which starts a second Startup-script while the first is running! In order to prevent task sharing from thrashing the disk drives up and down, the main script halts using WAIT for five minutes! At the end of the second script, BREAK stops WAIT in the first process. This seems a little pointless since the *first* script remains idle while the *second* runs. (This is discussed in more detail in *Mastering AmigaDOS 2 Volume One* – Startup-sequences.) For now though here is a neat little script to save typing the above example:

```
.key Command
.bra {
.ket }
STATUS >RAM:brk{$$} COM={Command}; find DIR command
BREAK >NIL: <RAM:brk{$$} ALL ?; and send it a break
```

This script just stops the first occurrence of the named CLI command and has proved its worth on many occasions.

Usage:

```
STOP <Command> ; (Set the S protection bit first!)
```

See also: EXECUTE, RUN, STATUS

BRU

Synopsis:

2.04: BRU -<C|D|E|G|H|I|T|X> [Control options] [Selection options] [files]

1.3: na

1.2: na

Templates:

2.04: specify mode (-cdeghitx)

1.3: na

1.2: na

Path:

Tools:

Use:

BRU is the Amiga's hard disk backup and restore utility, written by EST Inc. In many respects it is similar to the PD programs ZOO, ARC and LhARC – only much more powerful; powerful implies complex. BRU is so large that only the minimal options have been outlined here and the command has been given a section of its own in Volume 1. Basic usage is as follows.

To check how many disks are required:

```
1>STACK 50000   ; A large stack is essential
1>CD DHO:       ; for example
1>BRU -e        ; Estimate the number of disks
required
```

To back up a hard disk:

```
1>STACK 50000   ; A large stack is essential
1>CD DHO:       ; for example
1>BRU -c        ; Create new archive to default
drive
```

To restore a hard disk:

```
1>STACK 50000   ; A large stack is essential
1>CD DHO:       ; for example
1>BRU -x        ; Restore from default drive
```

Note: BRU formats disks as it goes, so there is no need to start with preformatted disks. You *must* keep a note of the number of each disk on the disk label since a complete backup could take more than 20 disks even for a small hard disk drive.

Options:

c Create a new archive using the specified files list.

d Check for differences between files already in the archive and the current files.

e Estimate the amount of disk space needed to create an archive with the specified files.

g Only give information from the archive header.

h Print extensive help information for BRU. We recommend that you send this output to a file which can be viewed at leisure using MORE or ED. That is:

```
BRU >RAM:Helpfile -h
ED RAM:HelpFile
```

i Check the named archive for consistency and integrity of data. Or, put another way, test the checksums.

t List the table of contents of files stored in the named archive.

x Extract file or files from the archive.

See also: COPY, DISKCOPY, *Mastering AmigaDOS 2 Volume One.*

CD

Synopsis:

2.04: CD [<directory>]

1.3: CD [<directory>]

1.2: CD [<directory>]

Templates:

2.04: DIR

1.3: DIR

1.2: DIR

Path:

Internal

C: <2.04

Use:

AmigaDOS operates under a hierarchical system of directories and CD stands for Change Directory, describing in a nutshell what this command does. As it turns out, the default action (with no parameters added) is to return the current directory. That is:

```
1>CD
Workbench1.3:devs/keymaps     ; where you are
```

With the introduction of the Shell (Workbench 1.3+) this function of CD was made largely obsolete because it is duplicated by the PROMPT command. There are times when it is still useful and it has been retained.

Changing directory is as simple as typing the name of the directory to move to – or the complete path. This is best explained by example thus:

```
1>CD DF0:             ; make df0: the current drive
1>CD pictures         ; enter the pictures drawer
1>CD SYS:Utilities    ; Move to boot disk, utilities
1>CD SYS:devs/keymaps    ; go to devs/keymaps
1>CD C:               ; go straight to C: (logical)
1>CD //devs           ; go to devs (indirectly)
```

Although these examples get more complex down the list, all but the last two should be obvious by now. CD C: makes the logical C (command directory) assignment the current directory. Thanks to ASSIGN this could be anywhere – not necessarily where you think it is! This is useful to know because it allows you to perform operations inside the system directories – as well as moving around the directories with remarkable ease.

The last example is more vague because it uses the directory separator "/". This symbol has another meaning to CD – move up one level of hierarchy. Each time the symbol is encountered, CD searches one level higher. Slash can be used many times and does not require a name.

New – AmigaDOS 2:

CD under the latest version of AmigaDOS allows the use of wildcard pattern matching in directory searches. This makes moving around the tree far simpler than ever before. Example:

```
1>CD SYS:devs/keymaps
```

becomes:

```
1>CD SYS:d#?/k#?
```

All the pattern matching options are available to CD but #? is the most useful.

Note: Changing between system directories no longer requires the use of CD! All you have to type now is the name of the directory (or logical assignment) and you're there! Here are just a few examples:

```
1>RAM:
1>CD
RAM Disk

1>FONTS:
1>CD
System2.04:Fonts

1>devs/keymaps
1>CD
System2.04:devs/keymaps
```

Any viable path can be used in this way making the whole system a lot faster to use. However, you *must not* specify wildcards in the name and the path must exist. If you need pattern matching, use CD. Also, when selecting disk drives, this feature expects to find the drive with a disk mounted. A small price to pay, we think.

Options:

DIR The new path or directory specification.

/ (Slash). Used as a separator or to move up one or more directory levels.

: (Colon). Used to denote the ROOT directory of the current drive.

See also: ASSIGN, PROMPT, *Mastering AmigaDOS 2 Volume One* – Understanding Directories.

CHANGETASKPRI

Synopsis:

2.04: CHANGETASKPRI <priority> [<process>]

1.3: CHANGETASKPRI <priority> [<process>]

1.2: CHANGETASKPRI <priority>

Templates:

2.04: PRI=PRIORITY/A/N, PROCESS/K/N

1.3: Pri/A, Process/K

1.2: Pri/A

Path:

C:

Use:

The Amiga is a multi-tasking machine and AmigaDOS is a multi-tasking disk operating system. It is important to realise the difference because, although the two go hand-in-hand, tasks are *not* the same as processes. This is an area where people frequently get confused. Any program started (launched) by AmigaDOS – or Workbench come to that – is a *process*. Processes are high-level functions which enjoy some privileges which are outside the remit of this manual.

Tasks on the other hand are much lower-level functions invisible to AmigaDOS (and you) without special software tools. The function CHANGETASKPRI should more accurately be called CHANGEPROCESSPRI which is what it does. Even so, a process is just a special form of task. The argument over the name could go on forever: but it's long enough already.

Every task, and therefore every process, has a priority which ranges (in theory anyway) from -128 to +127. This dictates how much time EXEC allocates to each task. In practice the range of priorities is much smaller, say from -5 for a low importance job to +20 for a hard disk SCSI handler. User processes should limit themselves still further to below about +5. If this limit is exceeded all sorts of things can start to go wrong – at worst the machine can seize up altogether. This command should be used with care.

With early versions of AmigaDOS this command only worked on the current CLI (or processes launched from it – siblings). Example:

```
1>CHANGETASKPRI 2           ; give me more time
```

A printer job is a background job of low speed – it doesn't need much time so:

```
1>CHANGETASKPRI -4        ; set priority of -4
1>RUN COPY RAM:texts/MyFile TO PRT:
                          ; start a printer job
1>CHANGETASKPRI 0         ; restore old priority
```

New – AmigaDOS 1.3:

From version 1.3 of AmigaDOS it is possible to allocate a priority to any running task. STATUS can be used to discover the task number required.

```
1>STATUS COM=DIR                ; who's doing DIR?
3                               ; aha, process #3!
1>CHANGETASKPRI -2 PROCESS=3    ; Less time for #3
```

Options:

PRI/A The new priority for the current process to run at. Range† +127..-128. Example to make this task "faster":

```
1>CHANGETASKPRI 1
```

† Useful range between –5 and +5

Options (>AmigaDOS 1.3):

PROCESS/K The process number to pass the new priority to. Note this is a keyword and must be supplied with the argument for the command to work. Example to give more time to task 2 (say a spreadsheet):

```
1>CHANGETASKPRI 4 PROCESS=2
```

See also: STATUS

CLICKTOFRONT

Synopsis:

2.04: CLICKTOFRONT [priority=<n>]

1.3: na

1.2: na

Templates:

2.04: CX_PRIORITY/K/N

1.3: na

1.2: na

Path:

Extras2: Tools/Commodities

Use:

This program solves another one of those annoying problems of working with windows: in order to bring a window to the front you have to find its depth gadget and click it. This can be a lot of bother and quite tricky if you have a lot of windows littering the desktop. Once CLICKTOFRONT is active, you can pull any window to the top of the pile by holding down either Alt key and double-clicking anywhere in the window. (AUTOPOINT can be useful here to ensure your pointer is in the activation rectangle.)

Basic usage is:

```
1>RUN CLICKTOFRONT
```

The program becomes active immediately. If you forget to enter RUN and get locked out of the Shell just press CTRL-E to quit and try again. If you wish to use this program from a Startup-sequence, you should use this version instead:

```
1>RUN >NIL: CLICKTOFRONT
```

That just makes sure the CLI window will close correctly when the startup script completes. This command should not be executed twice because the second invocation will QUIT the first and exit without starting itself. This feature is deliberate, but be aware of it.

Options:

CX_PRIORITY The priority passed to the program on startup. This is its priority over other CX programs – not the process priority shown by STATUS. By default all CX programs have a CX_PRIORITY of 0. Higher priority programs have the first grab at incoming messages – key presses and such like.

General Note – Commodities Exchange

The Commodities Exchange (CX) programs are normally stored on the Extras disk. However, to keep the examples simple, we'll assume you have already changed to the correct directory or set the correct path.

Important: Note that the CX programs *do not* return error conditions when an incorrect command line is entered. You can check they have launched correctly in scripts using STATUS.

See also: AUTOPOINT, BLANKER, EXCHANGE, FKEY, IHELP, NOCAPSLOCK

CLOCK

Synopsis

2.04: CLOCK [ANALOG or DIGITAL1 or DIGITAL2] [[=<X,Y>] [Width] [Height]] [12 or 24 Hour] [Seconds] [Date]

1.3: CLOCK [ANALOG or DIGITAL1 or DIGITAL2] [[=<X,Y>] [Width] [Height]] [12 or 24 Hour] [Seconds] [Date]

1.2: CLOCK [ANALOG or DIGITAL1 or DIGITAL2] [[=<X,Y>] [Width] [Height]] [12 or 24 Hour] [Seconds] [Date]

Templates:

2.04: [ANALOG | DIGITAL1 | DIGITAL2] [=<x>,<y>,[<width>,<height>]] [12HOUR | 24HOUR] [SECONDS] [DATE]

1.3: [ANALOG | DIGITAL1 | DIGITAL2] [=<x>,<y>,[<width>,<height>]] [12HOUR | 24HOUR] [SECONDS] [DATE]

1.2: [ANALOG | DIGITAL1 | DIGITAL2] [=<x>,<y>,[<width>,<height>]] [12HOUR | 24HOUR] [SECONDS] [DATE]

Path:

SYS:Utilities

Use:

CLOCK is a simple program to display an on-screen clock showing the current time (based on the system time) and optionally the date too. Three formats are available, an analogue variety is the default, but the two digital variations are much more useful to AmigaDOS users. CLOCK can be called from the Startup-sequence using:

```
RUN >NIL:.
```

To start the basic clock:

```
1>RUN CLOCK
```

Open a CLOCK display to fill the standard PAL (80 column) Workbench screen:

```
1>RUN CLOCK Analog=0,0,640,256
```

now add the seconds display:

```
1>RUN CLOCK Analog=0,0,640,256 seconds
```

A better clock for AmigaDOS usage:

```
1>RUN CLOCK DIGITAL2
```

Options:

ANALOG Note the American spelling. This option is default but must be supplied if you want to use X,Y co-ordinates. See examples.

DIGITAL1 If this option is specified, a small clock window appears at the top-left of the screen. A small space always appears below the time; and this is used for the optional date display.

DIGITAL2 This option forces Clock to display a clock on the menu bar at the right of the Workbench screen.

X and Y;=<x>,<y>
These arguments must be supplied together with one of those above. No spaces are permitted. X and Y are measurements in pixels from the Left and Top of the screen respectively.

,<width>,<height>
These arguments must follow X and Y settings and must not be separated by spaces. Measurement is in pixels and only affects the Analog mode.

12HOUR Selects 12 hour clock for digital display modes - default.

24HOUR Selects 24 hour clock for digital displays and suppresses the AM/PM display on the analog variety.

SECONDS Add this argument to the end of the command line if you want to display seconds. The argument is valid for all display modes.

DATE Add this argument to the command line to display the date. Date is displayed constantly on Analog and Digital1 modes or alternately in Digital 2.

CMD

Synopsis:

2.04: CMD <serial|parallel> <filename> [i] [s] [m] [n] [help]

1.3: CMD <serial|parallel> <filename> [i] [s] [m] [n] [help]

1.2: na

Templates:

2.04: [RUN] CMD devicename filename [opt i s m n]

1.3: [RUN] CMD devicename filename [opt i s m n]

1.2: na

Path:

SYS:Utilities

Use:

The Amiga's device infrastructure is based on some very hard and fast rules – it is these which enable utilities like CMD to be implemented. The purpose of this program is to grab output meant for either the printer or serial ports and send it back to a file. Incidentally, the name derives from the CMD_WRITE message sent to EXEC's device handlers which this program intercepts.

CMD with a Printer

CMD finds a use, for instance, when you want to produce a document for printing without actually having to print it yourself. This might be the case for those producing a disk-based magazine or a collection of PD software etc. You need a file which includes all the special printer control codes for things like *italic*, **bold** and so on. Most wordprocessors will not print to disk in this way – producing only 7-bit ASCII. CMD is the solution – here's how it works:

```
1>RUN CMD parallel RAM:print.me   ; multitask it!
[CLI 2]                  ; CLI confirms task running
1>COPY from MyBigDox to PRT: ; now start printing.
```

After a short while CMD responds:

```
Redirected nn bytes from parallel.device to
RAM:print.me
Cmd re-direction of parallel.device removed.
```

For this example we have simulated the use of a word processor by using COPY. Your software's normal print command will work in exactly the same way – provided that it obeys Commodore's conventions; most do. In the example output above 'nn' is the total number of bytes redirected.

CMD with the Serial Port

This is essentially exactly the same as for the printer port except that it works for serial transfers. You may find this useful for debugging problems with your comms software; then again, you may not. Installation is as follows:

```
1>RUN CMD serial RAM:send.me        ; multitask it!
[CLI 4]                             ; CLI confirms it
1>COPY from MyCommsPack to SER:
                                   ; now start sending
```

- If CMD is run without parameters it defaults to re-directing the parallel.device with the filename RAM:CMD_File

Options:

devicename	The device to patch with CMD. Default: parallel.device.
filename	The filename to send redirected device output to. Default: RAM:CMD_File – the case if run from the Workbench.
i	IGNORE: Using this option any file starting with four nulls is skipped.
s	SKIP: With this option in effect, any short initial writes, such as reset codes to the printer, are not redirected to the file.
m	MULTIPLE: By default CMD only works on one activation of the device it is tied to. Using this option CMD remains in effect until it receives a break code level C. Also, each file generated automatically has a unique number assigned to it.
n	NOTIFY: This option enables progress messages.
Help	HELP: Gives some extra help just in case you don't have this book to hand.

See also: BREAK, *Mastering AmigaDOS Volume One* – Devices.

COLORS

Synopsis:

2.04: COLORS [0|1|2|3]

1.3: na

1.2: na

Templates:

2.04: [planes mode]
(0=320 x 200, 1=64 x 200, 2=320 x 400, 3=640 x 400)

1.3: na

1.2: na

Path:

SYS:Tools

Use:

This is a simple command program that provides the facility to allow you to change the red, green and blue elements of the foremost screen. This is useful if an application does not provide such a facility.

Options:

0|1|2|3 COLORS only has one option – the planes mode. This appears to cover just basic NTSC resolutions and had no effect in all our tests! Note also, the American spelling of the command name. UK users can change this if they like – but remember to change the dot-info too if using CLI. Example:

```
1>COLORS
1>COLORS 3
```

Unless some use is discovered for this option, it's best left off – what the eyes don't see ...

See also: DISPLAY

CONCLIP

Synopsis:

2.04: CONCLIP [UNIT=<unit #>] [OFF]

1.3: na

1.2: na

Templates:

2.04: CONCLIP UNIT/K/N, OFF/S

1.3: na

1.2: na

Path:

C:

Use:

This command is normally started as part of the AmigaDOS 2 Startup-sequence and intended to provide the console (CON:) cut and paste operations. In fact, this facility is built into the 2.04 NEWSHELL command and is not usually required. Also, this command automatically starts its own asynchronous AmigaDOS process so it does not need to be RUN.

Options:

UNIT/K/N The console unit number to apply console clipboard facilities to. This is not usually used from the command line.

OFF Disable CONCLIP and remove it from the system. Only one CONCLIP process is possible at any time so the format is simply:

```
1>CONCLIP OFF
```

COPY

Synopsis:

2.04: COPY [FROM] <{name|pattern}> [TO] <name|pattern> [ALL] [QUIET] [BUF|BUFFER=nn] [CLONE] [DATE] [COM] [NOPRO]

1.3: COPY [FROM] <name|pattern> [TO] <name> [ALL] [QUIET] [BUF|BUFFER=nn] [CLONE] [DATE] [COM] [NOPRO]

1.2: COPY [FROM] <name|pattern> [TO] <name> [ALL] [QUIET]

Templates:

2.04: FROM/A/M, TO/A, ALL/S, QUIET/S, BUF=BUFFER/K/N, CLONE/S, DATE/S, COM/S, NOPRO/S

1.3: FROM, TO/A, ALL/S, Q=QUIET/S, BUF=BUFFER/K, CLONE/S, DATES/S, COM/S, NOPRO/S

1.2: FROM, TO/A, ALL/S, QUIET/S

Path:

C:

Use:

COPY, not surprisingly, is AmigaDOS's file duplication facility – even though, thanks to the machine's design, it can do much more than simply copy a file from one place to another. The basic format of the command could not be simpler:

```
1>COPY FROM "source file" TO "destination device:"
```

In this purely theoretical example, the FROM and TO options have been included for clarity and could be omitted; quotes have been used as separators – they need not be typed although they *must* be used if the destination or source file names include spaces. In general terms the inclusion of FROM and TO in command lines is purely personal taste, but we recommend they are used in scripts to enhance readability. The example above could have read:

```
1>COPY "source file" "destination device"
```

But this is less clear. These examples raise another point: that is, the destination device does not necessarily have to be a mass-storage unit like a disk drive. It can quite easily be any valid AmigaDOS device – physical or logical – some are more valid than others however. For this to work the device used must support write access. Here is an unusual instance:

```
1>COPY FROM SYS:S/Startup-Sequence TO CON:0/0/400/
200/Wow!
```

This opens a CON: window and copies the file "Startup-sequence" to it. A similar effect could be achieved by copying to the default console handle "*". Example:

```
1>COPY SYS:S/Startup-Sequence TO *
```

A more useful instance would be to copy a text file to the printer. Note: Don't try this unless you have a printer attached – and never attempt it with a binary (program/art/sound, etc.) file.

```
1>COPY SYS:S/Startup-Sequence PRT:
```

This example does the same thing but sends output to the printer. This technique can be easily combined with RUN to make use of the multitasking abilities of the Amiga.

Copying Multiple Files

It has already been mentioned that it's possible to copy more than one file using pattern matching. However, COPY provides an extra feature where one invocation of the command can copy several source files in one go – where pattern matching would not be suitable. The OR or bar character (|) is used to do this. Let's suppose you wanted to copy ASSIGN, COPY and MAKEDIR to RAM:. There is no fixed pattern in these names so you'd normally have to use COPY three times:

```
1>COPY COPY RAM:
1>COPY ASSIGN RAM:
1>COPY MAKEDIR RAM:
```

Using the bar character you can achieve the same effect for a fraction of the time and effort. We've used the optional "TO" keyword here to delimit the example:

```
1>COPY COPY|ASSIGN|MAKEDIR to RAM:
```

Pattern matching can be used in this way – in fact the two can be mixed if you require, here's a nice juicy example:

```
1>COPY DFO:C/M#?|C:ASSIGN|:Text to RAM:
```

You should be careful when mixing patterns in this way because the command can get confused. Remember, | is also used to mix patterns.

In AmigaDOS 2 the revised pattern matching requires that wildcards are grouped with parenthesis, ie:

```
1> COPY S:(sp#?|d#?) TO RAM:
```

Using COPY to Rename

AmigaDOS already has a renaming command – RENAME. This has the limitation that files cannot be renamed across devices. This is silly anyway, if you consider what it means. Instead you can use COPY to do the job for you since it can rename a file while it is being copied. Here's how:

```
1>COPY from RAM:My-Document to DF1:Chapter1
```

It is imperative to note here, that wildcards cannot be used for the source file for this type of copying. If they are used, AmigaDOS will assume a list of files is being copied to a new directory and create one on the destination. This is covered in more detail below.

Copying Directories

Copying a directory in AmigaDOS is a simple operation but the syntax for doing so is not as obvious as might at first appear. The problem stems from the fact that AmigaDOS tries to be all things to all men; and in its attempt to make things simpler they get more involved. This is no bad thing once you get used to it though. For instance – how do you copy the whole S: (logical) directory to RAM:?

```
1>COPY from S: to RAM:          ; try this yourself
```

What happens is this: AmigaDOS sees the directory and copies it to the RAM: disk file by file – which may have been what you wanted. It's certainly easier than using:

```
1>COPY from S:#? to RAM:
```

Which has precisely the same effect! But now try this:

```
1>COPY from S: to RAM:s
```

You might think – ah, but there's no S directory in RAM to copy to – and you'd be right. AmigaDOS thinks the same thing, naturally assumes that's what you intended to do in the first place, and creates the directory for you! This feature does not work in version 1.2.

This has its good and its bad points. On the plus side, this saves having to fiddle around creating the directories first. On the minus side: if you misspell a switch name, NPORO instead of NOPRO for instance, AmigaDOS creates a directory called NPORO then copies all the files into it! This can cause some unusual effects when copying large numbers of files quickly and is worth watching out for.

One other small point worth watching for is when attempting to copy directories with subdirectories, the subdirectories will *not* be created and copied unless you ask for them:

```
1>COPY from SYS:devs to RAM:devs
```

See the effect? This ignores the subdirectories KEYMAPS and PRINTERS. In order to copy all the files in their correct hierarchical order it is necessary to stipulate the ALL switch. To see this in action – how about this (albeit contrived) example. Here DEVS, KEYMAPS and PRINTERS are created – all files are copied: except the ones present in DEVS itself.

```
1>COPY from SYS:devs/(k#?|p#?) to RAM:devs ALL
```

One last point. You may remember, the * character is a pseudonym for the current console window allowing COPY to be used as a type command in special circumstances. AmigaDOS has another pseudonym for the current directory – "". this can be passed to copy as either a source or destination. Example:

```
1>CD                        ; find the current directory
RAM Disk:t
1>COPY from S:St#?-Se#? to"" ; now copy to it!
Startup-Sequence...Copied

1>COPY from "" to RAM:       ; copy files back too.
Startup-Sequence...Copied
```

Note: Using "" as a source is the same as using #? on the current directory – it's easier to type though.

New – AmigaDOS 2:

The advent of AmigaDOS 2 saw the introduction of the multi-argument command line parse and COPY is one of the commands to benefit from this. The syntax is exactly the same as for all previous examples except that now more than one source can be used. Again FROM and TO are optional:

```
1>COPY from File1 File2 File3 to RAM:
1>COPY from S:#? TEXTS:doc#? SOURCE:#?.C to PRT:
```

Options:

Note: The following examples all use FROM and TO in order to explicitly show what is going on – these are not required as keywords and can therefore be omitted if desired.

FROM/A — The source file, pattern, device or directory for COPY to take input from. A device can be just about any AmigaDOS device capable of generating output! PIPE:, CON: etc.

TO/A — The destination file, device, or directory to send copied output to. The device can be any AmigaDOS device capable of receiving input! CON:, PIPE:, PRT:, SER:, AUX: etc.

ALL/S — This facility copies ALL files from the source device to the destination – moving through the directory hierarchy. This should be used with some care since it can copy too much. Wildcards may be used to limit the search *but* these are used on subdirectory names, not individual files in those subdirectories. Example:

```
1>COPY from DEVS: to DF1: ALL
```

QUIET/S — This option suppresses output from COPY. It is mainly for use in script files. Example:

```
1>COPY from C:#? to RAM:c QUIET
```

This option should be used in preference to >NIL: since errors will be reported correctly. NIL: suppresses ALL output; QUIET only suppresses normal progress messages.

Options (>AmigaDOS 1.3):

BUF=BUFFER/K

This option defines the amount of temporary memory buffers used during the copy operation. Unlike ADDBUFFERS, this option caches files (or parts of them) *not* sectors. The default setting is 200 x 512byte buffers (100K) which is large enough for most operations. When copying files to the RAM: device the amount of buffer space can be reduced to decrease the likelihood of "Volume RAM: is full".

```
1>COPY from S:#? to RAM: BUF 50
```

CLONE/S — This switch is the same as using both DATE and COM options together. Example:

```
1>COPY from TOOLS:#? to DF1:c CLONE
```

DATES/S — If this switch is specified the copy of the file will retain the date and time stamp of the original. COPY defaults to stamping the file with the current settings.:

```
1>COPY from /S to :backups CLONE
```

COM=COMMENT/S

This switch is used expressly to ask COPY to retain any comments attached to the file using FILENOTE. It defaults to leaving files without a comment (to save disk space). Example:

```
1>COPY from S:#? to DF1:s COM
```

NOPRO/S — If this switch is used, COPY will use the default protection bits used for all files – RWED. The default is for the new file to adopt the bits of the old:

```
1>COPY from DF1:C to DF0:C NOPRO
```

This can be useful if you are copying command files to a temporary RAM: disk for instance and want to make sure the deletable flag is SET! This allows the script (or whatever) to clean up RAM: without having to fiddle around adding the DELETE flag.

Options (>AmigaDOS 2):

NOREQ — This switch is usually combined with the QUIET switch. It suppresses annoying requesters during the copying operation:

```
1>COPY from DF2:c to SYS:C quiet NOREQ
```

CPU

Synopsis:

2.04: CPU [CACHE] [BURST] [NOCACHE] [NOBURST] [DATACACHE] [DATABURST] [NODATACACHE] [NODATABURST] [INSTCACHE] [INSTBURST] [NOINSTCACHE][NOINSTBURST][FASTROM] [NOFASTROM] [TRAP] [NOTRAP] [NOMMUTEST] [CHECK=<fpu|mmu|68010|68020|68030|68040| 68881| 68882>]

1.3: na

1.2: na

Templates:

2.04: CACHE/S, BURST/S, NOCACHE/S,NOBURST/S, DATACACHE/S, DATABURST/S, NODATACACHE/S, NODATABURST/S, INSTCACHE/S, INSTBURST/S, NOINSTCACHE/S, NOINSTBURST/S, FASTROM/S, NOFASTROM/S, TRAP/S, NOTRAP/S, NOMMUTEST/S, CHECK/K

1.3: na

1.2: na

Path:

C:

Use:

CPU is intended for Amiga systems fitted with non-standard processor setups; any system fitted with a 68010 or above. Unless you have a third-party processor upgrade, (a 20-card for instance) this will only apply to the very latest machines like the A3000 and A3500. Even so, some of the information presented below may be of interest, if only as a matter of curiosity. At the time of writing this command is brand new to the Amiga system and very little accurate documentation exists for it, therefore the information supplied here is the result of experimentation and may be subject to change.

Overview of the Processors

68000: One word pre-fetch – constant tries to get the next instruction up while the current one is executing. This chaotic approach can actual slow down certain instructions.

68010: Two word pre-fetch – constant tries to get the next two instructions up while the current one is executing. Most effective in very short data transfer loops.

68020: 256-bytes instruction cache – speeds up long loops considerably. Not much general improvement in linear code.

68030: 256-byte instruction caches, plus 256-byte data cache. Like the 68020 but faster still. Enhances speed of linear code too.

68040: Twin-turbo version of 68030.

Note: The 68000 and 68010 are 16/32 bit processors while the 68020 and above are true 32-bit machines. This results in a most noticeable increase in speed.

Example Use:

If the command is run without any parameters it returns the current system settings, viz (on a vanilla A500):

```
>CPU
System: 68000  (INST: NoCache)
```

Whereas with the sort of system this command is intended for:

```
>CPU
System: 68030 68881 FastROM (INST: Cache Burst)
(DATA: Cache NoBurst)
```

The first two numbers indicate the processsor and floating point (if applicable) installed in the system. In this case: 68030 central processing unit (CPU) and 68881 floating point unit (FPU) sometimes called a maths co-processor – it means the same thing. Next up comes either FastROM or NoFastROM. This is used to indicate whether or not Kickstart has been copied into RAM – where it will run faster. Default on early systems is FastROM since Kickstart lives on the hard disk, not in ROM. If the machine is not fitted with a ROM Kickstart, this option cannot be turned off. The default setting on ROM Kickstart machines is likely to be NoFastROM. The remaining settings in brackets have a very large range of combinations. Each parameter is explained below.

INST: Cache	Instruction cache ON
INST: NoCache	Instruction cache OFF
INST: Burst	Instruction burst mode ON
INST: NoBurst	Instruction burst mode OFF
DATA: Cache	Data cache ON
DATA: NoCache	Data cache OFF
DATA: Burst	Data burst mode ON
DATA: NoBurst	Data burst mode OFF

Cache: The 68020/30/40 contain a small amount of on-chip memory which is used to store the last few instructions. This is used when the processor is executing a loop -the number of cached intructions in the loop depends on the processor. Using this method, the processor avoids the "fetch" cycle in loops, saving clock cycles, ram accesses, and therefore, time. This can result in a considerable increase in speed. It also precludes the use of "self-modifying code" used by some machine code programmers. The 68030 and 40 maintain a similar cache for data too.

Burst: Allows a much faster run access with certain (static column RAM) configurations.

Note: Data burst mode must be switched OFF for older expansion cards (designed for the Amiga 2000).

Options:

CACHE	Instruction and data caching are turned on.
BURST	Instruction and data burst mode are turned on.
NOCACHE	Instruction and data caching are turned OFF.
NOBURST	Instruction and data burst mode are turned OFF.
DATACACHE	Turn data cache ON, leave instruction cache unaffected.
DATABURST	Turn data burst mode ON, leave instruction burst mode unaffected.
NODATACACHE	Turn data caching OFF, leave instruction cache unaffected.
NODATABURST	Turn data burst mode OFF, leave instruction burst mode unaffected.
INSTCACHE	Turn instruction cache ON, leave data cache unaffected.
INSTBURST	Turn instruction burst mode ON, leave data burst mode unaffected.
NOINSTCACHE	Turn instruction caching OFF, leave data cache unaffected.
NOINSTBURST	Turn instruction burst mode OFF, leave data burst mode unaffected.
FASTROM	This option has no effect on machines with disk-based Kickstart. On ROM-based machines it copies Kickstart into RAM where it will work slightly faster. This requires an MMU to work.
NOFASTROM	This machine kills the effect of the FastROM switch, regaining user memory. It has no effect on machines with disk-based Kickstart.

TRAP	Sets up a trap handler which calls ROM-Wack (9600 baud serial debugger)† if any task accesses memory in the first 256 bytes or above the 16Mb range. This option is provided for developers *only* and should be avoided in normal use. At best the option will appear to have no effect, at worst it will cause a GURU.
NOTRAP	Switches the trap handler off.
NOMMUTEST	The effect of this switch is unknown.
CHECK	This keyword is used to check the system in scripts. It appears to check for the presence, type and integrity of the memory management unit, maths co-processor and CPU. If the specified unit is missing or inoperative, a WARN condition (RC=5) is returned. For example, to check for a 68882 co-processor:

```
CPU CHECK 68882
if warn
  echo "68882 missing or inactive"
endif
```

†Note: ROM-Wack is documented in the official documentation supplied by Commodore. Developers eager to try it should connect a 9600 baud 8-N-1 terminal (a PC will do at a pinch) to the serial port. When the power light starts flashing (just before the GURU starts to meditate) press the delete key on the remote – ASCII 127 – this triggers ROM-Wack. Press the ? key on the remote for help – be warned, there isn't much!

See also: 68000 series technical reference guide.

DATE

Synopsis:

2.04: DATE [<day>] [<date>] [<time>] [TO=VER <filename>]

1.3: DATE [<time>] [<date>] [TO=VER <filename>]

1.2: DATE [<time>] [<date>] [TO=VER <filename>]

Templates:

2.04: DAY, DATE, TIME, TO=VER/K/A

1.3: TIME, DATE, TO=VER/K

1.2: TIME, DATE, TO=VER/K

Path:

C:

Use:

The Amiga normally has two clocks – a battery-backed hardware unit, the other implemented in software. The A500 model is not supplied with a hardware clock as standard, but this is supplied with the "trapdoor" RAM expansion unit Commodore part# A501. Note: Some third-party RAM expansions do not feature a clock.

The purpose of DATE is to display or set the internal software clock; the hardware clock is discussed later in this section. DATE can also send the current date and time to the date stamp of a named file. This is usually left to SETDATE however. It should be noted also, that since the date sets only the software clock, any changes will not be retained after switching off.

For such a simple command, DATE has a surprising number of possibilities – some should be used with caution though. If the command is entered on its own it returns the current time and date. If date and/or time are supplied, the internal clock is reset. However, DATE can also take any of the following keywords too:

Yesterday, Tomorrow, Sunday, Monday, Tuesday, Wednesday, Thursday, Friday, Saturday.

These take the current date and work out the new date for you. All except "Yesterday" set the next possible date in advance of the current one. Keywords or dates can be mixed on the same command line as a file "touch" (using TO=VER) *but* the file receives the *current* date and time.

The format of the date and time in the UK and Canada is as follows:

DATE: DD-MMM-YY or DD/MMM/YY

TIME: HH:MM:SS

In America and some other countries an alternative is used:

DATE: MMM-DD-YY or MMM/DD/YY

Examples:

```
1>DATE
Saturday 07-Jul-90 09:43:09

1>DATE 10:42:20 9/jul/90
1>DATE
Monday 09-Jul-90 10:42:37

1>DATE 13:42
1>DATE
Monday 09-Jul-90 13:42:00

1>DATE yesterday
1>DATE
Sunday 08-Jul-90 13:43:19

1>DATE thursday
1>DATE
Thursday 12-Jul-90 13:44:25

1>DATE S/Startup-Sequence
1>LIST S/Startup-Sequence
Directory "Workbench1.3:s" on Thursday 12-Jul-90
Startup-Sequence           26---rw-d Today 13:50:23
1 file - 2 blocks used
```

Options:

DAY — Sets the current date to the DAY specified as a word. Unless "yesterday" or the current day is specified the new date is set in the future relative to current date.

DATE — The argument for the new date. Dates must be punctuated by hyphen or minus symbols (–). Months are supplied as the first 3 letters of the month name. Viz: Jun, Jan, Dec, etc. Invalid dates like 29-Feb-90, fail with returncode 20. In version 1.2 only, leading zeros must be supplied.

TIME — The new time. Takes an argument as HH:MM:SS or HH:MM if you do not want to supply seconds. In version 1.2 only leading zeros must be supplied.

TO=VER — This should be supplied as a keyword if the date command is being used in conjunction with SET DATE to "touch" a file's datestamp. If the file does not exist on the specified path it is created as a ASCII file consisting of DATE's output. This feature may be useful in scripts and prevents the need to use a redirection operator. This example uses the feature to add a date and time stamp inside an existing text file. A line by line breakdown of how this works has not been included for this simple example, beginners should study the chapters on scripts in Volume One.

```
.key MyFile/A,NewFile/A
.bra {
.ket }
ECHO >ram:1 "Created on: " NOLINE
DATE TO ram:2
JOIN ram:1 ram:2 {MyFile} AS {NewFile}
DELETE ram:1 ram:2
```

See JOIN for a better, multitasking version.

See also: SETDATE, SETCLOCK

DELETE

Synopsis:

2.04: DELETE <{name|pattern}> [ALL] [Q|QUIET] [FORCE]

1.3: DELETE <name|pattern>... [ALL] [Q|QUIET]

1.2: DELETE <name>... [ALL] [Q|QUIET]

Templates:

2.04: FILE/A/M, ALL/S, Q=QUIET/S, FORCE/S

1.3: ,,,,,,,,, , ALL/S, Q=QUIET/S

1.2: ,,,,,,,,, , ALL/S, Q=QUIET/S

Path:

C:

Use:

Briefly, DELETE attempts to erase the file(s) you specify. But read the following caveat carefully!

This is it folks: potentially the most dangerous command AmigaDOS provides. Even FORMAT (which is not strictly, AmigaDOS) offers some recourse before it completely "nukes" a disk. Under 1.2 DELETE was not too bad – but with advent of 1.3 and beyond it has become a veritable nightmare leaving destruction in its wake. The problem – especially for beginners is two-fold:

- First, there is a temptation to use pattern matching – which is fine provided the pattern only matches the files required. All too often it includes others too.
- Second, there is no going back, no escape route, no back doors. Once a file has gone it has gone for good. The file rescue utilities available in the Public Domain can sometimes recover things but many do not work on hard disks or with FFS. DISKDOCTOR supplied with AmigaDOS does not recover accidental deletions either. Even experts get it wrong sometimes so *take care.* Hint: test a pattern first using DIR!

The general format of the command allows from one to ten files to be deleted in one go. As always the complete path must be stated *unless* the file exists in the current directory. It is not possible to delete a subdirectory that already contains files unless the ALL switch is specified. Example:

```
1>DELETE temp          ; erase the file temp
```

Multifile deletes (deletes ALL) can be aborted using the CTRL+C break combination either from the keyboard or via BREAK.

- AmigaDOS does not offer an interactive version of DELETE (even in version 2!). If that is what you require DIR's interactive mode will usually suffice. See DIR for more details.

New – AmigaDOS 1.3:

Pattern matching was introduced in AmigaDOS 1.3 giving rise to the warning above. Example:

```
1>DELETE RAM:#?Doc#?   ; erase anything with "Doc"
RAM DISK:AmigaDoc1...deleted
RAM DISK:MyDoc...deleted
RAM DISK:Doc2...deleted
```

Multifile deletes using pattern matching or the ALL switch can be aborted using the CTRL+C break combination either from the keyboard or via BREAK.

Note: When attempting to erase a file containing a pattern matching string the escape character must be used to explicitly name the file or unexpected results can occur. The following example assumes you have a file named START#? in your S directory. This may have been produced by mistake, but attempting to erase it using DELETE would mean all files in the S directory starting with "START" would go. By definition this means the Startup-sequence script!

```
1>DIR S:start#?
Startup-sequence
START#?
1>DELETE start'#?
START#?...deleted
```

Notice the use of the escape character " ' " called tick or apostrophe. This switches off AmigaDOS pattern matching temporarily and comes in very useful in such situations. This is covered in more detail in the section on pattern matching in Volume One, but its inclusion here was felt necessary for reasons which should now be obvious.

New – AmigaDOS 2:

From AmigaDOS 2, DELETE uses the new command parser allowing any number of names or patterns to be used on the command line:

```
1>DELETE RAM:#? DF1:T/docs/tmp#? Myfile An_Other QUIET
```

Options:

ALL/S — This switch should be used with great care. It searches down through the directory hierarchy from where you are and deletes everything it comes to – unless the named files are protected from deletion. This is the only way to remove directories which contain files. Example:

```
1>DELETE DF2: ALL    ; wipe DF2:!
```

This would have been easier using format. Pattern matching can override the action of this switch to some degree – but again must be used with some care:

```
1>DELETE RAM:tem#? ALL
```

This example would delete any files starting with "tem" in the current directory. However, if it finds a directory starting with "tem" it will enter it and delete ALL the files it contains including directories. The pattern, therefore, is only valid for the current path.

QUIET/S With this switch in place DELETE generates no output. It finds use, for instance, in scripts when the program is cleaning up temporary files. Example:

```
DELETE RAM:tmp{$$}#? QUIET        ; Script use
1>DELETE RAM:tmp#? QUIET          ; Shell use
1>                                ; no output!
```

New – AmigaDOS 2:

FORCE/S Forces DELETE to remove files even if they have been protected against deletion with PROTECT. This is useful in scripts for example, to delete temporary work command directories. Commands copied from C: for instance may have been delete protected (which is wise) *but* removing temporary copies from RAM: can be a pain. (COPYing with the NOPRO option is another way around this – but it does *not* work for autoexecuting scripts.)

```
1>DELETE RAM:C/#? FORCE ; force deletion
```

This option *does not* work if the object is in use or is a directory which contains one or more files.

See also: DIR, PROTECT

DIR

Synopsis:

2.04: DIR [<dir|pattern>] [OPT A|I|AI|D|AD|F|AF] [ALL] [DIRS] [INTER] [FILES]

1.3: DIR [<dir|pattern>] [OPT A|I|AI|D|AD|F|AF] [ALL] [DIRS] [INTER] [FILES]

1.2: DIR [<dir|pattern>] [OPT A|I|AI|D|AD]

Templates:

2.04: DIR, OPT/K, ALL/S, DIRS/S, INTER/S, FILES/S

1.3: NAME, OPT/K, ALL/S, DIRS/S, INTER/S, FILES/S

1.2: DIR, OPT/K

Path:

C:

Use:

DIR is one of the most used commands in AmigaDOS – not altogether surprising considering it is the main way to find out a disk's contents. (What is more surprising though, is that it has been left in the C directory with release 2 and not made internal like so many of its brethren.) But saying DIR is only for listing a disk's contents is like saying you should drive an XR3i at 70mph. The metaphorical difference between the two, in case you haven't guessed, is it's legal with DIR.

DIR is used to get a sorted list of files from any disk, disk-like device, directory, logical assignment or path. Examples:

```
1>DIR                ; list the current directory
1>DIR df0:           ; list files on drive 0
1>DIR SYS:           ; root directory of boot disk
1>DIR S:             ; The S assignment
1>DIR :              ; This disk's root directory
1>DIR devs           ; devs sub-dir from root ONLY
1>DIR :devs/keymaps ; keymaps (from anywhere)
```

The output from DIR can be paused by pressing the spacebar and resumed by pressing backspace. The output can be terminated by pressing CTRL+C. Pattern matching can also be used to limit the output.

Examples:

```
1>DIR C:L#?              ; Commands starting with "L"
1>DIR S:#?-sequence      ; Startup scripts
1>DIR docs/chapt(2?|3?) ; Chapters 20+ & 30+
```

New – AmigaDOS 1.3:

The only change to the command was the introduction of pseudonyms: INTER, ALL, and DIRS to replace the OPT keyletters. These are explained below with the switch options. Also the FILES switch was added.

Options:

DIR — The argument which specifies the directory for the command to work on. Default for DIR is to search the current directory (and any levels below in the hierarchy if requested). DIR can be supplied as a keyword if required. Example:

```
DIR DIR=C:
```

ALL/S (opt A) — This switch puts DIR into a hierarchical search mode causing it to list all subdirectories below the specified path. It is important to realise therefore, that to get a list of all the files on a disk, it is necessary to either set the current directory to the root or to specify root in the path. Examples:

```
1>DIR OPT A          ; AmigaDOS 1.2
1>DIR ALL            ; AmigaDOS 1.3+
```

If a pattern matching search is used with this switch, only files and subdirectories in the current directory will be found. Files and subdirectories deeper in the hierarchy are *not* affected by the pattern.

DIRS/S (opt D) — This switch causes DIR to list just the subdirectories on the current path. It may be used with the ALL switch, if required, to list all subdirectories in the tree. Examples:

```
1>DIR OPT D               ; AmigaDOS 1.2
1>DIR DIRS                ; AmigaDOS 1.3+
1>DIR OPT AD              ; AmigaDOS 1.2
1>DIR DIRS ALL            ; AmigaDOS 1.3+
```

INTER/S (opt I) — This option can be very useful – it can also be very confusing until you get used to it. It puts DIR into interactive mode and, as we shall see later, probably explains why DELETE has no query option. Interactive mode has many options in its own right – these are explained below. The ALL switch may be specified for this command in all versions of AmigaDOS. Examples:

```
1>DIR OPT I               ; AmigaDOS 1.2
1>DIR INTER               ; AmigaDOS 1.3+
1>DIR OPT AI              ; AmigaDOS 1.2
1>DIR INTER ALL           ; AmigaDOS 1.3+
```

The various command keys recognised by the INTER option are listed and explained below.

B BACK: This ties to the ENTER option described below. It allows you to leave the sub–directory entered and go back to the previous level. This option is not available if:

•No sub-directories have been entered.

•The sub-directory has already run out of entries and the command has nipped back down the "tree".

DEL DELETE: Delete the file at the prompt. This command will fail if the file is protected from deletion and will kill the interactive directory listing. From release 1.3 commands can be executed from interactive DIR (see below) and this feature should be used to ensure the correct protection bits are set first!

C COMMAND: This option is only available from 1.3 onwards. It allows you to execute just about any general purpose command from within the interactive DIR. If C is entered on its own, DIR prompts for a command string. However, the command can be entered directly by enclosing it in quotes. Example:

```
1>DIR RAM: INTER
clipboards (dir) ?
env (dir) ?C "protect #? +d" ; enable deletes
```

Three caveats go hand-in-hand with this option:

1: *Never* issue a FORMAT from interactive mode. If this happens this disk will start formatting whilst another AmigaDOS task is trying to read it. This is like trying to read a newspaper while someone else sets fire to it!

2: Do not start another interactive DIR from here as the outputs will become unintelligible. This would be like two people trying to watch two different channels on the same TV.

3: If you must start another interactive command, start a new Shell first and then start the second interactive command from there.

E ENTER: At any (dir)? prompt this option can be used to enter the sub-directory and examine its contents. Similarly, if this directory also contains directories they too can be entered.

Q QUIT: This terminates interactive directory mode and returns you back to the command line. BREAK or CTRL+C can achieve the same effect.

T TYPE: Works just like the type command from AmigaDOS (although the extra command line options are not available). This should be used with care - typing a binary file to the console can have some curious effects.

? HELP. This works in exactly the same way as its counterpart in the rest of AmigaDOS. That is, it gives you a short aid-memoire to which commands are available. Of course, since you have *Mastering AmigaDOS Volumes One and Two* to hand at all times – you'll never need this option...

Options (>AmigaDOS 1.3):

FILES/S This switch is the direct opposite to DIRS – it causes DIR to list just the files on the specified path. This switch may be used with ALL to list all the files including those in subdirectories. If this is in effect the names of the subdirectories are suppressed. Examples:

```
1>DIR FILES         ; only list files on path
1>DIR FILES ALL     ; list ALL files
```

New – AmigaDOS 2

When DIR is used with a pattern which does not match any entries in the specified path it fails with error 232: no more entries in directory. This normally only affects scripts, and if it causes a problem, prefer LIST instead.

See also: CD, LIST, *Mastering AmigaDOS 2 Volume One* – Introducing Directories.

DISKCHANGE

Synopsis:

2.04: DISKCHANGE <device>:

1.3: DISKCHANGE <device>:

1.2: DISKCHANGE <device>:

Templates:

2.04: DRIVE/A

1.3: dev/A

1.2: dev/A

Path:

C:

Use:

In brief, DISKCHANGE informs AmigaDOS that a disk has been inserted into one of the "dumb" drives attached to it. This command only affects standard 5 1/4" units used mainly for the MS-DOS side and for some types of "removable media" unit – like a tape streamer. For these reasons, few of you will ever need to use it. The command only takes one argument – the drive number. Example:

```
1>DISKCHANGE DF1:   ; Tell AmigaDOS about the new disk
```

The command may also be used if you use RELABEL to change a disk's name and want to inform Workbench without having to remove and reinsert the disk. For the curious, the reasons behind all this are explained below. Most of you will neither need nor want this complication – just remember it works like that.

The Amiga design can accept several types of disk drive and AmigaDOS makes very few bones about how those drives are accessed. This is all due to some rather clever programming in the heart of Kickstart which we won't be covering here. Most Amiga floppy drives use a standard which allows the machine to sense when a disk is inserted or removed. The constant, irritating, clicking made by the drives is caused by the Amiga stepping the head of each in turn to find out if a disk has been inserted. This process is called polling.

The reason for the head movement is a feature of the drive – not the machine. Amiga drives are based on a modified version of the Shugart interface. This is a standard used the world over and one of the few that seems to actually work in practice – almost all micro-based drives use it. The problem (for the technically minded only) is this: The Shugart interface has a logic line to say a disk is present. When the disk is removed the line goes to logic 1 and is latched there. When a new disk is inserted the latch has to be reset before the line goes logic 0 – and the only way to do that is send a step pulse.

When the hardware senses that a disk has been inserted it wakes up Trackdisk (part of EXEC) – which in turn also sends a message to Intuition – which then passes it to anyone needing to know. This Intuition message DISKINSERTED is used by Workbench to recognise when disks are mounted. It is also the call intercepted by viruses (albeit, usually at a lower level) so they know when to replicate themselves.

Options:

DRIVE/A The only argument supplied to this command is required for it to work. The drive number is supplied as a device name and takes the form DF0:...DF3:.

```
DISKCHANGE DF1:
```

See also: RELABEL

DISKCOPY

Synopsis:

2.04: DISKCOPY [FROM] <drive>: [TO] <drive>: [NAME=<name>] [NOVERIFY] [MULTI]

1.3.2: DISKCOPY [FROM] <drive>: <TO> <drive>: [NOVERIFY] [MULTI] [NAME <name>]

1.3: DISKCOPY [FROM] <drive>: <TO> <drive>: [NAME <name>]

1.2: DISKCOPY [FROM] <drive>: <TO> <drive>: [NAME <name>]

Templates:

2.04: FROM/A, TO/A, NAME/K, NOVERIFY/S, MULTI/S

1.3.2: [FROM] <disk> TO <disk> [NOVERIFY] [MULTI] [NAME <name>]

1.3: [FROM] <disk> TO <disk> [NAME <name>]

1.2: [FROM] <disk> TO <disk> [NAME <name>]

Path:

SYS:System

Use:

DISKCOPY does just what its name implies – it copies disks. This command receives much less attention than it should, yet in reality, it is one of the most important on the whole Amiga system. There is no adequate way to describe the importance of DISKCOPY, but without it, it is possible to get into some very sticky situations. Just imagine what would happen if the Workbench disk failed for whatever reason. The Amiga would be rendered useless – in effect you could do nothing other than just play games!

It is possible to copy an entire disk using FORMAT and COPY, but this is a longwinded way of doing it. DISKCOPY blithely copies the complete disk track by track. It will not, however, copy protected disks. This is the reason they are protected after all! Neither will it copy a faulty disk – if this happens, the only recourse is to use DISKDOCTOR and COPY. However, if you had made good use of DISKCOPY in the first place there should be no need for this action. The fact is: In practice, very few of us ever do.

DISKCOPY is a remarkably easy command to use – as the examples below illustrate, it prompts the user at every step. The only point to note is that a drive device must be specified – not a volume name! Single drive copies may require several disk swaps on machines with less than 1Mb total RAM. DISKCOPY formats new disks during the copy process; there is no need to initialise them first.

Examples:

Using DISKCOPY with a single drive:

```
1>DISKCOPY DF0: to DF1:
Place SOURCE disk ( FROM disk ) in drive DF0:
Press RETURN to continue
reading xx, xx to go:
```

After the disk has finished reading, insert the new disk:

```
Place DESTINATION disk ( TO disk ) in drive DF0:
Press RETURN to continue
writing xx, xx to go:
```

Using DISKCOPY with dual drives:

```
1>DISKCOPY DF0: to DF0:
Place SOURCE disk ( FROM disk ) in drive DF0:
Place DESTINATION disk ( TO disk ) in drive DF1:
Press RETURN to continue
reading xx, xx to go:
```

- Dual drive DISKCOPYing is not possible between different disk capacities or drives of different type. You can DISKCOPY to the RAD: RAM disk provided it has been configured with the correct number of cylinders. DISKCOPYing between identical partitions of a hard disk is possible but not recommended.

CAUTION: Once you start a Shell you leave the protected environs of the Workbench. When a process is started from Workbench, it is impossible to diskcopy onto the disk the process was started from, without your consent. The same goes for any disks another process "owns". This is *not* true of Shell. If you issue a DISKCOPY the command will proceed without any warnings that something else is using the disk! The possible results range from inconvenience to disaster. If in doubt, use Workbench.

Note #1 DISKCOPY does an exact track by track copy – *but* at the end of a successful copy, the duplicate disk is given a unique prototype ID number. This is used by the system to identify which disks are in what drives and allows several otherwise unique disks to be mounted at once. Some "fast" DOS copiers do not modify the ID number potentially causing some very queer effects.

Note #2 The command can be multitasked but it should be run from a different Shell to the one in use. It can be started using RUN but this is not advisable because the output from the command smashes what is typed at the console. There is a way around this problem, of course, and for those with a thirst for the ridiculous, here's how to do it:

```
1>RUN DISKCOPY >CON:0/0/400/50/diskcopy DF0: to DF1:
```

The output redirection goes to the new console window so this prevents DISKCOPY treading all over what you are trying to type. The snag is input still comes from the original Shell console – so you have to press return a couple of times to get the command started. Re-direction to NIL: has much the same effect only you get even less information and the copy process begins *immediately!*

```
1>RUN DISKCOPY >NIL: DF0: to DF1:
```

Do not try this unless you are ready to start, DISKCOPY is in the RAM: disk and the PATH is set correctly. This is a dangerous but very effective method.

New - AmigaDOS 1.3.2:

This was one of several commands to receive a revamp in this release. It does not work correctly when operated from the Workbench environment. The main internal changes were as follows:

- Single drive copy on a 1Mb CHIP RAM machine works correctly.
- The command now uses FAST RAM if there is not enough CHIP available.
- Result2 is set correctly.
- Error messages are more informative.
- If the operation fails, the faulty cylinder number is displayed.
- The icon.library is only opened if required.

Note #3 This was one of several commands to receive a revamp in Workbench 1.3.2. It does not work properly when operated from the Workbench environment.

Options:

NAME With the name keyword, the destination disk can be given any name - subject to the usual AmigaDOS conventions and restrictions. Spaces are allowed, but the name string must be enclosed in quotes. Example:

```
1>DISKCOPY DF0: to DF1: NAME "MyDISK"
```

Options (>AmigaDOS 1.3.2):

NOVERIFY By default, DISKCOPY will attempt to verify that what is on the destination exactly reflects what is on the source. This process takes time – in effect, it has to read the complete disk. This switch turns verification OFF. We do not recommend this practice.

MULTI† DISKCOPY only tries to copy a single disk. If this switch is specified, it will make multiple copies of the source disk until the operation is aborted with CTRL+C (during duplication) or CTRL+D (after). This switch may be mixed with NOVERIFY to achieve a fast turnaround. We do not recommend this – however tempting it may be.

† This command doesn't work correctly under 1.3.2.

Note: in AmigaDOS 2, "TO" is no longer a keyword. Therefore the following is legal:

```
DISKCOPY DF0: DF1:
```

See also: BRU, COPY, FORMAT, *Mastering AmigaDOS 2 Volume One*

DISKDOCTOR

Synopsis:

2.04: DISKDOCTOR <drive>:

1.3: DISKDOCTOR <drive>:

1.2: DISKDOCTOR <drive>:

Templates:

2.04: DRIVE/A

1.3: DRIVE/A

1.2: DRIVE/A

Path:

C:

Use:

Disks go wrong – this is a fact of life. It is also the reason why we have spent a lot of time explaining DISKCOPY (above). However, mistakes can be made, and there are times when a copy of a file is either locked up in an archive somewhere or, perish the thought, a unique original. The latter can happen when the Amiga, for reasons known only to itself (or the local electricity board) decides to crash during a save operation. DISKCOPY is the AmigaDOS equivalent of an ambulance. It can help but only if it gets there in time. You should use DISKDOCTOR as soon as a disk starts to show any signs of getting "crabby". A typical example would be a requester stating:

```
KEY <nn> invalid, disk structure corrupt,
use diskdoctor to correct it.
```

It can even salvage disks when they have been partially formatted – ie, with format's QUICK option!

The syntax could not be simpler:

```
1>DISKDOCTOR df0:        ; fix disk in drive 0.
```

Before reading further – a few cautions:

- DISKDOCTOR should only be used as a last resort – it is meant for single drive machines and therefore cannot take advantage of a second drive. This implies that it has to work on the broken disk – and if anything should happen – poof. There are some more effective disk salvage utilities around for those lucky enough to own two drives. One of the best, Dave Haynie's excellent DISKSALV is included on the optional disk available with *Mastering AmigaDOS Volume One.*
- DISKDOCTOR should be used with extreme caution on FFS disks. For most users this will be a hard disk and it is vital to ensure the DOSTYPE keyword in the Mountlist (in DEVS:) is

correctly set to 0x444F5301 (ASCII for DOS1). Never use the DISKDOCTOR on a hard disk or other FFS disk unless you have checked the DOSTYPE!

The following errors and messages may be generated by DISKDOCTOR. We have arranged them in alphabetical order to ease location – you may, therefore, have to read the section more than once to grasp the meaning of some errors. The errors/messages are explained as if they had just happened:

ATTENTION: Some file in directory <name> is unreadable and has been deleted.

- A file in subdirectory <name> has been so totally corrupted by something it is now totally unreadable and even DISKDOCTOR can't find out what it was called. Files in this state can't be salvaged and are therefore discarded by the program.

Block zero failed to format – Sorry!

- In very dire circumstances track 0 may fail to format – which spells a seriously damaged disk. If this happens the disk is probably beyond saving (by DISKDOCTOR at any rate).

Cannot write root block – Sorry!

- Another fatal error insofar as DISKDOCTOR is concerned – it cannot recreate the disks root block – from which all other files are found.

Device <name> not found

- The device <name> could not be found or does not exist. This is usually caused by a typo. Have you entered the device name correctly?

DiskDoctor cannot be run in the background

- DISKDOCTOR is an interactive command and running it in the background would be silly. If you must multitask it, open another Shell window.

Disk must be write enabled

- DISKDOCTOR wants to write all over the source disk – that's the way it works after all. First make sure you are doctoring the right disk then close the "write enable" shutter.

Disk type mismatch – formatting block zero

- The disk ID is something AmigaDOS doesn't recognise. DISKDOCTOR is about to trash the track and start from scratch. This sort of damage is typical of virus infection but has other causes.

Delete corrupt files in dir <name>?

- DISKDOCTOR has found some dodgy files in the subdirectory <name>. You have the chance to leave them untouched or get rid of them. Command files should be discarded – it is unlikely they will work again. Text, picture and sound files may be recoverable and can be left for later examination.

Error: Unable to access disk

- This is just another way of saying: "Excuse me, but you forgot to put a disk in – just thought you'd like to know. . ."

Failed to read key <nn>

- Block <nn> could not be read – this was probably due to a hard error during the scan.

Failed to rewrite key <nn>

- Block <nn> could not be rewritten to the disk. The most likely cause is a physical error on the disk.

Hard error track <nn>

- Track <nn> appears to be physically damaged in some way. Recovery from this is not generally possible in DISKDOCTOR.

Inserting dir <name>

- Sub–directory <name> has been salvaged and is now being placed in the root directory.

Inserting file <name>

- File <name> has been recovered and is now being placed in the root directory. This happens when the subdirectory <name> belonged to has been destroyed by an error.

Key <nn> of <name> is out of range

- The block <nn> belonging to file <name> exceeds the range allowed for the device. This pointer error may be partially recoverable if DISKDOCTOR can find other fragments of the same file.

Key <nn> is unreadable

- The block could not be read – this block probably lives in a sector with a hard error.

Not enough memory

- DISKDOCTOR does not have enough memory to operate. In the unlikely event of this happening, shut down as many processes as possible or, preferably, reboot the machine. A curious bug in the program also causes this error when an invalid device name is specified: PAR:, SER: etc.

Now copy files to a new disk and reformat this disk

- This is DISKDOCTOR's handshake. It has done all it can to save the patient and now leaves you in charge of picking up the bits and salvaging what you can.

Parent key of <nn> is <yy> which is invalid

- The block <nn> cannot be connected to the list because its parent block <yy> has been irreparably damaged.

Replacing dir <name>

- The sub-directory <name> has been unaffected by any errors present on the disk and it is being reinstated where it was.

Replacing file <name>

- The file <name> has been unaffected by any errors present on the disk and it is being reinstated to its original position.

Root track failed to format – Sorry!

- The root track (39, upper side) is where all the main directory information lives on a disk. DISKDOCTOR has tried to format it in an attempt to pick up the bits and failed. It can do no more.

Unable to read disk type formatting block zero

- Block zero contains information like the boot sector and the disk type. If this information is missing due to a faulty track, DISKDOCTOR tries to format it and start over.

Unable to open disk.device

- This should never happen. The trackdisk.device is part of Kickstart and must already be open for the disks to be working.

Unable to write root – formatting root track

- There is a read/write error at the root track so DISKDOCTOR is going to reformat it. The disk will be renamed Lazarus – demonstrating its author's curious sense of humour.

Unexpected end of file

- Some file scanned turned out to be shorter than it should have been. Caused by a length error in the file's header block. Likely to be the result of a virus or user's meddling.

Unknown device <name>

- You have supplied a device <name> which is not attached to the system. Probably caused by a typo. Check that you have named the device correctly.

Warning: File <name> contains unreadable data

- A block or blocks belonging to <name> are on tracks affected by an error on the disk. This is fatal in many cases.

Warning: Loop detected at file <name>

- Some block pointers in <name> have become circular. This means the parent block (for instance) points to the child and the child points straight back at its parent. An attempt to read the file would result in the disk head continually thrashing between the two. Probable cause is virus or plain fiddling.

<name> is not a device

- DISKDOCTOR recognises <name> but reckons it isn't a device.

Nothing noticeable has changed between the 1.2, 1.3 and 2.04 commands, except the later versions work slightly better. From 1.3 onwards DISKDOCTOR can be used on the recoverable ramdrive.device – RAD:.

See also: The Mastering AmigaDOS 2 Volume One Programs Disk.

DISPLAY

Synopsis:

2.04: DISPLAY [[<file>]|[from=<file>]] [m|l|b|p|e|n|v] [t=n]

1.3: na

1.2: na

Templates:

2.04: <file> or from <file> opt <m>ouseadvance <l>oop <b>ack <p>rint <e>hb <n>otransb <v>ideo t=seconds

1.3: na

1.2: na

Path:

SYS:Utilities

Use:

This is one of those smashing little utilities the Amiga should have been supplied with years ago. At long last Commodore has provided a standard utility to display Amiga screen files and even produce simple slideshows, without having to resort to Shareware or Public Domain software. DISPLAY can be used to show any IFF compatible picture simply by specifying its name and path (if any). Once displayed, the picture can be "closed" by clicking once in the top left of the screen. slideshows can be created by specifying a list of pictures.

For example, to show a simple picture on the screen:

```
1>DISPLAY DRAWING
```

Creating a simple slideshow is almost as easy. This example creates the slideshow control file for you. Let's assume you have a directory of pictures called SHOTS:

```
1>LIST DF1:shots LFORMAT "%s%s" TO RAM:list
1>DISPLAY from RAM:list OPT LT=10
```

In this example we have used two extra options (outlined in more detail below) to provide a continuous slideshow with a ten second delay between each picture. The show can be stopped at any time using CTRL+D. Pressing CTRL+P causes the picture to be "dumped" to the default printer. Note, this uses the Preferences printer drives, so you should ensure that your printer is set correctly before starting!

Options:

FROM This keyword must be followed by the name of a file containing a list of pictures to display.

M Mouseadvance
When this option is specified, DISPLAY waits for a mouse click before progressing to the next picture. Left button goes to the next picture in the show, right button, the previous. Mouseadvance may be combined with the timed parameter to give an automatic display after a fixed amount of time.

L Loop
Repeat the display script in a loop until stopped with CTRL+D. This option can be used either on its own or with any combination of time and mouseadvance. Ideal for simple slideshows, for instance:

```
1>DISPLAY from DF1:show OPT L T=15
```

B Backdrop
Force the display screen behind all others – including Workbench. Used primarily while the Print option is in effect. See Print for an example.

P Print
Print the displayed picture. This can be triggered by pressing CTRL+P while the picture is displayed. If you're using this option to print a series of pictures in the background, the B option may also be specified, for example:

```
1>DISPLAY from DF1:show OPT PB
```

E EHB
Switch to extra half-brite mode. Forces screen selection into EHB.

N Notransb
Disable transparent backgrounds. Affects genlocking equipment only. See also OPT V.

V Video
Select video mixing mode. See also OPT N.

T Time
Wait for a specified time in seconds before showing the next picture in the sequence. This option can be combined with Mouseclick to give a timed display with mouse override. This example sets a 30 second delay between pictures with a mouse override:

```
1>DISPLAY from pix opt M T=30
```

See also: COLORS

DPAT

Synopsis:

2.04: DPAT <Command> <Pattern> <Directory> [<opt1>] [<opt2>] [<opt3>] [<opt4>]

1.3: DPAT <Command> <Pattern> <Directory> [<Opt1>] [<Opt2>] [<Opt3>] [<Opt4>]

1.2: na

Templates:

2.04: com/a,pat/a,dir/a,opt1,opt2,opt3,opt4

1.3: com/a,pat/a,dir/a,opt1,opt2,opt3,opt4

1.2: na

Path:

S:

Use:

DPAT is a script. Now we have got the shock of that over with, we can explain what this meta-command script does: Using LIST it adds the option of pattern matching to double argument commands – that is commands with FROM and TO arguments like SORT and RENAME. This example simulates a MOVE command by renaming files between two directories.

```
1>DPAT RENAME SYS:S/#? SYS:Scripts
```

DPAT takes three arguments – the other options have been provided for the sake of any commands which may need them. In this example they are:

```
com=RENAME ... RENAME adding pattern matching
pat=SYS:S/#? ... The pathname and pattern to use
dir=SYS:Scripts ... The destination directory
```

- It should be noted that, since DPAT relies on EXECUTE it is limited by the command parser supplied with that command. Therefore "" should not be used to refer to the current directory and * should not be used to refer to the console. (* can be used if you “escape” it with **). The current directory may be referred to using its full path description however. Also, if you need to output to a console window you should explicitly define one – as in this example:

```
1>DPAT SORT :temp/#? CON:0/0/600/200/Sorting...
```

New - AmigaDOS 2:

Most of the commands have had pattern matching added in any case, so DPAT is starting to look a little redundant. However, it does not take up much room on a disk and should not be deleted; it may come in useful for some third-party and PD software.

Options:

COM/A This is the command DPAT will execute for each file/ directory matching the pattern specification. This argument *must* be supplied.

PAT/A The pattern to match the files in the source directory. PAT may include a source path but pattern matching can only be used as the last part of the string. Note: This latter restriction has been lifted for release 2. This argument *must* be supplied.

DIR/A The destination directory to operate on. This can be any valid AmigaDOS path but does not include any pattern matching strings unless they are escaped with tick ('). This argument *must* be supplied.

opt1..4 These four option strings are passed directly to the command (COM/A). In the unlikely event of a command requiring more than four options, simply surround the OPTIONAL parts of the command line with quotes ("). This example uses a fictional command which has required keywords, START and END:

```
DPAT Fiddle S/#? RAM: "CASE START=2 END=21"
```

See also: SPAT

ECHO

Synopsis:

2.04: ECHO {string | $var} [NOLINE] [FIRST=<n>] [LEN=<n>] [TO=<file>]

1.3: ECHO [<string>] [NOLINE] [FIRST <nn>] [LEN <nn>]

1.2: ECHO [<string>]

Templates:

2.04: /M, NOLINE/S, FIRST/K/N, LEN/K/N, TO/K

1.3: , NOLINE/S, FIRST/K, LEN/K

1.2: ?

Path:

Internal

C: <2.04

Use:

This is the Amiga's print statement – akin to Printf in C, PRINT in BASIC, WRITELINE in FORTRAN, and SAY in ARexx. It can be used at any time but is most useful in script files for keeping the user informed of progress. The syntax is just like BASIC – the arguments are enclosed in quotes – so it is very easy to use. Used without an argument, ECHO produces a linefeed. The following works in all versions of AmigaDOS:

```
1>ECHO "This is just a simple example"
This is just a simple example
```

There are times however, when you may want to include a quote (") in ECHO's output. In BASIC this would mean surrounding the quote in quotes, arhum! In AmigaDOS the principle is much simpler, you just use the escape character, star (*) also called asterisk. For example:

```
1>ECHO " *" Now we can include quotes *" "
" Now we can include quotes "
```

The escape sequence here is just *". In the event that you wanted to include the star in your command line it can be escaped itself:

```
1>ECHO "This is how to include a star – **"
This is how to include a star – *
```

Just to confuse matters, AmigaDOS has another escape character tick (') or apostrophe which is used to make pattern matching strings into literal strings. That is turning the pattern matching off. The two should not be confused and are not interchangeable!

Another useful escape sequence is the *n combination which forces a newline. This is far better than using ECHO more than it needs to be in scripts prior to release 2 when the command was made resident. In the second example – two of these sequences have been mixed. Spaces, as this demonstrates, are not required – and since they are printed, may not even be desirable:

```
1>ECHO "Mastering AmigaDOS*nThe only one you need!"
Mastering AmigaDOS
The only one you need!

1>ECHO "Beware of*n*"journalists*"*nwearing hats!*n"
Beware of
"journalists"
wearing hats!
```

Colours and other effects may be incorporated into the printed string by incorporating special ANSI escape sequences. The escape key (marked <Esc> in the list) is simulated by the *e sequence. The complete list is described in *Mastering AmigaDOS 2 Volume One.* Try these examples yourself – almost anything is possible but avoid using too many styles in a single line.

```
1>ECHO "*e[7mHow about this *e[0m then?"
1>ECHO "*e[41mEven funny backgrounds*e[0m!"
1>ECHO "*Or some *e[3mItalics?*e[0m"
```

Like most AmigaDOS commands, ECHO can send output to a specified device via the redirection operators. This is also the only (efficient) way of getting control characters into a file:

```
1>ECHO >RAM:example "This will go to a file..."
1>ECHO >>RAM:example "in v1.3+ this will be added on
to it!"
```

New – AmigaDOS 2:

The command can take multiple strings as arguments, viz:

```
1>ECHO "First" "Middle" "Last"
First Middle Last
```

or even:

```
1>ECHO  1 2 3
1 2 3
```

Option:

TO This has been added in the latest release of AmigaDOS 2 and works very much like the TO keyword in LIST. It writes ECHO's output to a file, removing the need for redirection which can become confused under certain circumstances. These examples achieve the same end:

```
ECHO "This is a new file" TO File ; AmigaDOS 2>
ECHO >File "This is a new file" ;  AmigaDOS 1.3
```

The second example will *not* work with AmigaDOS 2 unless you also specify a file path such as T:. For instance:

```
ECHO >T:File "This is a new file"
```

Options (>AmigaDOS 1.3):

NOLINE/S This switch suppresses ECHO's default setting which is to produce a line feed at the end of everything it prints. This option is only of any real use inside a script or, perhaps, during a redirection operation. Example:

```
1>ECHO >RAM:temp "This is all part " NOLINE
1>ECHO >>RAM:temp "of the same sentence!"
1>TYPE RAM:temp

This is all part of the same sentence!
```

FIRST/K This option normally ties to the LEN keyword, but can be used on its own. It is used to perform a limited string parsing akin to BASIC's RIGHT$. Used on its own, FIRST skips the first <n> characters of the string. The first character of the substring is counted as ZERO! See LEN for an example of using the two together:

```
1>ECHO "1234567890" FIRST=5
67890
```

If a value of 256 is supplied, ECHO returns the last character in the string. Example:

```
1>ECHO "System1.3:" FIRST=256
:
```

LEN/K LEN ties to FIRST but can be used on its own; in this case it prints the last <n> characters of the string. Example:

```
1>ECHO "23456789" LEN=3
789
```

If the command is used with FIRST the result is similar to BASIC's MID$. The effect is to print characters starting at position FIRST <n> and going on for LEN <n> characters:

```
1>ECHO "123456789" FIRST=2 LEN=3
345
```

In practice the use of the FIRST and LEN options is somewhat limited. It seems likely that they were introduced for use in scripts for enhancing the programming language as a way of editing strings. This is only speculation of course, but, at the time of writing we cannot get anything more useful than cute value from them. One possible use could have been:

```
1>ECHO >RAM:text "*"This is some text*" "
1>ECHO <RAM:text FIRST=0 LEN=5


1>
```

The first line just prepares the example string for use; note the escaped quotes – *". The second one attempts to redirect input to echo from the file. Result? Nothing. The only way to get the command to work the way one might expect in this instance is to use the ? operator to put it into interactive mode (see the examples using EVAL) first. This gets the command to spit out its command line too. Redirection to NIL: is not possible because the command would not display anything!

```
1>ECHO >RAM:text "*"This is some text*""
1>ECHO <RAM:text FIRST=0 LEN=5 ?
,NOLINE/S,FIRST/K,LEN/K:This
```

Not a lot of use really. One possible way around this is in a script, and to call the script recursively – sending string to be edited as an argument to the script. This forces AmigaDOS to do the expansion (of the string to be edited) for you. Here is a slightly contrived – although usable – example; anything more would be too complex. This should be saved as WhatIs – you give it a CLI number and it returns the name of the process using it:

```
.key process,s1,s2,s3,s4,s5,s6,s7
.bra {
.ket }

if "{s1}" EQ ""
echo >ram:qwe{$$} "{process} " noline
status >>ram:qwe{$$} {process}
execute <ram:qwe{$$} >nil: whatis ?
endif

if "{s1}" NOT EQ ""
echo "{s1}{s2}{s3}{s4}{s5}{s6}{s7}" first=16
endif
```

Example:

```
1>execute WhatIs 2
Edit
```

The entire script revolves around producing a string to be expanded during the execute phase – hence the recursion. The first "pass" constructs a string something like this:

```
2 Process 2 loaded as command: Edit
```

The first "2" is passed back as the "process" argument, the rest of the string is passed to options s1..s7. These are then echoed in the second "pass" (after being expanded by execute) and the command name is parsed out using first=16. The whole thing then "unwinds" itself invisibly; that's what the IFs are for.

From release 2, a better solution would be to use environmental variable expansion of the string. The WhatIs script therefore becomes a great deal simpler:

```
.key process
.bra {
.ket }
status >env:qwe{$$} {process}
echo "$qwe{$$}" first=31
```

This sets an environment variable to the current status of the process and expands it immediately using "$". The result is parsed in the same way.

See also: TYPE, *Mastering AmigaDOS 2 Volume One* – Scripts.

ED

Synopsis:

2.04: ED [FROM] <filename> [SIZE <nn>] [WITH] [WINDOW] [TABS] [WIDTH] [HEIGHT]

1.3: ED [FROM] <filename> [SIZE <nn>]

1.2: ED [FROM] <filename> [SIZE <nn>]

Templates:

2.04: FROM/A, SIZE/N, WITH/K, WINDOW/K, TABS/N, WIDTH=COLS/N, HEIGHT=ROWS/N

1.3: FROM/A, SIZE

1.2: FROM/A, SIZE

Path:

C:

Use:

ED is one of three editors supplied with the Amiga. Due to the complexity and importance of ED, we have devoted a chapter to it in *Mastering AmigaDOS 2 Volume One* and will be limiting ourselves to just the command line options and some of the more important updates here.

New – AmigaDOS 2:

The old version of ED is not compatible with the new Kickstart and this version has several extra features. Most obvious is the use of the mouse – ED now responds to a mouse click. Also, shifted cursor keys are now allowed. And, wait for it, ED now has menus!

Under the surface, ED has received a number of enhancements, some of which are described below. More important, ED now supports the function keys; with shifted options available this gives an extra 20 possible user-programmable commands. The default settings are stored in ED's config file – S:ED-Startup (surprise, surprise). ED may also be controlled from ARexx where its port is called – ED!

Options:

FROM/A ED must have a file to work with – even if that file does not actually exist. This is used to provide ED with a default filename that the text will be saved under when the command-X (exit and save) option is chosen. Example:

```
1>ED S:MyNewScriptFile
```

SIZE This option can be used to define the maximum file size (in bytes) ED can work with. ED uses this argument to request the amount from the free memory pool. There must be a large enough chunk to fulfil the request or ED will exit. The default setting, if a value is not supplied, is 40,000 bytes; amounts less than this cause ED to complain. The SIZE keyword can be omitted. Examples:

```
1>ED DF0:Source/MyBigProggy SIZE 50000
1>ED SYS:Textfile 100000
```

Options (>AmigaDOS 2):

WITH/K By default ED looks for its initial configuration file ED-Startup in the S: assignment. Using this argument one of many startup configurations can be supplied depending on different requirements. The file can also contain any number of ED's extended mode commands which, in effect, means that you could create autoexecuting ED programs to do almost anything. This has an interesting side effect that if a QUIT command was inadvertently left in ED's startup file, the program would never run! Example:

```
ED RAM:test WITH S:My-ED-Config
```

WINDOW/K

This defines the new window boundaries for ED to work in. This can be any valid AmigaDOS window or interactive device – including the current console and the serial device AUX:. This makes ED considerably more user friendly than it used to be. The first example opens a small ED window in the current Shell console – the second one uses a remote serial link. It worked up to a point. We used an ANSI–BBS emulation on a Commodore PC-20:

```
1>ED RAM:test WINDOW=*
1>ED S:spat WINDOW=AUX: WIDTH=80 HEIGHT=20
```

WIDTH/K This defines the width of the terminal window in use. It does not affect the size of the console window – but this should be made large enough. It is a keyword and must be specified. See WINDOW for an example.

HEIGHT/K

This affects the height of the pseudo-terminal like WIDTH. See WINDOW for an example.

TABS/N Sets the number of spaces the cursor moves to the right every time the TAB key is pressed. The default value is 3. ED does not insert tabs into the text however.

See also: EDIT, MEMACS

EDIT

Synopsis:

2.04: EDIT [FROM] <filename> [[TO] <filename>]
[WITH <filename>] [VER <filename>]
[[OPT P <lines>|W <chars>]
| PREVIOUS <lines>|WIDTH <chars>

1.3: EDIT [FROM] <filename> [[TO] <filename>]
[WITH <filename>] [VER <filename>]
[OPT <option>]

1.2: EDIT [FROM] <filename> [[TO] <filename>]
[WITH <filename>] [VER <filename>]
[OPT <option>]

Templates:

2.04: FROM/A, TO, WITH/K, VER/K, OPT/K, WIDTH/N, PREVIOUS/N

1.3: FROM/A, TO, WITH/K, VER/K, OPT/K

1.2: FROM/A, TO, WITH/K, VER/K, OPT/K

Path:

C:

Use:

EDIT is a strange beast and almost like a scaled down version of ED. It is a line editor of the type most often encountered on MS-DOS machines. EDIT has no Intuition menu interface – and no Intuition window either. EDIT communicates everything with the console. This may seem a little outdated and out of context but it can be surprisingly useful.

EDIT does not read the entire file at once and therefore can deal with extremely large amounts of source. This also has the added advantage that binary content, physically included in the file, will remain unaffected by actions performed in ED. The best feature though is that EDIT can be used remotely over a serial link to another machine – say another Amiga. Total masochists could use this technique to write, assemble and test code over the phone.

EDIT is started thus (FROM is optional):

```
1>EDIT FROM S:Startup-Sequence
Editor
:
```

The rest of its options and commands are described below. EDIT is best used over a serial link (in the multi-user environment) or for its automatic editing functions in a script. We have used this feature extensively in scripts chapters in *Mastering AmigaDOS 2 Volume One*. If you have the choice – ED is generally a better option.

Options:

FROM/A This is ED's only required argument and should be the name of an existing file. In the absence of a TO argument, EDIT creates a temporary file in T: which is used to store the changes. When the W (windup) command is issued, EDIT modifies the original file. Example:

```
1>EDIT FROM S:Startup-Sequence
```

EDIT attempts to rename a work file stored in the T: assignment (or :T directory) to the name of the original file. This constitutes a move and since moves across devices are not possible, this can cause EDIT to fail. This would happen for instance, if the T: is in RAM: (where it should be) and the destination file is on a floppy disk. Better to use the TO option described below.

TO This optional keyword is used to specify the file EDIT should create when it exists. If this option is used the original file is left untouched and a new file is created containing the edits. Example:

```
1>EDIT S:OldFile TO NewFile
```

WITH/K This keyword should be specified to put EDIT into auto mode. The WITH file is just a text file containing EDIT commands which will be executed when the program starts. This file will normally be terminated with a W command. Example:

```
1>EDIT S:MyText WITH S:AutoCom
```

VER/K This keyword specifies the destination of the messages EDIT produces. If this option is not specified output defaults to the current terminal. Any valid AmigaDOS device can be used. Example using the printer for hard copy:

```
1>EDIT S:Spat VER PRT:
```

OPT/K This option keyword has been superceded by the two arguments described below. OPT should not be mixed with the PREVIOUS or WIDTH keywords in AmigaDOS 2:

```
OPT P <nn> = PREVIOUS <nn>
OPT W <nn> = WIDTH <nn>
```

Options: (>AmigaDOS 2):

PREVIOUS/K

This ambiguous sounding argument defines the number of previous lines available to the program. It replaces the

OPT P argument in older versions. See WIDTH below. Default=40.

WIDTH/K Sets the maximum line width to be edited to the integer value supplied. It replaces the OPT W argument in older versions. EDIT uses a combination of this and the WIDTH value to calculate the amount of working store – PREVIOUS*WIDTH. This gives EDIT the ability to work with very large files – much larger than ED can handle and yet use very little memory. Default=120. This example increases the amount of memory used by EDIT:

```
1>EDIT Darts PREVIOUS=180 WIDTH=180
```

Edit Commands

Following is a brief description of all EDIT's commands. The best way to learn them is by use – although, once learnt, experts claim EDIT can be faster and more powerful than ED. Caveat: When experimenting with EDIT always work on a copy of something – never the original!

- Version 2 of EDIT creates a T: directory for itself if one does not exist already.

Key:

/string/ Slash delimited (qualified) character string: The "/" characters work as delimiters (or qualifiers). Both terms are in different references – it depends on the author's preference. Delimiters are used so EDIT can find spaces and white space. The default delimiter can be changed as required, see below. Examples:

```
/ABC/, /abc/, /Bruce/, /Mark Smiddy/
```

text String: A string of characters. Strings must not contain spaces. Examples:

```
ABC, abc, Bruce, Mark
```

x A number. Line numbers can be * (last line) or "." current line.

n A number indicating how many times the following command is executed.

bool Boolean switch: + = ON; – = OFF.

Edit Commands:

' Repeat command
Do the previous A, B or E (line command) again.

=x Goto Line
Resume editing at line x.

; Command separator
When using more than one command in the same line use

this to indicate where each starts. Akin to : in BASIC and ; in C.

n(...) Repeating Multiple Command
Execute the command(s) enclosed in brackets n times. If n=0 repeat forever (or until an error occurs).

n< Move Pointer Left
Move n positions along the current line. Default 1 position if n is omitted.

n> Move pointer right Move n positions in along the current line. Default 1 position if n is omitted.

? Verify
Display the current line.

! Verify
Display the current line but show invisibles and capital letters too.

n# Delete
Wipe n characters from the current pointer position. Default 1 character if n is omitted.

n$ Force Lower Case
Change n characters from the current pointer position into lower case. Default 1 character if n is omitted.

n% Force Upper Case
Change n characters from the current pointer position into upper case. Default 1 character if n is omitted.

n_ Typeover Delete
Overwrite n characters with spaces. Default 1 character if n is omitted.

A/string/text
[insert] After
Searching just the current line, find the string "/string/" then replace it with the string "text". Caveat: Trailing spaces are read from the replacement "text". This function does *not* move the pointer. (See also AP.)

AP/string/text
[insert] After Pointer
Searching just the current line, find the string "/string/" then replace it with the string "text". Caveat: Trailing spaces are read from the replacement "text". This function moves the pointer. (See also A.)

B/string/text
[insert] Before
Searching backwards on the current line, find the string "/string/" then replace it with the string "text". Caveat:

Trailing spaces are read from the replacement "text". This function does *not* move the pointer. (See also BP).

BP/string/text
[insert] Before Pointer
Searching backwards on the current line, find the string "/ string/" then replace it with the string "text". Caveat: Trailing spaces are read from the replacement "text". This function moves the pointer. (See also B).

BF/string/
Backwards Find
Search for the string "/string/" starting from the current pointer position. If the string is not found on the current line, move backwards through the file until either the string is located or input is exhausted. (See also BP).

C .text. Command
Execute the command file "text". Note: the period "." symbol is used to delimit filenames.

CF .text. Close File
Close an open file named "text". Note: the period "." symbol is used to delimit filenames.

CGx Cancel Global
Clears the global operation x from the workspace – does not undo what has been done though. If x is omitted, all globals are cleared. (See also SHG.)

CL/string/ Concatenate Lines
Join the current line, "/string/" and the next line. A null string can be used (//) to join two lines. Caveat: there must be a next line (even if it's blank) for this function to work.

D Delete [line]
Delete the current line! Do not confuse this with # which deletes just the current character. (See also DF, #.)

DF/string/
Delete Find
Search for the string "/string/" moving from the current pointer position – and deleting lines as they are passed. If the string is not found on the current line, move through the file until either the string is located or input is exhausted. Use with care! (See also DFA.)

DFA/string/
Delete Find After
Find "/string/" on the current line, move the pointer to the next position and delete the rest of the line. A string must be supplied or this function fails. (See also DF.)

DFB/string/
Delete Find Before
Find "/string/" on the current line and delete everything from the start "/string/" to the end of the line. A string must be supplied or this function fails. (See also DFA.)

DGx Disable Global
Prevents the global x from having any effect but retains it for future use. If x is omitted, all globals are switched off. (See also CG.)

DTA/string/
Delete sTart After
Delete everything from the beginning of the line to after "/ string/". (See also DTB.)

DTB/string/
Delete sTart Before
Delete everything from the beginning of the line to the last character before "/string/". (See also DTA.)

E/string/text
Exchange
Find "/string/" and replace it with "text". This function does not affect the character pointer. (See also EP.)

EGx Enable Global
Enable the global operator x. Enable all global operators if x is omitted. The global must be defined. (See also DG.)

EP/string/text
Exchange Pointer
Find "/string/" and replace it with "text". This function also moves the character pointer. (See also E.)

F/string/ Find
Search for the string "/string/" moving from the current pointer position. If the string is not found on the current line, move through the file until either the string is located or input is exhausted.

FROM From
Take input (source) from the original file.

FROM .text.
From
Take input (source) from the file "text". Note: the period "." symbol is used to delimit filenames.

TO To
Send output to the original destination specified in the command line argument.

TO .text.
To
Send output to the file named "text". Note: the period "." symbol is used to delimit filenames.

GA/string/text
Global After
Globally place "text" after "/string/". Works just like A (After) but takes effect when EDIT scans the source. In Workbench 2, the scan starts immediately. (See also GB.)

GB/string/text
Global Before
Globally place "text" after "/string/". Works just like B (Before) but takes effect when EDIT scans the source. In Workbench 2, the scan starts immediately. (See also GA).

GE/string/text
Global Exchange
Globally exchange "/string/" with "text". Works just like E (exchange) but takes effect when EDIT scans the source. In Workbench 2, the scan starts immediately.

Hx
Halt
Set the halt (fence) at line x. If line=* (the current line) then halt and clear h. Used for EDITing files containing binary data.

I
Insert
Insert characters from terminal. Press CTRL+C <Return> to stop the operation. Pressing <Return> whilst in insert mode inserts blank lines.

I .text.
Insert [from file]
Insert lines or text from filename "text" into the current file. Note: the period "." symbol is used to delimit filenames.

Mx
Move relative
Move forward x lines. There must be enough lines in the file to satisfy the request or EDIT complains "input exhausted".

M+
Move forward
Move to highest line currently in memory – not necessarily the end of the file.

M-
Move backwards
Move to first line currently in memory – not necessarily the start of the file.

N
Next
Go to the next line in the file.

P
Previous
Go the previous line in the file.

PA/string/
Pointer After
Move pointer to position after "/string/". Multiple feature not reliable under Workbench 2 – use:

```
n(pa/string/;>)
```

PB/string/
Pointer Before
Move pointer to position before "/string/". Multiple feature not reliable under Workbench 2 – use:

```
n(pb/string/;<)
```

PR
Pointer Reset
Move pointer to beginning of the current line. (See also PA.)

Q
Quit
Exit from command level. Usually, this implies exiting EDIT too (using W). The same applies when an autoexecuting EDIT falls off the end of its command file.

R
Replace
Replace characters from terminal. Press CTRL + C <Return> to stop the operation. Pressing <Return> whilst in replace mode moves to the next line in the file.

R.text.
Replace [from file]
Replace lines or text from filename "text" into the current file. This operation may not work under early versions of Workbench 2.

REWIND Move back to the start of the file.

SA/string/
Split After
Move the pointer to the position after "/string/" and split the line. The pointer moves to the new line.

SB/string/
Split Before
Move the pointer to the position before "/string/" and split the line. The pointer moves to the new line.

SHD
SHow Data
List information on the current settings. (See also SHG.)

SHG
SHow Globals
List all the currently defined globals. (See also SHD.)

STOP
Stop
Leave EDIT leaving the original file unchanged.

T
Type
Display all lines in the file starting with the current line and moving to the end of the file.

Tn	Type Number Display n lines in the file starting with the current line. (See also TL.)
TLn	Type Lines Number Display n lines in the file starting with the current line but display line numbers too. (See also TN.)
TN	Type uNtil Display lines in the file starting with the current line, until the buffer has been changed. (See also T, TL.)
TP	Type Previous Move to the top of the text in memory (M-) then display all the lines in the file. (See also T).
TR bool	Trailing space Removal TR+ switches it on; TR-switches it off.
V bool	Verification switch V+ switches verification (echo result of last command) on. V– turns it off.
W	Windup Stop editing, keep changes.
Z text	Set input terminator to "text"

* Version 2 of EDIT creates a T: directory for itself if one does not exist already. Also a bug in early releases of AmigaDOS 2 prevents the period "." delimiter working in filenames – this is very rarely needed anyway.

See also: ED, MEMACS, *Mastering AmigaDOS 2 Volume One.*

ELSE

Synopsis:

2.04: ELSE

1.3: ELSE

1.2: ELSE

Templates:

2.04: ?

1.3: ?

1.2: ?

Path:

Internal

C: <2.04

Use:

ELSE can only be used from inside a script file. It is supplied as an optional part of the IF...ENDIF construct. If the IF part fails, control jumps to the ELSE part and executes from there until an ENDIF is reached. The command takes no arguments and is meaningless outside an IF...ENDIF. In nested IF...ELSE...ENDIF constructs, ELSE ties to the latest IF encountered.

Example in a script fragment:

```
IF EXISTS RAM:ENV
  ECHO "The ENV directory seems safe and sound..."
ELSE
  ECHO "Oh, no! The ENV directory is missing!
ENDIF
```

Example of nesting in a script fragment. ELSE ties to the second IF:

```
IF <filename> NOT EQ ""
  IF EXISTS <filename>
        ECHO "I have found <filename>"
  ELSE
        ECHO "<filename> seems to be missing"
  ENDIF
ENDIF
```

- Early versions of AmigaDOS have to load this command from disk every time it used. In AmigaDOS 1.3 it is wise to make this command RESIDENT either in complex scripts where it can be removed on exit or, preferably RESIDENT all the time if you use scripts a lot. The command is already resident in AmigaDOS 2.

See also: IF, ENDIF, *Mastering AmigaDOS 2 Volume One.*

ENDCLI

Synopsis:

2.04: ENDCLI

1.3: ENDCLI

1.2: ENDCLI

Templates:

2.04: ,

1.3: ,

1.2: ,

Path:

Internal

C: <2.04

Use:

This command is used to terminate the current CLI. It has been superceded by ENDSHELL in later versions. The two commands do the same thing however.

- If using this in a script, the "CLI nn ending" message may be suppressed thus:

```
ENDCLI >NIL:
```

See also: ENDSHELL, NEWCLI

ENDSHELL

Synopsis:

2.04: ENDSHELL

1.3: ENDSHELL

1.2: na

Templates:

2.04: ,

1.3: ,

1.2: na

Path:

Internal

Use:

This command can be used like ENDCLI to terminate the current Shell or CLI process, free up any resources it may have claimed and close the current console window. Example:

```
1>ENDSHELL
```

The command is implemented internally prior to release 2 as:

```
ALIAS EndShell EndCLI
```

It is important to note, ENDSHELL always works *but* sometimes has to wait until all the commands it has launched are terminated. This is not always the case though. Why? The description following is meant mainly for hackheads – beginners can proceed to the next command, in the firm and certain knowledge: "It just works that way – that's the way it is and there's no perfect way around it."

Now we have your attention: When you start a child process from the Shell using RUN, AmigaDOS gives it a couple of handles – one for input and one for output. These usually default to the current console window – which is one reason some commands seem to refuse to multitask properly or even at all. Every child process receives the same two handles no matter how many processes are started – up to the maximum number allowed: 20 prior to release 2. The actual handles sent to a program can be changed using the redirection operators < and >. This is how redirection works, incidentally.

The upshot of all this is: once a child process has started the Shell cannot close the console until the child lets go of the handle. If it did, the handles would vanish, the child would fall off (no jokes about the NSPCC, please) and the Amiga would crash.

There are cases when this can be avoided. The first is to pass the program a pair of dummy handles to NIL: like this:

```
RUN <NIL: >NIL: Sleepy
```

Since "Sleepy" does not make any grabs for the console handles at any time, the Shell can shut down normally. The same is not true for some C programs which seem to make claims for console access and must be terminated first.

The second instance where a process can be started and the Shell exited is a bit of a red herring and has less to do with the Shell and more to do with EXEC. Programs like this start their own resident "task" which has no connection with AmigaDOS at all. In fact, tasks cannot access the dos.library at all but they can do just about anything else – including opening Intuition windows. VirusX v4 appears to be an example of this.

See also: ENDCLI, NEWSHELL

ENDIF

Synopsis:

2.04: ENDIF

1.3: ENDIF

1.2: ENDIF

Templates:

2.04: ,

1.3: ,

1.2: ,

Path:

Internal

C: <2.04

Use:

ENDIF is the terminator for an IF...ENDIF or IF...ELSE...ENDIF construct and closes the last IF encountered. It may only be used in script files and is meaningless without at least one IF to tie to. Example:

```
IF WARN
ECHO "A warning condition was generated!"
ENDIF
```

- Early versions of AmigaDOS have to load this from disk every time it's used. In AmigaDOS 1.3 it is wise to make this command RESIDENT either in complex scripts where it can be removed on exit or, preferably RESIDENT all the time if you use scripts a lot. This command is resident in AmigaDOS 2.

See also: IF, ELSE, *Mastering AmigaDOS 2 Volume One* – three chapters on Scripts.

ENDSKIP

Synopsis:

2.04: ENDSKIP

1.3: ENDSKIP

1.2: na

Templates:

2.04: ,

1.3: ,

1.2: na

Path:

Internal

C: <2.04

Use:

ENDSKIP can be used to terminate a SKIP block and is only used inside script files. When the command is encountered the WARN condition flag is set which can be tested for using IF. This may be used to return a condition flag to another script file as this fragment demonstrates:

```
SKIP jail  ; Go straight to Jail - do not pass GO
.
.          ; Some other code goes in here
.
LAB GO     ; A fictional label
ENDSKIP    ; Generate a Return Code (RC) =5
LAB exit   ; Get here for a normal exit
IF WARN    ; Test which RC to send.
QUIT 5     ; Return a WARNing to the calling script
ENDIF
QUIT 0     ; Return all clear to the calling script
```

- Early versions of AmigaDOS have to load this from disk every time it's used. In AmigaDOS 1.3 it is wise to make this command RESIDENT either in complex scripts where it can be removed on exit or, preferably RESIDENT all the time if you use scripts a lot. In AmigaDOS 2 the command is already resident.

See also: SKIP, LAB, *Mastering AmigaDOS 2 Volume One* – three chapters on Scripts.

EVAL

Synopsis:

2.04: EVAL <Value1> [<operator>] [{value2}] [TO=<file>] [LFORMAT=<format string>]

1.3: EVAL <value1> [<operation>] [<value2>] [TO <file>] [LFORMAT=<string>]

1.2: na

Templates:

2.04: VALUE1/A, OP, VALUE2/M, TO/K, LFORMAT/K

1.3: VALUE1/A, OP, VALUE2, TO/K, LFORMAT/K

1.2: na

Path:

C:

Use:

This command is one of the least understood in AmigaDOS, partly because it seems to offer a bewildering range of options – but mostly because some subtle buggettes frequently wreak havoc with expected results. EVAL is very useful in script files as it can perform some simple integer calculations and base conversions to denary (base 10); conversions to other bases are slightly more involved.

- To define a hexadecimal number prefix it with 0x or #x
- To define octal, prefix with either "0" or #0
- To convert character codes to ASCII prefix with '

Be careful not to prefix decimal numbers with 0 or they will be interpreted wrongly. The basic syntax is simple as these examples demonstrate:

```
1>EVAL 0xFF    ; convert hexadecimal &FF to decimal
255

1>EVAL 077     ; convert octal 77 to decimal
63

1>EVAL 'c      ; the character code of lower case "c"
99

1>EVAL 2 + 2   ; add 2 and 2
4
```

Note the use of spaces in the last example? There is a single space after the first 2 and before the second 2. This is the most common area where beginners find difficulty with the command since the spaces are vital to its operation. If one or both are omitted some very curious results can be obtained:

```
1>EVAL 2+2
2
```

Humm? Users of AmigaDOS 1.3.2 and 2.04 will be pleased to discover this bug has been fixed and the command now yields the correct result. The following script tries to fix the bugs in early versions by supplying an error code if the spaces are missing. To keep it short, there is no support for extended options but this is not beyond the realms of possibility. By setting the S bit in the resulting file protection, this can be used, more or less, like the existing EVAL. Of course, the error checking relies on EXECUTE so you have to supply all the arguments correctly spaced – base conversion is possible (by adding 0) but that's better handled by EVAL.

```
.key val1/a,op/a,val2/a          ; The calc script!
EVAL <val1> <op> <val2>          ; do sum
```

New – AmigaDOS 1.3.2:

The input restrictions have been overcome and EVAL now works like a proper calculator. It's therefore no longer necessary to supply just two numeric arguments plus an operator. In fact the command works just like a proper calculator.

```
1>EVAL 2+2+4
8
```

You can supply as many numeric arguments as required – spaces are not necessary. The command follows the correct arithmetic precedence rules so order of calculation is not important. Therefore 2+2*4 yields 10 *not* 16! Brackets have been added to allow you to specify the order of calculation. Brackets are *always* expanded first. Here are a few simple examples:

```
1>EVAL 2+2*4
10
1>EVAL (2+2)*4
16
1>EVAL (3+2)*4+(12/3)
24
```

New – AmigaDOS 2:

EVAL now works with environmental variables using the dollar operator rather than needing to work with redirection, to wit:

```
1>EVAL <ENV:Count >NIL: to=RAM:tmp VALUE2=1 OP=+ : ?
1>TYPE RAM:tmp
```

is virtually equivalent to:

```
1>EVAL $Count + 1
```

The difference is, in the first instance a temporary file is created and the new value stored in it. In the second the value is printed straight away. The file could be created if required however:

```
1>EVAL >RAM:tmp $Count + 1
```

Finally, in this release,it is possible to read and write a variable at the same time. Previously it has been necessary to write results to an intermediate file, then copy the temporary result back to the variable, for instance:

```
1>EVAL <ENV:Count >NIL: OP=+ VALUE2=1 to ENV:tmp ?
1>COPY ENV:tmp to ENV:Count
```

This was caused by a feature of re-direction which keeps the file open until the command exits. Thanks to the new environment handling, this is no longer necessary and almost anything is possible. Here is a small selection:

```
1>EVAL $Count + 1 to ENV:Count
1>EVAL $Count+1 to ENV:Count
1>EVAL ($Count+$Var) * 2 to ENV:Count
```

Options:

VALUE1/A The only argument required by EVAL. This must be numeric. On its own, this may be used to convert TO decimal from other number bases. Example:

```
1>EVAL 0xFF    ; convert FF (Hex) to decimal
```

OP This (OPeration) defines the operator EVAL will use when making the calculation. The command understands a vast range of operators but can only use one at a time. The operators recognised are as follows:

+,-,*,/ The arithmetic operators work in the same way as their counterparts in BASIC and most other languages. Only division "/" is different because the fractional part of the result is truncated without rounding. That is: 7.2 would be the same as 7.6.

mod Modulo: Returns the remainder after a division of value1 and value2.

& Ampersand: Value1 is ANDed bitwise with value2.

| Bar: Value1 is bitwise ORed with value2.

~ Tilde: Value1 (or value2) is bitwise NOTed.

There are several negation operators as well:

xor   Exclusive OR: Value1 is XORed bitwise with value2.

eqv   The bits in value1 are tested for logical equivalence with the bits in value2 and the resulting bits set accordingly.

New in AmigaDOS 1.3.2

()   Brackets added to explicitly define the order of calculation. Overrides the internal */+- (My Dear Aunt Sally) calculation order. For instance:

```
1>EVAL (2+2)*3
12
1>EVAL 2+2*3
8
```

VALUE2   This is just the second number sent to EVAL. It can be omitted if the operator is not specified. Example:

```
1>EVAL VALUE1=2 VALUE2=3 OP=+    ;  2+3!
```

TO   Defines the name of a file the result of the calculation should be sent to. This forms the heart of EVAL's use in script loops. For reasons best not explained here it is not possible to route output to and from the same filename (or device) at the same time through normal redirection or use more than two redirection operators on the same line. This helps to overcome the problem. This example has been adapted from the script loop in *Mastering AmigaDOS 2 Volume One* – "Evaluating and Manipulating":

```
EVAL <env:count<$$> >NIL: TO=t:qwe<$$> value2=1 op=+ ?
TYPE >env:count<$$> qwe<$$>
```

The first redirection takes VALUE1 from env:count<$$>, and second sinks screen output into no-man's land. This is because for the input redirection to work EVAL must be in interactive mode – using ? – or otherwise its template output would appear on the screen. TO now sends the result of the calculation to a temporary file qwe<$$> which is then put back into env:count<$$> by the TYPE command. The <$$> appended to the variable name ensures the example multitasks correctly by appending the current process number to it. Phew!

LFORMAT   This is the grand manipulator of EVAL's output and works in an similar manner to the same option in LIST. C programmers will have met this technique before. LFORMAT defines EVAL's output in terms of a format string. Results are placed in the string at the points you define according to fairly standard Printf rules, where:

%x	Print the result in hexadecimal.
%n	Print the result in decimal.
%o	Print the result in octal.
%c	Print the result as a character.

When using the %X and %O options, it is possible to define the number of characters displayed thus: %X4 gives four hex characters. The example above for improving 1.3's EVAL could be enhanced using this:

```
EVAL <val1> <op> <val2> LFORMAT "The answer is %x4*n"
```

Which gives the result as a four digit hex string. The *n is borrowed from ECHO and supplies an extra carriage return. Note also, leading zeros will be displayed but this option should be used or misleading results can occur. Try this to see what we mean:

```
EVAL %xEEEF LFORMAT "Where did EEE go %x?*n"
```

To KEYWORD or not to KEYWORD?

The question must be raised: whether it is better to explicitly include non-keyword options when they are required or omit them as normal. Over the rest of AmigaDOS, optional words are just that -optional. With EVAL though, there seems to be an argument for including options like VALUE2 and OP. In very simple command lines, they make no difference but in more complex ones they can mean the difference between the command working and falling over. The following examples illustrate this – the first works, the second, well you try it for yourself. (Just to confuse matters further still, the last example works correctly.) This primarily affects just AmigaDOS 1.3.

```
1>SETENV count 1
1>EVAL <ENV:count >NIL: TO=RAM:tmp OP=+ VALUE2=1 ?
1>TYPE RAM:tmp
2                                     ; 1+1 =2
1>EVAL <ENV:count >NIL: TO=RAM:tmp + 1 ?
1>TYPE RAM:tmp
11                                    ; Pardon?
1>EVAL <ENV:count >NIL: TO=RAM:tmp 1 + ?
2                                     ; Correct!?
```

- EVAL only handles numbers up to 16-bits wide. That is: +32767...–32678.

See also: Mastering AmigaDOS Volume One - three chapters covering on scripts.

EXCHANGE

Synopsis:

2.04: EXCHANGE [Hotkey="hotkey(s)"] [display=<no>] [priority=<n>]

1.3: na

1.2: na

Templates:

2.04: CX_POPKEY/K, CX_POPUP/K, CX_PRIORITY/K/N

1.3: na

1.2: na

Path:

SYS:Utilities

Use:

This opens the main Commodities Exchange manager and allows you to alter or unload currently selected Commodities programs. For most purposes you will just need to call this program directly like this:

```
1>EXCHANGE
```

and operate it from Intuition. More information can be found in the options list. If you RUN-launch EXCHANGE and put it in the background (from Startup say) it hangs around in memory until you explicitly tell it to quit. Startup-sequence launches are accomplished like this:

```
RUN >NIL: EXCHANGE CX_POPUP=NO
```

Options:

CX_POPKEY The *hotkey* used to awaken EXCHANGE and open its configuration screen. By default this is Alt-Help.

```
RUN >NIL: Exchange "CX_POPKEY=Alt F1"
```

POPKEY extensions are as follows:

Shift	–	Either Shift key
Control	–	The Ctrl key
Alt	–	Either Alt key
F<n>	–	Function key N: F1, F2

CX_POPUP

This keyword takes a yes or no argument which tells EXCHANGE whether or not to display its main screen. If this option is not supplied, YES is assumed – strictly, this option should be a switch. It's usually only used like this to alter the EXCHANGE's internal priority at startup:

```
RUN EXCHANGE CX_POPUP=NO CX_PRIORITY=5
```

CX_PRIORITY

The priority passed to the program on startup. This is its priority over other CX programs – not the process priority shown by STATUS. By default all CX programs have a CX_PRIORITY of 0. Higher priority programs have the first grab at incoming messages – key presses and such like.

General Note — Commodities Exchange

The Commodities Exchange (CX) programs are normally stored on the Extras disk. However, to keep the examples simple, we'll assume you have already changed to the correct directory or set the correct path.

Important: the CX programs *do not* return error conditions when an incorrect command line is entered. You can check they have launched correctly in scripts using STATUS.

See also: AUTOPOINT, BLANKER, CLICKTOFRONT, FKEY, IHELP, NOCAPSLOCK

EXECUTE

Synopsis:

2.04: EXECUTE <command file> [{arguments}]

1.3: EXECUTE <command file> [arguments]

1.2: EXECUTE <command file> [arguments]

Templates:

2.04: (Dependent on script being executed)

1.3: (Dependent on script being executed)

1.2: (Dependent on script being executed)

Path:

C:

Use:

This command is used to "run" script files. A script is just a sequence of AmigaDOS instructions optionally proceeded by a series of arguments. This makes EXECUTE look like a very powerful command, because it can, in effect produce meta-AmigaDOS programs tailored to your own needs. Scripts are so important we have dedicated three chapters to them in *Mastering AmigaDOS 2 Volume One.* for this reason we will limit ourselves to just a description of the EXECUTE command.

This is a very simple command to use. All you do is supply the name of the file to be executed and any arguments it requires – see below. There is no need to supply a path if the script lives in either the current directory or the S: assignment (usually SYS:s):

```
1>EXECUTE Copyfiles
1>EXECUTE DF1:Scripts/install-sleepy df0:
```

New – AmigaDOS 1.3:

The "S" protection bit introduced for this release allows scripts to be executed directly without using execute. What actually happens is this: when AmigaDOS attempts to run a file and finds the required header is missing, it checks the "S" bit. If this is set, EXECUTE is loaded and run automatically – with the complete command line passed internally. This removes the need to specify EXECUTE distinctly and allows the construction of complete commands you can use like any other. On the down side, EXECUTE must be present either in the C: assignment or already resident.

Options:

Strangely enough, this is one command which has no external options of its own instead taking everything from inside the script file. Direct commands are prefixed with a period or dot "." and are explained below. If you need to use dot commands in a script, and most will, then the first command in the script must be one of these dot commands.

< and > The angle brackets are used to indicate where an argument should be substituted for the argument string. This was an unfortunate choice since it conflicts with the redirection operators. These can be changed to something else – which is what we'd recommend. This example (which is complete incidentally) substitutes the users drive number with a device spec.:

```
.key number/a
DIR df<number>:
```

.BRA <char> Replaces <char> for the opening bracket. We recommend using { but this is mainly personal taste. You *must* use this if the script uses re-direction operators!

.KET <char> Replaces <char> for the closing bracket – BraKet (get it?). We recommend using } but again, this is just personal taste. You *must* use this if the script uses re-direction operators!

.DOLLAR <char>

Replaces the dollar sign with <char>.

.KEY <args> Is the most powerful operator as it lets you define a command line which can be interpreted by AmigaDOS in the same way as any normal command! In fact, if the user sends a ?, EXECUTE spits out the command line just like a real command. Command lines are subject to the same conventions and restrictions but parsing is limited to the /A and /K arguments – see the description at the head of this section. Example:

```
.KEY drive/a, TO=AS/K, dest
```

.DEF <argument>

Gives a default argument to an argument string if one was not supplied as a command line argument. Example:

```
.DEF device df0
```

An alternative, and perhaps, a better way to do this is to use the dollar directive where the command is substituted thus:

```
<device$PRT>:
```

Here if the string "device" is null (empty) PRT is substituted instead. You can use a mixture of these two systems but it's wiser to choose one and stick with it.

Options (>AmigaDOS 2):

.<space> A remark – this can be the first line of a script if you want to use dot-commands but include details of what the script does.

```
. The multi-copy script
; This script copies loads of stuff
.KEY source/a,dest/a
```

.\ A blank remark. This does nothing except to inform EXECUTE to embark on a scan for embedded arguments.

In the true spirit of saving the best for last there now follows a description of EXECUTE's lower level operation. This it not intended for beginners but that should not put them off – in fact, a very useful debugging script appears here which can make everyone's life a lot simpler.

When EXECUTE starts it reads the first byte of the file and if this is a dot it creates a temporary file in the T: assignment or the :T directory. If the file cannot be created for some reason, the albeit rare error "Can't create T:Command-00-01" is generated. This temporary file is created by scanning the entire script and copying it with the argument substitutions made.

This file can be useful for de-bugging scripts because it allows you to see just where the substitutions are being made and read the script more like AmigaDOS does. But EXECUTE throws this file away at the end of a run. Also, the name seems to be made up thus: Command-NN-PP, where NN is the nesting level and PP is the process number calling execute. This results in a unique number every time no matter how many scripts are executing. Now *Mastering AmigaDOS 2* shows you how!

```
.KEY NOARGS
LIST >RAM:ShowMe<$$> T:COM#? LFORMAT "RUN ED %s%s"
EXECUTE RAM:ShowMe<$$>
```

This script is incredibly simple but it can save an awful lot of headaches. It relies on the multi-tasking capability of the Amiga and would not be possible on a lesser machine. To use it, simply insert "EXECUTE SHOW-ME" near to the start of a script:

```
.KEY arg1/a,arg2/a,opt1,opt2
EXECUTE SHOW-ME
```

Here is how it works: When the first script starts executing, EXECUTE scans the first byte and finds a dot. Now it builds a temporary file in the T: assignment. When SHOW-ME is executed it lists all the temporary command files in T: and creates (yet) another script in RAM: which reads like this – the actual names will vary of course:

```
RUN ED T:Command-02-00
RUN ED T:Command-00-01
```

The second line now executes the script – snapshotting the various "command" files into multiple EDs – before EXECUTE gets control back and deletes them! Neat, huh? These command files can then be studied at leisure. If you want to keep them simply use the *X option to leave ED AFTER the scripts have finished and copy them onto a spare disk.

Note: This command may not work in AmigaDOS 2. Use this instead:

```
; Show-Me V2.0
TYPE >>ram:test   T:#?
ED ram:test
```

New – AmigaDOS 2:

In addition to the standard argument parsing of /A and /K, EXECUTE now supports the following arguments correctly:

/F Final. The remainder of the command line is read and loaded into a variable. This option must not be used when there may be a chance of other aruguments parsing incorrectly. For safety, other args should be made keywords or switches. Example:

```
.key      First/K, Last/F
echo      "<first>"
echo      "<last>"
```

/S Switch. The variable contains the argument name if supplied and is empty if not. Example:

```
.key      ON/S
IF "<on>" NOT EQ " "
 echo "The switch was <on>"
ELSE
 echo "The switch was not supplied"
ENDIF
```

Limited support is given to the numeric argument, /N, although it will be checked, it is not inserted in the parsed script.

See also: Mastering AmigaDOS 2 Volume One – three chapters on scripts.

FAILAT

Synopsis:

2.04: FAILAT [<n>]

1.3: FAILAT [<n>]

1.2: FAILAT [<n>]

Templates:

2.04: RCLIM/N

1.3: RClim

1.2: RClim

Path:

Internal

C: <2.04

Use:

FAILAT displays or sets the failure condition limit at which a script will be terminated. In the template RCLIM stands for the Return Code LIMit returned by many commands on exit. The actual limit can be set to just about any integer value but Commodore recommends values of 5 (WARN), 10 (ERROR), and 20 (FAIL) are adhered to. The syntax is very simple:

```
1>FAILAT              ; read the current fail limit
Fail limit: 10
1>FAILAT 20           ; Set failure at 20 and above
```

This command can be very useful for debugging scripts – especially new or modified Startup-sequences. For instance, the following line could be added as the first line of a new Startup-sequence before the machine is rebooted:

```
FAILAT 21
```

This will ensure the script will continue to execute no matter what happens – even if a fatal error occurs. Unless redirection to the NIL: device is in effect, any commands returning errors will report normally *but* the script will continue to execute. This has its good and bad points.

On the plus side, you will normally be returned to the Workbench no matter what goes wrong (in the absence of a *Guru*). This allows much easier access to the editors and other features of the system.

On the minus side, errors early in the script can give rise to other errors later on even though the actual command is correct. Take the following example:

```
FAILAT 21
MAKEDIR RAF:TEMP            ; This line is wrong
 .
 .                          ; more commands here
 .
ASSIGN TEMP: RAM:TEMP       ; This is OK.
```

Both of these commands generate an error. The first puts up a request for volume RAF to be inserted in any drive. This can be cancelled at which point MAKEDIR will return a fatal error – but when the script reaches ASSIGN since RAM:TEMP does not exist this will also generate an error. Because of this you should always debug scripts from the top downwards fixing each bug before progressing to the next.

When AmigaDOS executes a script, the current fail limit as set by FAILAT from the Shell is adopted for that run only! Once the script exits the failure limit is returned to 10. There may be cases however when you want to vary the failure limit throughout the script, returning to the Shell limit at various times. This is less than straightforward, but still possible - using the automatic EDIT macro defined below and some judicious use of redirection.

First, the EDIT macro:

```
12#                     ; Delete "Fail limit: "
```

This macro is defined in the script using echo. See EDIT and PROTECT. Now the two script fragments:

First get the current fail level. Then use EDIT to delete the "Fail limit:" string.

```
ECHO >RAM:fail-ED{$$} "12#"
FAILAT >RAM:fail{$$}    ; Get the CURRENT fail level
EDIT RAM:fail{$$} TO RAM:fail{$$} WITH RAM:fail-ED{$$}
```

Next reset the failure level from the modified file:

```
FAILAT <RAM:fail{$$} >NIL: ? ; Reset the entry fail level
```

Note this example uses the interactive mode of FAILAT to gain input from the file and sends template information to NIL: so it does not mess up the output in the script.

Options:

RClim (RCLIM/N)

If supplied, this argument defines the new return code limit for script failure. Values in excess of 20 prevent all fatal AmigaDOS command errors from stopping a script. Use this with care!

See also: QUIT, *Mastering AmigaDOS 2 Volume One* – Scripts

FASTMEMFIRST

Synopsis:

2.04: na

1.3: FASTMEMFIRST

1.2: FASTMEMFIRST

Templates:

2.04: na

1.3: ,

1.2: ,

Path:

SYS:System

Use:

The Amiga's memory map is split into two major parts – that which can be accessed by the custom chips and that which can't. The problem with the custom chips is they can prevent processor (for very short periods) access to certain parts of RAM. This prevents some programs from running at full speed. This command, which has been removed from Workbench 2, tells EXEC to use "fast" memory (which the custom chips cannot access) whenever a program requests some memory of unspecified type. If fast memory is not available this command has no effect. Example:

```
1>FASTMEMFIRST
```

This command is usually only called once in the Startup-sequence. In Kickstart 2 it has been removed since the revised EXEC memory mapping always tries to allocate FAST first.

New – AmigaDOS 1.3.2:

The CHIP RAM test was incorrect. This has now been fixed – the command works correctly either way.

See also: NOFASTMEM

FAULT

Synopsis:

2.04: FAULT {error code}

1.3: FAULT <error code>...

1.2: FAULT <error code>...

Templates:

2.04: /M/N

1.3: ,,,,,,,,,

1.2: ,,,,,,,,,

Path:

Internal

C: <2.04

Use:

FAULT is one of those unusual commands that seems to be lacking in purpose. It returns an explanation for error codes returned by the system. AmigaDOS will only generate an error code if FAULT is not in the current C: directory or assignment.

The only place you are likely to encounter actual fault numbers is from the Workbench where they appear across the title bar! (In Workbench 2 the error code and description appear.) This then means you have to open a CLI or Shell and ask FAULT to give you the description. For some other reasons best known to the Amiga's designers, FAULT can return explanations of up to 10 error codes separated by either commas or spaces. If fault does not recognise the code it returns an error.

Examples:

```
1>DIR M:
Could not get information for M:
Error code 218
1>FAULT 218
Fault 218: device (or volume) not mounted

1>FAULT 105 106 214
Fault 105: task table full
Fault 106: Error 106
Fault 214: disk write protected
```

See also: WHY, Appendix A Error Codes

FF

Synopsis:

2.04: na

1.3: FF [-0] [-N]

1.2: na

Templates:

2.04: na

1.3: –0/S, –N/S

1.2: na

Path:

C:

Use:

FASTFONTS (FF) was introduced in Workbench 1.3 to help speed up text flow in windows. Technically, FF re-vectors a call in the graphics.library responsible for text printing to its own much improved routines. The introduction of Kickstart 2 has seen this particular routine enhanced and speeded up anyway so there is no need for the command. Also, the new release has seen the introduction of scaleable fonts which FF does not support. FF is usually used in a startup script:

```
FF >NIL: ; Speed up text
```

FF offers limited support for fixed size 8x8 bitmapped fonts like the pearl and topaz fonts. The complete font name must be specified:

```
FF pearl.font ; speed up text (and switch to pearl.font)
```

Options:

O/S	Switch on FASTFONTS. Default.
N/S	Switch the FASTFONTS program off and clean up.

- FF was written by Charlie Heath of Microsmiths who are also responsible for the standard file requester present in the new operating system and the improved pattern matching routines. These are part of the new asl.library – previously known as ARP.

FILENOTE

Synopsis:

2.04: FILENOTE [FILE] <File | Pattern> [Comment=<comments>] [ALL] [QUIET]

1.3: FILENOTE [FILE] <file> [COMMENT <remarks>]

1.2: FILENOTE [FILE] <file> [COMMENT <remarks>]

Templates:

2.04: FILE/A, COMMENT, ALL/S, QUIET/S

1.3: FILE/A, COMMENT/A

1.2: FILE/A, COMMENT/A

Path:

C:

Use:

This very useful command attaches a comment line of up to 79 characters to any file. The comment itself only appears during LIST listings and does not affect the normal directory function. If a file is specified without a comment string any existing comments are removed. Spaces and literal quotes may be included in the comment string but in this case the entire comment *must* be enclosed in quotes.

Options:

ALL/S Adds the comment string to all the files in the current directory and any sub-directories below it. (Pattern matching can be used to limit the search on the first level only.) The following example could be used to flag the date you backed up your hard drive (remember to use the right apostrophe!):

```
FILENOTE DHO: "Backed up `date`" ALL
```

QUIET/S Tells FILENOTE to suppress the "...Done" progress message. Note: this only appears when the ALL switch (described above) is specified or a wildcard is used.

Examples:

```
1>FILENOTE SOURCE:Sleepy.S assembler

1>FILENOTE S:Startup-sequence "The startup script"

1>FILENOTE DOCS/MyText "This is *"Chapter1*" of the book"
```

New - AmigaDOS 2:

From AmigaDOS 2 onwards, pattern matching has been added to this command so the same comment can be added to a rash of files in one sweep.

Example:

```
1>FILENOTE SOURCE:S1#?.S "Sleepy -devpac source- file"
Sleepy.S...Done
Sleepy2.S...Done
Sleezy.S...Done
```

Note: the protection flags are not affected by FILENOTE.

Options:

FILE/A The file to receive the new comment string – see below. Note: pattern matching has been added to this argument for AmigaDOS 2.

COMMENT/A

The comment to attach to the specified file. Comment strings must not exceed 79 characters in length. Escaped quotes and ANSI escape codes may be used but they are counted as multiple characters – not as single displayed characters.

See also: LIST

FIXFONTS

Synopsis:

2.04: FIXFONTS

1.3: FIXFONTS

1.2: na

Templates:

2.04: ,

1.3: ,

1.2: na

Path:

SYS:System

Use:

FIXFONTS must be used whenever you have changed the contents of any of the font directories in the FONTS: assignment. It changes the ".font" font files to reflect the contents of the directories. If this command is not performed after new font sizes have been added or others deleted, the Amiga will become confused as to which sizes are actually available. This is because when the system performs a font scan (while loading NotePad for instance) it uses the .font files in the directory assigned to FONTS: and not the contents of the font subdirectories. The command takes no arguments and is executed thus:

```
1>FIXFONTS
```

If you modify disk fonts other than those on the system disk (or the the current FONTS: disk) you must reassign FONTS: temporarily to that disk for the command to work:

```
1>ASSIGN FONTS: DF1:fonts   ; Make DF1:fonts current
1>FIXFONTS                  ; fix the font.info files
1>ASSIGN FONTS: SYS:fonts   ; now back to normal
```

FIXFONTS may Guru if it finds an empty font directory with non associated .font header.

See also: ASSIGN

FKEY

Synopsis:

2.04: FKEY [F<n>="new string"] [SF<n>="new string"] [Hotkey="hotkey"] [display=<no>] [priority=<n>]

1.3: na

1.2: na

Templates:

2.04: KEY/M, CX_POPKEY/K, CX_POPUP/K, CX_PRIORITY/K/N

1.3: na

1.2: na

Path:

Extras2:Tools/Commodities

Use:

This command opens the Commodities function key helper, redefines its settings or alters its priority. This particular program is intended to make repetitive tasks, like entering AmigaDOS commands, easier by assigning them to function keys. Quite how useful this is, is not a subject for debate here. If you do use it, may we suggest you make a paper key strip and stick it to your keyboard above the function keys. There's nothing worse than hitting Shift-F1 and getting DELETE #? when you meant to press F1 and get DIR #?. Like all the Commodities programs FKEY can be invoked simply by entering its name:

```
1>FKEY
```

However, this will lock the Shell and the command must be terminated by entering CTRL-E. A better solution is to use RUN thus:

```
1>RUN FKEY
```

At this point the program will open and display the list of function keys with the strings currently assigned to them. The program will become active when you click either the USE or SAVE gadgets. You must click SAVE to remember any changes. (The settings are stored in the icon file so any changes you make will be available from the Workbench too.)

Options:

KEY/M The key (or keys) whose strings you wish to define or change. The string should be terminated with \N if you wish to add a return – this is akin to *N in AmigaDOS. Here's an example:

```
RUN FKEY F1=DIR\N F2=Status\N SF1=MORE\N
```

CX_POPKEY

The *hotkey* used to awaken Exchange and open its configuration screen. By default this is Alt-F1.

```
RUN >NIL: FKEY "CX_POPKEY=Shift F1"
```

POPKEY extensions are as follows:

Shift	–	Either Shift key
Control	–	The Ctrl key
Alt	–	Either Alt key
F<n>	–	Function key N: F1, F2

CX_POPUP

This keyword takes a yes or no argument and tells Exchange whether or not to display its main screen. If this option is not supplied, YES is assumed – strictly, this option should be a switch. In this example, Shift-F1 is altered without displaying the FKey requester:

```
RUN FKEY SF1=Status\N CX_POPUP=NO
```

CX_PRIORITY

The priority passed to the program on startup. This is its priority over other CX programs – not the process priority shown by STATUS. By default all CX programs have a CX_PRIORITY of 0. Higher priority programs have the first grab at incoming messages – key presses and such like.

General Note - Commodities Exchange

The Commodities Exchange (CX) programs are normally stored on theExtras disk. However, to keep the examples simple, we'll assume you have already changed to the correct directory or set the correct path.

Important: The CX programs *do not* return error conditions when an incorrect command line is entered. You can check they have launched correctly in scripts using STATUS.

See also: AUTOPOINT, BLANKER, EXCHANGE, CLICKTOFRONT, IHELP, NOCAPSLOCK

FONT

Synopsis:

2.04: FONT [[FROM=]<file>] [EDIT] [USE] [SAVE] [WORKBENCH] [SCREEN] [SYSTEM]

1.3: na

1.2: na

Templates:

2.04: FROM, EDIT/S, USE/S, SAVE/S, WORKBENCH/S, SCREEN/S SYSTEM/S

1.3: na

1.2: na

Path:

SYS:Prefs

Creates:

ScreenFont.prefs; SysFont.prefs; WbFont.prefs

Use:

This command is one of the new Preferences suite. It opens the FONT Preferences tool, changes the current system fonts, or directly alters the defaults from saved files.

Preferences files are stored as IFF of type FORM PREFS/FONT. So you can examine them like this:

```
1>TYPE SYS:Prefs/Presets/FONT.PRE HEX
```

and if you do, the following information may be of use:

```
Font name at offset $003E
Font size at offset $003C
```

The font size is a two byte long hex digit. It can be converted back to real numbers using EVAL thus:

```
1>EVAL $000D
13
```

Only one font (the last one edited) is stored in the Font Presets file. This can be applied to other areas of the screen by applying the relevant switch – see below. The following files are stored in ENVARC:Sys and control the three user-defined system fonts. If these are missing, Topaz is assumed.

ScreenFont.prefs:	The screen font (titles etc) font.
SysFont.prefs:	The system (windows) default font.
WbFont.prefs:	The Workbench windows font.

Options:

FROM The full path and filename of a file to use for the font preferences. If FONT is being executed from a Startup-sequence this should be combined with USE – see below. The file should have been previously created by FONT using "Save As..." from the project menu. Example:

```
1>FONT FROM SYS:Prefs/Presets/NiceFonts USE WORKBENCH
```

EDIT/S Open the preferences editor screen when the command runs. This switch is implied in the current release (unless USE or SAVE is specified) but it should be retained in scripts for future compatibility. Example:

```
1>FONT FROM SYS:Prefs/Presets/Font.Pre EDIT USE
```

USE/S Supply this switch to open a FROM file and use the preferences settings from that file immediately. The FONT preferences editor window is not opened unless the EDIT switch is also supplied.

```
1>FONT FROM SYS:Prefs/Presets/Font.Pre USE
```

SAVE/S Specify this switch to save the settings defined in the FROM file to the correct file in ENV-ARCHIVE:Sys.

```
1>FONT FROM SYS:Prefs/Presets/HiResFont WORKBENCH SAVE
```

WORKBENCH/S

When this switch is supplied the font change is applied to the Workbench screen – even if the original file was saved with screen preferences. This option can be used safely from the Shell.

SCREEN/S

When this switch is supplied the font change is applied to all the currently opened screens. This option should *not* be used from Shell because the IPrefs Daemon will complain and you will have to close all open Workbench applications in order to make the change.

SYSTEM/S

When this switch is supplied the font change is applied to the System windows (new Shells etc) – even if the original file was saved with Workbench preferences. This option can be used safely from the Shell.

FORMAT

Synopsis:

2.04: FORMAT [DRIVE <drive>:] [NAME <name>] [FFS] [NOICONS] [QUICK]

1.3.2: FORMAT [DRIVE <drive>:] [NAME <name>] [FFS] [NOICONS] [QUICK]

1.3: FORMAT [DRIVE <drive>:] [NAME <name>] [FFS|NOFFS] [NOICONS] [QUICK]

1.2: FORMAT [DRIVE <drive>:] [NAME <name>] [NOICONS] [QUICK]

Templates:

2.04: DRIVE/K/A, NAME/K/A, FFS/S, NOICONS/S, QUICK/S

1.3.2: DRIVE <disk> NAME <name> [NOICONS] [QUICK] [FFS]

1.3: DRIVE <disk> NAME <name> [NOICONS] [QUICK] [FFS|NOFFS]

1.2: DRIVE <disk> NAME <name> [NOICONS] [QUICK]

Path:

SYS:System

Use:

This command initialises a new disk so AmigaDOS can read it. It is directly equivalent to Workbench's Initialise menu option (which calls FORMAT incidentally). However, it is a much more powerful command from Shell. The syntax of format may seem slightly clumsy at first since it is necessary to define both the device to format and a name. This is probably because there is no going back from the command once it is started – see below for a more technical explanation of what it does. Note that under AmigaDOS 1.2 format can only initialise physical (floppy and hard) disk drives. The basic syntax (all versions) is:

```
1>FORMAT DRIVE DF0: NAME Empty
```

The screen will respond with the message:

```
Insert disk to be formatted in drive df0: and press RETURN
```

Both DRIVE and NAME are keywords and *must* be specified or the command will fail and spit out its command line template. Also, if you specify a nondisk device (PIPE:, SER:, etc.) FORMAT will drop out before you press Return and give a "no disk in drive" error. A similar situation exists if you attempt to format the RAM: disk.

It is possible to enter spaces in the name string by enclosing it in quotes. Actual quotes should be "escaped" using the * character; ANSI sequences cannot be used.

```
1>FORMAT DRIVE DFO: NAME "My *"Devpac*" diskette!"
```

Like DISKCOPY, FORMAT is a command which should not be multitasked using RUN – otherwise constant messages from the command interfere with your console interactions. This is possible if the command is given its own console window to work in:

```
1>RUN FORMAT >CON:0/0/400/40/Formatting DRIVE DFO: NAME Empty
```

A better solution would be to use the NIL: device or just open a new Shell window. If FORMAT is RUN launched with redirection to NIL: formatting of the specified drive starts *immediately*! Do *not* use this if you are at all unsure of the consequences. In any case, FORMAT should be in the RAM: disk (unless a hard disk is in use) and the PATH set correctly. This is a very efficient way to format several disks at once leaving you to carry on – but it is potentially disastrous. *YOU HAVE BEEN WARNED!*

```
1>RUN FORMAT <NIL: >NIL: DRIVE DF1: NAME Empty   ; DANGER!!
```

CAUTION: Like DISKCOPY, once you leave the protective environs of the Workbench you enter a world where you have ultimate power over the machine. This is rather like a BASIC programmer going over to assembly level code. The extra power has its cost and the cost here as it is in programming – is one of safety. Once you issue a FORMAT command from Shell the Amiga assumes you meant to do it even if you didn't! Once the command starts there is very little you can do to stop it – even though FORMAT responds to CTRL+C or BREAK, the damage may already have been done! The same applies to hard disks too.

This means in effect, AmigaDOS would quite happily let you format, and effectively destroy the boot disk! This is possible from Workbench but if something is using the disk marked for formatting Workbench should warn you first – in practice *it probably will not!*

New – AmigaDOS 2:

It is at last possible to format floppy and RAD: disks using FFS. The boot sectors of the disks can be installed as either independently of the rest of the disk. It is not worth formatting RAD: for FFS since it should be fast enough anyway!

Options:

DRIVE — This keyword *must* be supplied and takes an argument which is the drive to format. For floppy disks this will be the device number df0:..df3:. For hard disks the partition name should be supplied. There is no going back once this command starts so ***never*** experiment on a hard disk partition.

```
FORMAT DRIVE DFO: NAME empty
```

NAME — Like DRIVE, this keyword must be supplied. It takes as an argument the disk label for the new disk. Spaces may be included if the name is surrounded by quotes. Example:

```
FORMAT DRIVE DFO: NAME "Backups 21-7-90"
```

QUICK — When this switch is used FORMAT does a very quick format of the destination drive. That is it initialises just the boot sectors at track 0 side 0 and the root directory sectors at track 39 side 0. This is a very fast way of wiping old disks *but* should only be used if the disk is known to be in good condition. It can be freely mixed with the other switches. Example:

```
1>FORMAT DRIVE DFO: NAME Free QUICK
```

NOICONS — This switch stops FORMAT creating a "Trashcan" subdirectory and the trashcan.info file. Example:

```
1>FORMAT DRIVE DF1: NAME blank NOICONS
```

Note: The trashcan icon that appears on each disk is copied from the the current SYS: assignment – usually the boot disk.

Options (>AmigaDOS 1.3):

NOFFS — This switch was introduced in 1.3 and rapidly removed with 1.3.2. It does nothing – the default is to format a disk without the Fast Filing System.

FFS — When this switch is used it attempts to format the specified drive using the new Fast Filing System. Note: prior to Kickstart 2, it is not possible to format a floppy disk using FFS. It just won't work because there is no support for it in the trackdisk.device. The command may appear to work at first but the results can be, well, interesting. The next example formats the first partition on the hard disk. *Do not try this.*

```
1>FORMAT DRIVE DHO: NAME FastBench FFS
```

See also: DISKCOPY, INSTALL, RELABEL, and *Mastering AmigaDOS 2 Volume One* – Formatting and Copying.

GET

Synopsis:

2.04: GET <variable>

1.3: na

1.2: na

Templates:

2.04: NAME/A

1.3: na

1.2: na

Use:

This command works just like GETENV described elsewhere, but it retrieves the value of a *local* environmental variable. Local environmental variables are stored locally to the process which created them and cannot be accessed via ENV:

It is possible to have a local and global variable with the same name, but the local variable receives precedence when used on the command line directly with the dollar operator:

```
1>SETENV Test Global
1>SET Test Local
1>ECHO "Test is $test"
Test is Local
```

Options:

NAME/A The name of the local variable to display. Case is ignored.

GETENV

Synopsis:

2.04: GETENV <name>

1.3: GETENV <name>

1.2: na

Templates:

2.04: NAME/A

1.3: NAME/A

1.2: na

Path:

Internal

C: <2.04

Use:

This command is used to retrieve the value of an environmental variable. By default the output of this command is sent to the screen but can be redirected in the usual manner:

```
1>GETENV Editor            ; Where is MORE'S editor?
SYS:Tools/Memacs
```

New – AmigaDOS 2:

Environmental variables can be read and displayed in command lines using the dollar ($) operator. Example:

```
1>ECHO "The path for MORE's editor is $EDITOR"
The path for MORE's editor is Extras:Tools/Memacs
```

This feature suggests another, rather useful feature – indirection. This means using a single variable to retrieve the value of *any* other! All you have to do is set the indirection variable to the name of the variable to read and use GETENV $. This is better explained by a simple example:

```
1>SETENV counter 2         ; Set up a variable
1>SETENV IND counter       ; This will point to counter
1>GETENV $IND              ; gets counter!
2
```

Here the variable IND is being used to *indirectly* retrieve the value of the variable: counter.

There are a couple of points to watch out for:

- The names of the environmental variables are *not* case sensitive. That means EDITOR, editor and EdItOR all have the same meaning and hold the samc value.
- Be very careful when using the dollar operator with GETENV or you might get to see the Amiga's extra special "FIREWORKS-DISPLAY" mode.

Options:

NAME/A The name of the variable to retrieve. An error occurs if the variable does not exist. Example:

```
1>GETENV counter
```

See also: SETENV

GRAPHICDUMP

Synopsis:

2.04: GRAPHICDUMP [tiny|small|medium|large|xdots:ydots]

1.3: GRAPHICDUMP [tiny|small|medium|large|xdots:ydots]

1.2: na

Templates:

2.04: [tiny | small | medium | large | xdots:ydots]

1.3 [tiny | small | medium | large | xdots:ydots]

1.2 na

Path:

SYS:Tools

Use:

GRAPHICDUMP is used to print the contents of any Amiga screen to a printer. When the command is started, it waits for ten seconds then prints the frontmost screen – this gives you some time to start the command then use the depth gadgets arrange the screens so the one you want to print is at the front. This command takes its printer settings from the current Preferences settings, so it is vital to ensure all settings for colour, smoothing and so on are set correctly before proceeding. Typically this command is called directly from Workbench, from Shell it can be called thus:

```
1>GRAPHICDUMP medium   ; print a medium sized image
1>GRAPHICDUMP  ; print a full image at top of form
```

Options:

tiny — The screen is printed approximately 1/4 original width. The height is adjusted to maintain the original aspect ratio of the screen.

small — The screen is printed approximately 1/2 original width. The height is adjusted to maintain the original aspect ratio of the screen.

medium — The screen is printed approximately 3/4 original width. The height is adjusted to maintain the original aspect ratio of the screen.

large — The screen is printed to the maximum size allowed by the printer – this is the default setting.

xdots:ydots — The width and height in dots to use within the confines of the printer; both figures must be specified. This option must be used with care otherwise the aspect ratio of the picture may be distorted.

ICONTROL

Synopsis:

2.04: ICONTROL [[FROM=]<file>] [EDIT] [USE] [SAVE]

1.3: na

1.2: na

Templates:

2.04: FROM, EDIT/S, USE/S, SAVE/S

1.3: na

1.2: na

Path:

SYS:Prefs

Creates:

ICONTROL.prefs

Use:

This command is one of the new Preferences suite – it opens the ICONTROL Preferences tool, changes the current settings or directly alters the defaults from saved files. ICONTROL is used to set certain Intuition functions such as the keyboard options for requester confirmations, coercion and so on.

Preferences files are stored as IFF of type FORM PREFS/ICTL. So you can examine them like this:

```
1>TYPE SYS:Prefs/Presets/ICONTROL.PRE HEX
```

The following information will only be of use to hackers and is provided *as-is* to get you started:

```
$0033 Verify timeout (1 byte) T/.02 seconds
$0035 Mouse screen drag bits
$0039 Coercion and misc flags (lower nybble only)
$003A WB to front alpha-qualifier
$003B Front screen to back alpha-qualifier
$003C Requester OK alpha-qualifier
$003D Requester CANCEL alpha-qualifier
```

Options:

FROM The full path and filename of a file to use for the font preferences. If ICONTROL is being executed from a Startup-sequence this should be combined with USE – see below. The file should have been previously created by ICONTROL using Save As... from the project menu. Example:

```
1>ICONTROL FROM SYS:Prefs/Presets/MyKeys USE
```

EDIT/S Open the editor screen when the command runs. This switch is implied in the current release (unless USE or SAVE is specified) but it should be retained in scripts for future compatibility. Example:

```
1>ICONTROL FROM SYS:Prefs/Presets/Icontrol.Pre EDIT USE
```

USE/S Supply this switch to open a FROM file and use the preferences settings from that file immediately. ICONTROL's editor window is not opened unless the EDIT switch is also supplied.

```
1>ICONTROL FROM SYS:Prefs/Presets/Icontrol.Pre USE
```

SAVE/S Specify this switch to save the settings defined in the FROM file to the correct file in ENVARC:Sys.

```
1>ICONTROL FROM SYS:Prefs/Presets/IC.Settings SAVE
```

ICONX

Synopsis:

2.04: ICONX

1.3: ICONX

1.2: ICONX

Templates:

2.04: ?

1.3: ?

1.2: ?

Path:

C:

Use:

ICONX (ICON eXecute) is only used from the Workbench since it is used to allow scripts to run from the Workbench. The options available in the Project icon's Tool Types display are detailed below:

Options:

(These are in the tooltypes array from the Workbench.)

The options here *are* case sensitive as opposed to the rest of AmigaDOS and must be entered in capitals complete with an equals sign.

WINDOW= This allows you to define a window specification for ICONX to open when it executes the script. Any valid window or device may be used:

```
WINDOW=CON:0/0/400/200/Install_script
WINDOW=AUX:
```

This last one does work (we've tried it) but has some strange effects since it sends all output to the serial port. See *Mastering AmigaDOS 2 Volume One – Multi-user Machine.*

DELAY= Defines the number seconds ICONX will wait before closing the console window. If a delay of 0 is specified, the program waits for a CTRL-C combination.

See also: EXECUTE

IF

Synopsis:

2.04: IF [NOT] [WARN] [ERROR] [FAIL]
[<string> EQ|GT|GE <string>] [VAL] [EXISTS <file>]

1.3: IF [NOT] [WARN] [ERROR] [FAIL]
[<string> EQ|GT|GE <string>] [VAL] [EXISTS <file>]

1.2: IF [NOT] [WARN] [ERROR] [FAIL]
[<string> EQ <string> [EXISTS <file>]

Templates:

2.04: NOT/S, WARN/S, ERROR/S, FAIL/S,, EQ/K, GT/K, GE/K,, VAL/S, EXISTS/K

1.3: NOT/S, WARN/S, ERROR/S, FAIL/S, , EQ/K, GT/K, GE/K, VAL/S, EXISTS/K

1.2: NOT/S, WARN/S, ERROR/S, FAIL/S, , EQ/K, EXISTS/K

Path:

Internal

C: <2.04

Use:

This is the heart and soul of the script languages condition testing; the head of the IF...ELSE...ENDIF construct. IF can only be used in scripts and is meaningless if used on its own. Prior to AmigaDOS 2, this command must be loaded from disk every time it is used. If you use scripts much IF should be either copied to the RAM: disk or (from release 1.3) made resident. The basic syntax is simple:

```
IF <condition>
...                     ; AmigaDOS commands
ELSE                    ; this is optional
...                     ; more AmigaDOS commands
ENDIF
```

The <condition> can be one of several described below. If the condition succeeds, control proceeds at the next line until either (a) an ENDIF is met or (b) an ELSE is met. When ENDIF is encountered control jumps out of the IF...ENDIF construct and down to the next level (if one exists). If ELSE is met, control jumps to the next ENDIF.

If the condition fails, control jumps to either the next ENDIF or the next ELSE statement if one is available. Many IFs can be nested *but* each one must be terminated with a corresponding ENDIF or the EXECUTE interpreter will become confused. We recommend you indent your scripts with tabs so you can easily follow the flow of control. In this example the multiple nested IFs can clearly be seen and the flow of control easily followed:

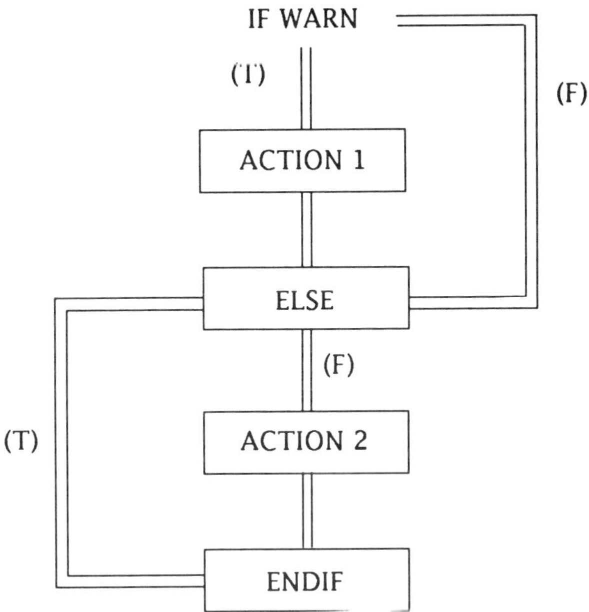

New – AmigaDOS 1.3:

The command has been generally improved and allows direct access to the environmental variables using the dollar operator (see GETENV). It is possible therefore, to read an environmental variable thus:

```
IF $count GT 5
ECHO "Count has exceeded 5!"
ENDIF
```

As an alternative means of achieving the same result you may use:

```
IF <ENV:count >NIL: GT 5 ?; the long way round!
```

This technique is worth remembering however because it can be used to retrieve a value from any interactive AmigaDOS device like RAM: or even the PIPE:! Examples:

```
IF <RAM:temp >NIL: EQ 0 ? ; Use a temporary RAM file
IF <PIPE:a >NIL: GT 7 ?   ; Use the PIPE: device.
```

Note: In some releases of the Shell, placing a remark (;) on the same line as an interactive IF (as above) causes IF to fail!

Options:

STRING (,,) This is the string which some IF options use to test against known strings. If you are expanding an argument (which is likely) the expansion should be enclosed in quotes. This example tests if a device argument has been supplied:

```
IF "{device}" EQ ""
```

NOT/S — This switch is used to negate the action of any boolean flag tested for with IF. This seems slightly confusing at first but it really is quite straightforward once you get used to it. Every test performed by IF returns a boolean flag:

```
TRUE=test succeeded.
FALSE=test failed.
```

Therefore NOT <test> just reverses the outcome, making TRUE=FALSE and FALSE=TRUE. For convenience, the switch actions below are described as boolean results – so if you need the opposite action, just specify NOT:

```
IF NOT EXISTS RAM:t
ECHO "Can't find RAM:T!"
ENDIF
```

WARN/S — This switch should be specified to test for a warning (RC=5) condition. The boolean flag is set to TRUE if the last command resulted in a warning. Example:

```
IF WARN
ECHO "Something is amiss!"
ENDIF
```

ERROR/S — This switch should be specified to test for an error (RC=10) condition. The boolean flag is set to TRUE if the last command resulted in an error. Note: execution will terminate at the erroneous command unless FAILAT is set >10. Example:

```
IF ERROR
ECHO "Something went WRONG!"
ENDIF
```

FAIL/S — This switch should be specified to test for a fatal error (RC=20) condition. The boolean flag is set to TRUE if the last command resulted in a fail condition. Note: execution will terminate at the faulty command unless FAILAT is set >20. Example:

```
IF FAIL
ECHO "This is it, we're going to die!"
ENDIF
```

EQ/K — EQUAL: This option is used to test for logical equivalence between strings or values. For instance to check that something has been entered for an argument:

```
IF <arg> EQ ""
ECHO "OI! you forgot something"
ENDIF
```

There are better ways of achieving the same objective but this shows the point. From release 1.3 EQ can also be used to test for equivalence with values from environmental variables. Example:

```
IF $count EQ 5
ECHO "count now equals five"
ENDIF
```

EQ returns boolean TRUE if the values match. Use NOT EQ if you require not-equal (< >).

EXISTS/K This option takes an argument corresponding to a file, directory or device name. If the device is found, boolean TRUE is returned and execution continues at the next line. If the device does not exist (or cannot be found) AmigaDOS puts up a requester giving the user chance to remedy the situation. In the case of disk drives, EXISTS returns FALSE if the drive is empty. Use NOT if you need to test for the absence of a file.Examplcs:

```
IF EXISTS df1: ; test for mounted disk in DF1:
IF EXISTS <device>  ; Check for argument of device
IF EXISTS SYS:S     ; Finds "boot" :S
IF NOT EXISTS T     ; TRUE if T missing
```

If you want to check for the presence of a logical assignment use ASSIGN EXISTS instead and test the WARN condition. See above.

Options (>AmigaDOS 1.3):

GT/K GREATER THAN (>). This option returns boolean TRUE if the number on the LEFT or the keyword is larger than the number on the RIGHT. Used with environmental variables in loops, etc. If you need less than (<), use NOT GE.

GE/K GREATER THAN OR EQUAL (>=). This option returns boolean TRUE if the number on the LEFT or the keyword is larger than OR equal to the number on the RIGHT. Used with environmental variables in loops, etc. Use NOT GT if you need less than or equal to (<=).

VAL/S VALUE. This switch is supposed to be used as a modifier to explicitly test for numeric values in environmental variables. The dollar operator indicates a numeric value. VAL is used alongside EQ, GT, GE. This example tests for a number in the evironmental variable "count" which is LESS than 10:

```
IF VAL $count NOT GE 10
```

See also: ELSE, ENDIF, ENDSKIP, EXECUTE, LAB, QUIT, SKIP and also *Mastering AmigaDOS 2 Volume One* – three chapters covering Scripts.

IHELP

Synopsis:

2.04: IHELP [priority=<n>] [CycleWindow="hotkey(s)"] [MakeBig="hotkey(s)"] [MakeSmall="hotkey(s)"] [CycleScreen="hotkey(s)"] [ZipWindow="hotkey(s)"]

1.3: na

1.2: na

Templates:

2.04: CX_PRIORITY/K/N, CYCLE/K, MAKEBIG/K, MAKESMALL/K, CYCLESCREEN/K, ZIPWINDOW/K

1.3: na

1.2: na

Path:

SYS:Utilities

Use:

This command opens Commodities Intuition helper, redefines its settings and priority. The idea is to assign certain Intuition functions to key strokes. Like all the Commodities programs it can be invoked simply by entering its name.

```
1>IHELP
```

Used in this way, IHELP will lock the Shell and the command must be terminated by entering CTRL-E. A better soluton is to use RUN thus:

```
1>RUN IHELP
```

A better solution, one which must be used if the command is executed from a Startup-sequence, is to redirect output to NIL:

```
1>RUN >NIL: IHELP
```

This prevents IHELP getting a lock on the Shell window and preventing it from closing.

You can redefine the keys employed by IHelp by passing the function as a parameter. Typical examples are listed in the options below. If you intend using normal letters, modifier keys must be used – entered as follows:

Shift	–	Either Shift key
Control	–	The Ctrl key
Alt	–	Either Alt key
F<n>	–	Function key n: F1, F2
Help	–	The Help key

and the key/modifier combination must be enclosed in quotes. Alpha keys are case sensitive: "a" and "A" will be read separately.

Options:

CYCLE/K The *hotkey* used to cycle through any windows open on the current screen and activate them. When a window is activated, it's pushed to the front of the display. By default this is allocated to F1.

```
RUN >NIL: IHELP "CYCLE=Alt F1"
```

Note: this facility doesn't affect disk and drawer windows.

MAKEBIG/K
Defines the *hotkey* used to expand the window to fill the available screen area. By default this is F2. To change it to Ctrl-B, you would use:

```
RUN >NIL: IHelp "CYCLE=Control B"
```

Note in this case, you would have to use SHIFT-CTRL-B because the command is case sensitive.

MAKESMALL/K
Defines the *hotkey* used to shrink the window to its minimum size. By default this is F3. To change it to CTRL-S, you would use:

```
RUN >NIL: IHelp "CYCLE=Control s"
```

Unlike the example given above, a lower-case "s" is used so you should not combine this with Shift.

CYCLESCREEEN/K
The *hotkey* used to cycle through active screens. This is usually F4, so we'll add the Alt modifier.

```
RUN >NIL: IHelp "CYCLE=Alt F4"
```

ZIPWINDOW/K
This *hotkey* is used to emulate the *zoom* gadget. It's usually F5, but in this case CTRL-Z will be used:

```
RUN >NIL: IHelp "CYCLE=Control z"
```

CX_PRIORITY
The priority passed to the program on startup. This is its priority over other CX programs – not the process priority shown by STATUS. By default all CX programs have a CX_PRIORITY of 0. Higher priority programs have the first grab at incoming messages – key presses and such like. You must take this into account when using more than one Commodity at a time; especially IHelp and FKey.

General Note — Commodities Exchange

The Commodities Exchange (CX) programs are normally stored on the Extras disk. However, to keep the examples simple, we'll assume you have already changed to the correct directory or set the correct path.

Important: The CX programs *do not* return error conditions when an incorrect command line is entered – be aware of this. You can check they have launched correctly in scripts using STATUS.

INFO

Synopsis:

2.04: INFO [<device>:]

1.3: INFO [<device>:]

1.2: INFO

Templates:

2.04: DEVICE

1.3: DEVICE

1.2: ,

Path:

C:

Use:

INFO is used to list a lot of helpful information about the filing system and disk devices currently mapped onto the system. The early versions of this command merely listed all the information currently available:

```
1>INFO
Mounted disks:
Unit Size  Used Free Full  Errs Status      Name
RAM: 80K   80   0    100%  0    Read/Write  Ram Disk
DF0: No disk present
DF1: 879K  1744 14   99%   0    Read Only   Workbench

Volumes available:
Workbench1.2 [Mounted]
Workbench1.3
Ram Disk [Mounted]
```

The meaning of these being:

Unit	The physical unit number – DF0:, RAM: etc.
Size	The amount of formatted storage available in total.
Used	The amount of storage in use by files and directories in blocks. 1 block = 512 bytes.
Free	How much storage is remaining and available for use. Expressed in blocks.
Full	How full the device is as a percentage.
Errs	The number of disk errors.

Status Whether the unit is write enabled or not.

Name The name of the disk if one is present.

Volumes Available
This list is similar to the one output by ASSIGN. A disk marked as available but not "[Mounted]" has probably launched a program or been opened by the Workbench.

New – AmigaDOS 1.3:

With the 1.3 release an option was added to allow you to stipulate which device you wanted information on. This saves cluttering the screen with a lot of useless information. The default output from the command remains the same as before however so we will not reiterate it here. When listing specific devices though, some quite different things can happen.

```
1>INFO DF1:
Mounted disks:
Unit  Size Used Free Full Errs Status    Name
DF1:  879K 1744 14   99%  0    Read Only Workbench2.0
```

If Workbench2 is available and mounted you may get information on it by name:

```
1>INFO Workbench2:
Mounted disks:
Unit        Size Used Free Full Errs Status    Name
Workbench2: 879K 1744 14   99%  0    Read Only Workbench2
Volumes available:
Workbench2 [Mounted]
```

Or, if the disk is not in any drive *but* AmigaDOS knows about it.

```
1>INFO Workbench2:
Mounted disks:
Unit   Size   Used   Free   Full   Errs   Status  Name


Volumes available:
Workbench2
```

In this last case information as such is not available but AmigaDOS lists it anyway since it knows the device in question is, in fact, a volume. It is not possible to get info on pseudo-devices or assignments like PIPE: or T:. This will not cause an error, incidentally; you can use ASSIGN to get more information about these.

Options:

DEVICE Added for Workbench 1.3 optionally define which device or volume to get info on. All device and volume names *must* be followed by a colon (:). Example:

```
1>INFO DF1:
```

See also: ASSIGN

INITPRINTER

Synopsis:

2.04: INITPRINTER

1.3: INITPRINTER

1.2: na

Templates:

2.04: ,

1.3: ,

1.2: na

Path:

SYS:Utilities

Use:

This command is included here for the sake of completeness only. It sends a reset code to the currently selected Preferences printer and readies it for printing. The printer's internal buffer will be cleared and it will enter its on-line state (provided paper is loaded). The command will fail if a printer is not currently attached, but it does not return any testable conditions or warnings.

If you need to check for the presence of a suitably configured printer, use COPY instead. This example creates a file containing a single NULL (no operation) then attempts to send it to the printer. If a printer is not attached or on-line, COPY fails with ERROR:

```
FAILAT 11
EVAL >T:PrintTest 0 LFORMAT "%c"
COPY >NIL: T:PrintTest TO PRT:
IF ERROR
  ECHO "Your printer is off-line or dead"
ENDIF
```

In AmigaDOS 2 and higher, you can suppress the "printer not responding error" too:

```
FAILAT 11
EVAL >T:PrintTest 0 LFORMAT "%c"
COPY >NIL: T:PrintTest TO PRT: QUIET NOREQ
IF ERROR
  ECHO "Your printer is off-line or dead"
ENDIF
```

INPUT

Synopsis:

2.04: INPUT [[FROM=]<file>] [EDIT] [USE] [SAVE]

1.3: na

1.2: na

Templates:

2.04: FROM, EDIT/S, USE/S, SAVE/S

1.3: na

1.2: na

Path:

SYS:Prefs

Creates:

Input.prefs

Use:

This command is one of the new Preferences suite. It opens the Input Preferences tool, changes the current settings or directly alters the defaults from saved files.

Preferences files are stored as IFF of type FORM PREFS/INPT. So you can examine them like this:

```
1>TYPE SYS:Prefs/Presets/INPUT.PRE HEX
```

No readable (alpha) information is contained in this file. The following information will only be of use to hackers and is provided *as is* to get you started.

Offset	Meaning
$0033	Mouse speed (1 byte)
$0038	Double-click speed (4 bytes) * 1,000,000
$0040	Key repeat delay (4 bytes) * 1,000,000
$0048	Key repeat rate (4 bytes) * 1,000,000
$004C	Mouse acceleration (1 byte where $80 = ON)

Options:

FROM The full path and filename of a file to use for the font preferences. If INPUT is being executed from a Startup-sequence this should be combined with USE – see below. The file should have been previously created by INPUT using Save As... from the project menu. Example:

```
1>INPUT FROM SYS:Prefs/Presets/Mouse.set USE
```

EDIT/S Open the editor screen when the command runs. This switch is implied in the current release (unless USE or SAVE is specified) but it should be retained in scripts for future compatibility. Example:

```
1>INPUT FROM SYS:Prefs/Presets/Input.Set EDIT USE
```

USE/S Supply this switch to open a FROM file and use the preferences settings from that file immediately. INPUT's editor window is not opened unless the EDIT switch is also supplied.

```
1>INPUT FROM SYS:Prefs/Presets/Input.Pre USE
```

SAVE/S Specify this switch to save the settings defined in the FROM file to the correct file in ENV-ARCHIVE:Sys.

```
1>INPUT FROM SYS:Prefs/Presets/Input.Set SAVE
```

INSTALL

Synopsis:

2.04: INSTALL [DRIVE] <DF0|DF1|DF2|DF3>: [NOBOOT] [CHECK] [FFS]

1.3: INSTALL [DRIVE] <DF0|DF1|DF2|DF3>: [NOBOOT] [CHECK]

1.2: INSTALL [DRIVE] <DF0|DF1|DF2|DF3>:

Templates:

2.04: DRIVE/A, NOBOOT/S, CHECK/S, FFS/S

1.3: DRIVE/A, NOBOOT/S, CHECK/S

1.2: DRIVE/A

Path:

C:

Use:

The main use of this command is to prepare boot disks. These are ordinary, formatted disks, made special in that they have a customised bootblock at track 0 side 0 blocks 1 and 2. When the Amiga is reset it checks the "boot sectors" to see if a valid boot program can be found. If it can, the program is executed and the machine starts. If not, the disk icon (disk animation for Kickstart 2) reappears and the machine completely refuses to do anything until a valid boot disk is inserted. To install a new disk simply supply the device name; "volumes", as such, cannot be installed:

```
1>INSTALL DF1:          ; put a bootblock on drive #1
1>INSTALL System1.3:    ; this is NOT legal
```

It is important to realise though, that merely installing a disk does not constitute a complete Workbench disk which requires a lot more files and directories. The result of booting a newly formatted and installed disk is a CLI prompt which can be very confusing. *Mastering AmigaDOS 2 Volume One* describes what makes a boot disk and how to create one.

As well as writing the boot block, INSTALL adds an ASCII sequence to the bootblock identifying it as a DOS disk. This allows the Amiga to distinguish between DOS disks and special Kickstart disks used on Amiga 1000s and other "development" machines.

Options:

DRIVE/A The floppy disk drive to install. A disk must be mounted in the drive and this argument must be supplied. Range df0:..df3:

Options (>AmigaDOS 1.3):

NOBOOT/S This switch tells INSTALL to remove the boot block from an installed disk. Note: this always tries to write something and will write a boot block on a non-DOS disk. Example:

```
1>INSTALL DF0: NOBOOT
```

CHECK/S Is used to determine if the disk has a valid bootblock or not. On early systems this option reports the presence of a bootblock; with release 2 it also reports the type of bootblock in use. This should not be relied upon to identify viruses however:

```
1>INSTALL DF0: CHECK
```

Appears to be normal 1.2/1.3 bootblock

When used in scripts, the command returns a WARN condition if the disk is *non-standard*! Example:

```
FAILAT 11
INSTALL >NIL: DF0: CHECK
IF WARN
ECHO "May now be a virus in DF0:"
ENDIF
```

Note: At the time of writing the version 2 INSTALL does *not* return WARN for nonstandard disks! The 1.3 install works *but* the FAILAT condition must be higher than 10 even though a WARN condition can be tested.

Options (>AmigaDOS 2):

FFS/S This explicitly asks install to write a FFS bootblock. By default the bootblock will use the old filing system (OFS). It is unwise to use this option on OFS disks however. See also CHECK/S above.

```
1>INSTALL DF2: FFS
```

• The test for a boot disk is performed by a special checksum routine in Kickstart. This allows legitimate authors to create customised disk startups without resorting to fancy Startup-sequence scripts. Of course, the program must be written in assembler and has to be very short – about 1K – but this is quite sufficient to allow either a simple scrolling message or a custom disk loader. The boot sectors are also the inroad for many of the dangerous (and preventable) viruses kicking around the Amiga circuit.

See also: Appendix B – The Virus Menace.

JOIN

Synopsis:

2.04: JOIN <{oldfiles|pattern}> AS|TO <newfile>

1.3: JOIN <file1> <file2>... AS|TO <newfile>

1.2: JOIN <file1> <file2>... AS <newfile>

Templates:

2.04: FILE/M, AS=TO/K/A

1.3: ,,,,,,,,,,,,,, , TO=AS/K

1.2: ,,,,,,,,,,,,,, , AS/K

Path:

C:

Use:

This is one of those strange commands. Its sole purpose in life is to join a list of files together as one. Curiously enough it can join any type of file to any other type of file. This means you could join a couple of commands to an IFF sampled sound and the startup-sequence. Of course, no one in their right mind would do that because it's silly. Needless to say too, most file formats have a built-in file ID which will be corrupted by JOIN. One possible example is:

```
1>JOIN Chapter1 Chapter2 Chapter3 Chapter4 AS Chapters1-4
```

So the question is why? And indeed, why not? JOIN may not be a lot of use on its own, but it can be used to great effect in scripts as the following 1.3/2 compatible example shows. This creates two files, takes one as an argument and joins the whole lot together as a fourth. Why? This script allows you to add a creation date and time to almost any text file. It should *not* be used on 1.3 scripts, however, unless they are edited afterwards.

```
.key MyFile/A,NewFile/A
.bra {
.ket }
ECHO >ram:1.t{$$} ". Created on: " NOLINE
DATE TO ram:2.t{$$}
JOIN ram:1.t{$$} ram:2.t{$$} {MyFile} AS {NewFile}
DELETE ram:1.t{$$} ram:2.t{$$}
```

Options:

,,... (FILE/M) The list of files to concatenate into a single file. Up to 15 files can be joined.

New for 2 : This restriction has been removed so it's now possible join as many files as will comfortably fit on one line! It is even possible to use pattern matching! Example:

```
JOIN Cha#? Appx#? AS TheWholeBook
```

AS/K This keyword must be supplied. It names the destination file which will produced as the result of joining all the other files together.

Options (>AmigaDOS 1.3):

TO/K This is essentially just a pseudonym for AS. However, it may be better supplied in scripts if the destination file is itself, being joined TO.

LAB

Synopsis:

2.04: LAB <string>

1.3: LAB <string>

1.2: LAB <string>

Templates:

2.04: ?

1.3: ?

1.2: ?

Path:

Internal

C: <2.0

Use:

This command is part of the script languages SKIP...LAB...ENDSKIP construct and is meaningless outside a script file. It defines a label (hence LABel) where the SKIP is to jump to. The label text may be any reasonable length and can start with any nonscript characters. That is: you couldn't use the .BRA or .KET characters (< and >) or a period (.). In practice a simple, *short* text string will suffice. Labels are local to the script currently executing, so the same label may be used in several scripts without contention. The same is not true of the environmental variables.

Example:

```
SKIP buck               ; start a skip section
...
LAB buck                 ; The buck stops here. Uumm?
```

• Early versions of AmigaDOS have to load this from disk every time it is used. In AmigaDOS 1.3 it is wise to make this command resident either in complex scripts where it can be removed on exit or, preferably resident all the time if you use scripts a lot. The command is already resident in AmigaDOS 2.

Options:

TEXT — The label name. Don't use spaces or any queer characters no matter what they are escaped with!

This is actually optional – if the label is omitted, SKIP jumps to the nearest blank label. Neat.

See also: SKIP, ENDSKIP

LIST

Synopsis:

2.04: LIST [dir | pattern] [P|PAT <pattern>] [KEYS] [DATES] [NODATES] [TO <filename>] [SUB <substring>] [SINCE <date>] [UPTO <date>] [QUICK] [BLOCK] [NOHEAD] [FILES] [DIRS] [LFORMAT <format string>]

1.3: LIST [dir|pattern] [P|PAT <pattern>] [KEYS] [DATES] [NODATES] [TO <filename>] [SUB <substring>] [SINCE <date>] [UPTO <date>] [QUICK] [BLOCK] [NOHEAD] [FILES] [DIRS] [LFORMAT <format string>]

1.2: LIST [dir] [P|PAT <pattern>] [KEYS] [DATES] [NODATES] [TO <filename>] [SUB <substring>] [SINCE <date>] [UPTO <date>] [QUICK] [BLOCK] [NOHEAD]

Templates:

2.04: DIR/M, P=PAT/K, KEYS/S, DATES/S, NODATES/S, TO/K, SUB/K, SINCE/K, UPTO/K, QUICK/S, BLOCK/S, NOHEAD/S, FILES/S, DIRS/S, LFORMAT/K

1.3: DIR, P=PAT/K, KEYS/S, DATES/S, NODATES/S, TO/K, SUB/K, SINCE/K, UPTO/K, QUICK/S, BLOCK/S, NOHEAD/S, FILES/S, DIRS/S, LFORMAT/K

1.2: DIR, P=PAT/K, KEYS/S, DATES/S, NODATES/S, TO/K, SUB/K, SINCE/K, UPTO/K, QUICK/S, BLOCK/S, NOHEAD/S, FILES/S, DIRS/S, LFORMAT/K

Path:

C:

Use:

This must surely be one of the most powerful commands on the Amiga – and even though it offers a bewildering range of options it can be used with great ease. Dubbed by some "The script creator" we have used this command many times for creating complex scripts: automatically saving time, effort and – most important of all – errors!

At its simplest the command is just:

```
>LIST
```

Which lists the current directory contents. This can be limited by judicious pattern matching with the PAT argument:

```
1>LIST S: PAT=s#?
Directory "S:" on Tuesday 10th-Jul-90
Startup-Sequence 629 -s-- rwed Today      12:10:02
StartupII        327 -s-- rwed Today      12:12:55
Shell-Startup    928 -s-- rwed <Invalid> <Invalid>
3 files - 7 blocks used
```

The information output from LIST is very comprehensive – although this can be limited, if required, by the switches described below. By default the command lists the most useful stuff.

New for 1.3:

From this release pattern matching is usually included in the directory specification. The two must *not* be mixed. Example:

```
1>LIST S:s#?          ; This is OK
1>LIST S:st#? PAT=s#? ; This IS NOT!
```

New – AmigaDOS 2:

The new NOT wildcard (~) operator can be used for pattern matching everything but what the pattern matches:

```
1>LIST S:~(st#?|sh#) nohead
SPAT   243  -s--  rwed   12-Dec-89   12:10:02
DPAT   668  -s--  rwed   Today       14:12:55
PCD    206  -s--  rwed   Yesterday   17:46:12
```

For this release you may specify more than one source directory or device, for instance, you can now enter:

```
1>LIST SYS: DF1: RAM: T:
```

Which is the equivalent of:

```
1>LIST SYS:
1>LIST DF1:
1>LIST RAM:
1>LIST T:
```

The following options are now available in the LFORMAT string:

- %A Attributes: The file's protection bits.
- %B Blocks: The size of a file in blocks.
- %C Comment: Inserts any attached comment string.
- %D Date: The file's date stamp.
- %K Key: The file's key block (where it is on the disk).
- %L Length: The file's length in bytes.
- %N Name: The filename.
- %P Path: The file's path.
- %T Time: The file's time stamp.

Additionally, these operators can be further modified by inserting field width operators between the "%" and the "X". This new option should not be used with %S, which was retained for upward compatibility and it doesn't work as you might expect.

Using %N as an example, the two operators are as follows:

```
%<xx>.<yy>N
```

where:

<xx> is the field width and

<yy> is the number of characters in the field. This is optional.

Let's take an example, assuming you had a file with such an odd name. (Escaped quotes are used for output clarity, they are not important.) First, the standard output:

```
1>LIST ABCDEFGHIJKLMN LFORMAT "*"%N*""
ABCDEFGHIJKLMN
```

Now, let's put that in a field 20 characters wide:

```
1>LIST ABCDEFGHIJKLMN LFORMAT "*"%20N*""
"   ABCDEFGHIJKLMN"
```

and finally limit our name to the first 5 characters in a 20 character field:

```
1>LIST ABCDEFGHIJKLMN LFORMAT "*"%20.5N*""
"               ABCDE"
```

This might not look very interesting, yet. But consider this gives you the power to determine LIST's output without necessarily faffing around with EDIT. Better still, you can make the output much more predictable for functions such as SORT.

Note: One limitation of this procedure is that it's not possible to use environmental variables as part of the formatting string. For instance:

```
1>SET WIDTH 20
1>LIST #? LFORMAT "%$widthN"
```

is not legal. It just confuses the parser. However, the following is:

```
1>SET WIDTH %20N
1>LIST #? LFORMAT "$width"
```

Options:

By way of a slight departure for this command, we have found it better to use more than one switch on a command line. This allows us to show more pertinent examples and demonstrate how some of the switches interact with each other. Optional switches are shown as lower case to separate them from the rest of the example.

DIR — By default LIST searches the current directory. This allows you to specify the directory to be searched.

```
LIST SYS:; List the root of the boot!
```

In release 1.3, the directory specification may include pattern matching. Pattern matching can be applied to the current directory by just stipulating the pattern. See LIST PAT.

```
LIST #?.info  ; info files in this dir
```

P=PAT/K This is used for defining a pattern to be used during the file search. PAT is a keyword which takes any combination of standard AmigaDOS wildcard characters. From release 1.3 this option is not required but has been retained mainly for compatibility. Example:

```
1>LIST SYS: P=#?.info ; list info files
```

KEYS/S When this switch is specified LIST outputs the starting block number of the file *header*. This block points to the file and is not the start of the file's actual data. This information can be useful for recovering partly destroyed files when using a disk editor. The block or KEY numbers are surrounded in square brackets. Note: this information is invalid for the RAM: device. This example also uses NOHEAD and NODATES described below to suppress needless information:

```
1>LIST S:SPAT KEYS nohead nodates

SPAT      [ 1058]      229 -s--  rwed
```

From this we can deduce that SPAT's file header block is at track 48 sector 2.

DATES/S By default, LIST always tries to specify the weekday and time of a file's creation (assuming the file was created recently). This switch tells it to display the exact date the file was last MODIFIED. In this example the NOHEAD and QUICK switches suppress needless information:

```
1>LIST RAM:T DATES nohead quick

E01-WK1  13-Jul-90 21:01:02

E01-WK2  13-Jul-90 21:01:12
```

NODATES/S This switch suppresses the date and time information. It makes no sense to supply this option on the same line as the DATES switch. If you do try, AmigaDOS returns a helpful message about what to do with mutual admiration. Well, what did you expect? For this example we have used the NOHEAD switch to exclude some excess information.

```
1>LIST RAM:T NODATES nohead
E01-WK1         3    --rwe-
E01-WK2        15    --rwe-
```

TO/K — This may be used to define a file for LIST's output to be sent to. TO is a keyword and takes the filename as an argument. This option is most often used in conjunction with LFORMAT to create scripts. This avoids the need to use redirection although this is just as valid. Note: It is not possible to send output to two devices at once by mixing TO and ">" except >NIL:. This is an internal limitation of AmigaDOS. This example sends the listing to a PIPE and then sorts it. A detailed explanation appears at the foot of this section:

```
1>LIST SYS: TO PIPE:a; LIST to a pipe
1>SORT PIPE: *        ; sort to console
```

SUB/K — May be used if you want to limit the search pattern still further by specifying a SUBstring. SUB is a keyword and takes the string as an argument. Only files which match the pattern supplied *and* contain the substring are displayed. This example uses NOHEAD and QUICK to limit the output. It looks for any files in S: using the "st" substring to limit the search just to, say, Startups. Note: The search is *not* case sensitive – so "st" also matches "ST" and "St":

```
1>LIST S: nohead SUB=st quick
Startup-sequence
Shell-Startup
StartupII
```

SINCE/K — This keyword takes *any* valid date as an argument and restricts the display files created (or modified) *on* or *after* that date. Dates may include keydays like monday, yesterday – see DATE. SINCE may be mixed with UPTO to window the search between two dates. In versions up to 1.3 leading zeros must be supplied. Example:

```
1>LIST DEVS: SINCE 01-Jan-89 nohead dates quick
mountlist               11-Apr-89 02:38:48
printers                31-Jan-89 21:57:31
clipboards              10-Apr-89 23:40:57
system-configuration    01-Feb-89 00:58:28
```

UPTO/K — This keyword takes *any* valid date as an argument and restricts the display files created (or modified) *upto* and *including* that date. Dates may include keydays like thursday, tomorrow – See DATE. UPTO can be mixed with SINCE to window the search between two dates. UPTO's date must come after SINCE's for this to work. Examples:

```
1>LIST DEVS: UPTO TODAY nohead dates quick
mountlist                11-Apr-89 02:38:48
printers                 31-Jan-89 21:57:31
clipboards               10-Apr-89 23:40:57
system-configuration     01-Feb-89 00:58:28
```

Put it all together and use UPTO and SINCE as a window:

```
1>LIST DEVS: SINCE 11-Apr-89 UPTO 12-Apr-89 dates quick
Directory "Fastbench1.3:Devs" on Sunday 15-Jul-90
mountlist                11-Apr-89 02:38:48
clipboards               10-Apr-89 23:40:57
2 directories - 2 blocks used
```

QUICK/S This option is used to limit the output of list to the bare minimum. By default this is just the filename list, dates can be added if explicitly requested. Refer to the examples above for more information. QUICK does not imply using the NOHEAD option which must be specified if required. Example:

```
>LIST T QUICK nohead
E01-WK1
E01-WK2
```

BLOCK/S By default, when LIST gives size information about a file it does so in bytes – this option causes the output to show how many 512k blocks the file is using. Caution: do not confuse this with the KEYS option (above). This example suppresses date and time information:

```
1>LIST T nohead BLOCK nodates
E01-WK1            1     --rwed
E01-WK2            1     --rwed
TEMP           empty     --rwed
```

NOHEAD/S This switch has been used extensively throughout the examples here – it causes LIST to suppress output of the headers and footers (Directory of... and XX files...) it normally produces.

Options (>AmigaDOS 1.3):

FILES/S This switch causes LIST to suppress outputting subdirectory names and information – listing just the files instead. Files listed are subject to other specifications entered on the command line however. This example makes use of the "dev" substring to match only the devices:

```
1>LIST DEVS: FILES sub=dev quick nohead
printer.device
serial.device
clipboard.device
narrator.device
```

DIRS/S This switch is the direct opposite of FILES, causing just subdirectory information to be listed. Example:

```
1>LIST DEVS: DIRS nohead nodates
printers            Dir   --rwed
keymaps             Dir   --rwed
```

LFORMAT/K This keyword is the grand master of them all and is the main reason every user should be at least conversant with the other features of the command. LFORMAT allows you to specify a listed output tailored to your needs in such a way that it can create entire script files. This aspect of operation is covered fully in *Mastering AmigaDOS 2 Volume One*. It is sufficient here to give only the briefest overview.

There are two golden rules to remember when LFORMAT is in effect.

1) The output descriptor switches: DATES, NODATES, and so on are disabled. The entire output of the command is generated using the LFORMAT string.

2) The search switches (PAT, SUB, etc) remain in effect. This offers ultimate control of what the LFORMAT created file ultimately shows.

Other than those, the file and path name can be included twice in the output string replacing %s in the format description:

%s	Filename only
%s%s	Path and filename
%s%s %s	Path and filename, filename
%s%s %s%s	Path and filename, same again...

Example (from a script):

```
LIST >RAM:qwe<$$> T:co#? "RUN ED %s%s"
```

Note for AmigaDOS 2: After using %s four times, every new occurrence is replaced by the filename.

Options (>AmigaDOS 2):

ALL/S Just like the ALL switch in DELETE and DIR, this causes LIST to search downwards through the directory hierarchy from the current or specified directory. This has very far reaching consequences for script files – it could be used to write a script to back up a whole disk! Pattern matching only works on the top level of the search.

• By default LIST does not sort its output like DIR does and this can be a bit of a nuisance sometimes. The following example shows how to correct this:

```
1>LIST >PIPE:a

1>SORT PIPE:a *
```

This sends sorted output to the screen. All the normal options are available and should be added after the command redirection. If you need to send sorted output to a file, simply replace the * (current window) with the required filename.

See also: DIR, PROTECT, FILENOTE, SETDATE.

LOADWB

Synopsis:

2.04: LOADWB [DELAY | -DEBUG] [NEWPATH] [CLEANUP]

1.3: LOADWB [DELAY], [DEBUG]

1.2: LOADWB [DEBUG]

Templates:

2.04: DELAY/S, -DEBUG/S, NEWPATH/S, CLEANUP/S

1.3: ,

1.2: ,

Path:

C:

Use:

This command loads and activates the Workbench program. It is important to note, however, that LOADWB is not the complete Workbench program–this command only activates it. A considerable amount of work is still performed internally by Kickstart. For instance, the Workbench screen is always opened on startup even if the actual Workbench itself is not being used.

The command is normally executed as part of the Startup-sequence script. At this point it "snapshots" the current path settings and uses them to locate its extended commands like Initialise. These settings are passed to all Shells launched from the Workbench unless overridden by a PATH command in the Shell-Startup script. LOADWB can be started from the Shell with care!

```
1>LOADWB
```

The problem is this: when the Workbench is restarted it does *not* reset AmigaDOS. Any programs which happened to have a lock on the disks available at the time of the re-start (see INFO) will still have a lock afterwards. However, Workbench is reset and has a new lock on the same disks. This causes some confusion with Workbench constantly throwing up requesters to "Insert volume XX in any drive". In release 2 this problem has been overcome by the reset Workbench command which tests for any Workbench launched programs before closing down.

New AmigaDOS 2:

Preferences files are stored as IFF of type FORM PREFS/WBCF. So you can examine them like this:

```
1>TYPE ENVARC:Sys/Workbench.prefs HEX
```

These settings are determined directly from the Workbench. The original WBCONFIG tool is no longer used, although it may still appear in older versions of the software distributed with the Amiga 3000.

Options:

DEBUG This is provided for development purposes. It activates a hidden menu with two options: DEBUG and FlushLibs. The DEBUG option activates ROM Wack, the serial debugger. FlushLibs causes Workbench to free up memory, diskloaded libraries and resources still mapped to the system but marked for purging. Example:

```
LOADWB -debug
```

This option cannot be combined with DELAY.

DELAY The delay switch is provided to make Workbench wait for three seconds before starting. This allows all other disk activity (as might have been caused by previous script commands executing) to stop first. It prevents a lot of disk thrashing, and therefore, wear on the drives and your ears.

Options (>AmigaDOS 2):

NEWPATH/S:

This switch can be used with LOADWB at any time to re-snapshot the current path settings. It's a good idea to do this if you change paths a lot and launch Shells from Workbench; otherwise this option is pretty useless.

CLEANUP/S:

This switch does a CleanUp as soon as the Workbench starts. It can only be used when the Workbench has been unloaded (quit) or before it starts in the normal boot sequence. The effect of this switch is to override the current snapshot settings of the desktop icons.

LOCK

Synopsis:

2.04: LOCK <drive>: [ON|OFF] [<passkey>]

1.3: LOCK <drive>: [ON|OFF] [<passkey>]

1.2: na

Templates:

2.04: DRIVE/A, ON/S, OFF/S, PASSKEY

1.3: Drive/A, On/S, Off/S, Passkey

1.2: na

Path:

C:

Use:

LOCK was introduced as part of the FFS package from release 1.3 and is provided to inhibit write access to FFS partitions on hard disks. For this reason it cannot be used to write protect floppy disks which use OFS. The command is used thus:

```
1>LOCK DH1: ON        ; No writes to partition #1
DH1: locked
```

Once the lock is operational no command can write to the disk until it is removed. However, a couple of points must be understood. LOCK only provides a software write protect – which means the lock is *only* valid until the next system reboot or it is explicitly removed. Also, it only stops AmigaDOS access to the affected partitions or devices. Most applications software goes through AmigaDOS and will behave as expected.

Important: LOCK offers no protection against viruses or other non-AmigaDOS write access.

New – AmigaDOS 2:

With AmigaDOS 2, LOCK has been considerably improved and extended and now works on all disk partitions regardless of filing system. Also, it is now possible to lock OFS and FFS floppies as well as the system assignments†:

```
1>LOCK DF1: ON
DF1: locked
```

However, for removable media, LOCK only locks the DEVICE, not individual media units. That is: the example above stops write access to *all* disks inserted into DF1: until the lock is removed – regardless of the status of an individual disk's write protect tabs.

†System assignments are slightly more complex still. Example:

```
1>LOCK C: ON
C: locked
```

What has this done? The message "C: locked" seems to confirm C: is write protected. But you can't really prevent writing to an assignment – so LOCK, locks the device the assignment belongs to. In this case: Workbench2.x/C. You should also note that, when an assignment is moved the lock *does not* move with it. Example:

```
1>ASSIGN FONTS: DF1:fonts        ; move FONTS: to DF1:
1>LOCK FONTS: ON                 ; lock FONTS:
FONTS: locked                    ; confirmed
1>COPY Siesta.font to FONTS:     ; try to write to
FONTS:
Can't open Siesta.font for output – disk write
protected
```

Move the FONTS: assignment back to the default and see what happens:

```
1>ASSIGN FONTS: SYS:fonts        ; move FONTS: to DF1:
1>COPY Siesta.font to FONTS:     ; write to FONTS:
Siesta.font...copied             ; Write confirmed
1>COPY Siesta.font to DF1:       ; Now try DF1:
Can't open Siesta.font for output – disk write
protected
```

This has its good and bad points – but it isn't a bug. One man's bug is another man's pet flea called Cuthbert. If you didn't understand this, the chances are it doesn't affect you anyway. Think of it like this: devices are like doors, assignments are notes pinned to the door. The lock is on the door *not* on the note. The note can be moved to another door, *but* the lock must remain (fixed) where it is. QED.

Options:

DRIVE/A — Specifies the device LOCK will operate on. Hard disk partitions may be named *but* the name must be followed by a colon (:)

ON/S — Set a lock (write access) on the specified device.

OFF/S — Remove the lock on the named device – see below.

PASSKEY — A password. Once this is set the lock cannot be removed until the correct password is supplied. Note also, passwords are limited to a maximum of four characters but they are case sensitive (thus, Abcd, AbcD and ABCD are seen as different passwords.) and can contain control characters. For example:

```
1>LOCK DHO: ON Keep
DHO: locked
1>LOCK DHO: OFF
Attempt to change lock failed
1>LOCK DHO: OFF Keep
```

MAGTAPE

Synopsis:

2.04: MAGTAPE [DEVICE=<device name>] [UNIT=<unit #] [RET | RETENSION] [REW | REWIND] [SKIP=<skip #>]

1.3: na

1.2: na

Templates:

2.04: DEVICE/K, UNIT/K/N, RET=RETENSION/S, REW=REWIND/S, SKIP/N/K

1.3: na

1.2: na

Path:

C:

Use:

This is a new command in AmigaDOS 2, so new in fact no documentation exists describing it. At the time of going to press, the best we can suggest is this command is used to drive SCSI tape streamers directly. More information will probably be made available when the associated hardware appears. For the moment this command is a white elephant.

MAKEDIR

Synopsis:

2.04: MAKEDIR <{new name}>

1.3: MAKEDIR <new name>

1.2: MAKEDIR <new name>

Templates:

2.04: NAME/M

1.3: /A

1.2: /A

Path:

C:

Use:

This command creates a new sub-directory in an existing directory. It does not create an .info file for Workbench however. If you need one, it's faster to DUPLICATE the empty drawer using Workbench, or use the Create Drawer option on Workbench 2; or use the ICONED program to create a new icon. Creation of a new directory is as simple as specifying the name. Here are a few examples:

```
1>MAKEDIR Book    ; create new dir in this directory
1>MAKEDIR :Book   ; create new dir in the root of this disk!
1>MAKEDIR DF1:Book  ; Create new dir on DF1:
1>MAKEDIR DF1:Book/Chapters ; Create new sub-dir in DF1:Book
```

This command has a few limitations, remaining pretty much unchanged throughout the revisions covered in this handbook. The main problem with MAKEDIR is that it will not create more than one directory at a time and it cannot create sub-directories within sub-directories in one fell swoop. For instance the following creates a path – :Upper/Middle/Lower

```
1>MAKEDIR :Upper
1>MAKEDIR :Upper/Middle
1>MAKEDIR :Upper/Middle/Lower
```

This would have been easier to produce in one go (using just the last line) – but such is life. It is possible that this feature may be added in future revisions of course. Note: When COPY is being used it will create any new subdirectories it requires automatically. See COPY.

Choice of names for directories is subject to the usual AmigaDOS limitations. If the name requires any form of punctuation, it must be enclosed in quotes. Literal quotes must be escaped with an asterisk:

```
1>MAKEDIR "My left thumb"
1>MAKEDIR "From *"beginner*" to *"expert*""
1>MAKEDIR "RAM:      "      ; even this is possible!
```

We used the last example to show what can be done. Spaces can be a useful way of preventing prying eyes poking into your directories. Unless you have a good reason to use white space, *don't*.

New – AmigaDOS 2:

The command has been enhanced using the new multiargument parser so that any number of directories may be created at once. The deficiency above can be partially solved, albeit slightly clumsily, thus:

```
1>MAKEDIR :Upper :Upper/Middle :Upper/Middle/Lower
```

On a more useful level, you can use this to create many directories at once, say, in a Startup-script. Better still, if the command finds a directory already exists, it does not "fall over" straight away, preferring instead to complete the command line. This avoids the need to test for the existence of certain directories first. This example deliberately forces an error to show what we mean:

```
1>MAKEDIR RAM:t RAM:env RAM:t RAM:c RAM:contents
RAM:t already exists
```

Note: Unlike some disk operating systems, AmigaDOS uses DELETE to remove empty directories and files; there is no separate command.

Options:

/A, (NAME/M)

The name of the new directory. This may include any legal path but only one directory level can be created at any time.

For this releaseof AmigaDOS 2 , multiple arguments are allowed there are no restrictions as to how many directories can be created with one command.

See also: ASSIGN, CD

MAKELINK

Synopsis:

2.04: MAKELINK [FROM] <file> [TO] <file> [HARD] [FORCE]

1.3: na

1.2: na

Templates:

2.04: FROM/A, TO/A, HARD/S, FORCE/S

1.3: na

1.2: na

Path:

C:

Use:

This is a curious command which creates a file to provide an indirect "link" to another file which must be executable. When the FROM filename is given, the real executable file is called instead. LINKs do not obey the PATH, that is: a link file in SYS: can only be called when the current directory is SYS. In this example the FROM and TO options have been included, they are optional though.:

```
1>MAKELINK FROM index TO C:LIST   ; Link INDEX to list
1>INDEX
Directory of SYS: on Sunday 15-Jul-90
...
etc.
```

For this command to work, the FROM file (the link) must not already exist.

Options:

FROM/A The source file which will be linked to the TO file. LINK creates this file. It must not already exist. Must be supplied.

TO/A The destination file to be linked to the source file. Must be supplied.

HARD/S By default, MAKELINK creates soft links, that is files which link across volumes. In this way the LINKed file could be on a different disk. This option prevents this.

```
1>MAKELINK FROM index TO C:DIR HARD
```

• In the current release, soft links (which can link between volumes) are not supported. If you try to create a soft link, a hard link (or error) will be produced.

• Linked files and directories are flagged in the directory listing thus:

```
1>DIR
Devlink <hl>
```

• Under normal circumstances, links only take 1 block of disk space, although they display the file size allocated to the file they are linked to.

Where HL= Hard Link. Presumably SL will be used for a soft link, but only time will tell. Note: <hl> is not shown by LIST, although the link files will be.

Curiously enough, links can link to each other like this:

```
1>ECHO >T:Test "This is a linked test"
1>MAKELINK LNK1 T:TEST
1>MAKELINK LNK2 LNK1
1>MAKELINK LNK3 LNK2
1>MAKELINK LNK4 LNK3
1>TYPE LNK4
"This is a linked test"
```

Now, see what happens if you delete a link:

```
DELETE LNK2
1>TYPE LNK4
"This is a linked test"
```

You can even delete the original file:

```
DELETE T:Test
1>TYPE LNK4
"This is a linked test"
```

Neat, eh? In fact the data remains valid as long as at least one link remains.

IMPORTANT: If you modify the file or any of the links connected to it the links are removed and the links become files in their own right.

You could use links to create new directories of commands, where the links point to many different directories, as this script fragment shows:

```
MAKEDIR Commands
CD Commands
LIST >T:ExFile C: LFORMAT "Makelink %N %P%N"
LIST >>T:ExFile SYS:System LFORMAT "Makelink %N %P%N"
LIST >>T:ExFile SYS:Utilities LFORMAT "Makelink %N %P%N"
EXECUTE T:Exfile
```

Options:

FORCE This option is required if you want to create a link to a directory. For instance:

```
1>MakeLink Devlink TO DEVS: FORCE
```

MEMACS

Synopsis:

2.04: [<file>] [GOTO nn] [OPT W]

1.3: [<file>] [GOTO nn] [OPT W]

1.2: na

Templates:

2.04: ,

1.3: ,

1.2: na

Path:

Extras:Tools (floppy disk)

SYS:Tools (Hard disk)

Use:

MEMACS is an Amiga-ed version of David Conroy's excellent Public Domain µEmacs (pronounced Micro Emacs) Editor. For most purposes, MEMACS is the only editor you will ever need. Far more powerful than ED and far friendlier than EDIT. Here we are limiting ourselves to the command line options.

The program can be started from a Shell without a filename:

```
1>Extras1.3:Tools/Memacs
```

or:

```
1>Extras2.04:Tools/Memacs
```

Hard disk users have it a bit easier because the TOOLS directory is already in the PATH (at least it should be).

```
1>MEMACS
```

Note: to floppy users (especially those with two drives). You can add the TOOLS to the path if you are doing a lot of editing with MEMACS like this:

```
1>PATH Extras1.3:Tools ADD
```

If you have two drives and your Extras Disk normally lives in DF1: the following will do the trick. This can be added to the Startup-sequence if desired – we don't recommend it since every reset the machine will ask for a disk to be inserted in DF1:.†

```
1>PATH DF1:Tools ADD
```

The following examples all assume MEMACS is available in the current path, or the current directory. To edit a named file from the Shell you can supply either a name or complete name and path:

```
1>MEMACS User-Startup
1>MEMACS RAM:DPAT
1>MEMACS DF1:S/Startup-sequence
1>MEMACS :T/qwe1
```

† A better way around this problem is possible with ALIAS. This example should be added to the Shell-Startup script:

```
ALIAS Emacs Extras1.3:Tools/MEMACS
```

Options:

,	The file to edit would normally be supplied here but MEMACS does not specify a keyword for it. A filename is not required to start the program.
GOTO nn	This option opens the MEMACS window and loads the file – nn specifies the first line number it should display. `1>MEMACS S:Startup-sequence GOTO 20`
OPT W	With this added, the program opens a window in the Workbench screen instead of opening a private screen which is the default. This may be useful if memory is tight – otherwise this option should be ignored. `1>MEMACS S:Shell-Startup OPT W`

See also: ED, EDIT.

MERGEMEM

Synopsis:

2.04: na

1.3: MERGEMEM

1.2: MERGEMEM

Templates:

2.04: na

1.3: ?

1.2: ?

Path:

SYS:System

Use:

If you have additional memory (over 1Mb) added to your machine it usually lives in separate blocks or pools of 512k. In certain cases it may be desirable to have all the blocks memory mapped as one contiguous chunk instead of several smaller ones. MERGEMEM attempts to do this – but it can only work with memory blocks of the same attributes. If the command fails, it lists the current configuration with the attributes of each block. This example shows the command running on a 3Mb A3000:

```
>MERGEMEM
RAM Configuration
Memory node type $A, attribute $105, from $7F00000 to $7F7F000
Memory node type $A, attribute $303, from $400 to $FFFFF
No Merging possible
```

New – AmigaDOS 2:

This command has been removed in release 2.

MORE

Synopsis:

2.04: MORE [<file | pipename>]

1.3: MORE [<file | pipename>]

1.2: na

Templates:

2.04: ?

1.3: ?

1.2: na

Path:

SYS:Utilities

Use:

MORE is AmigaDOS's ASCII file viewer. Like TYPE it can show any ASCII file such as the ubiquitous READ.ME files found on so many PD disks and commercial applications. You can also use MORE to view files in the S: assignment too. Typically, the format for this command is:

```
1>MORE filename
```

or:

```
1>MORE
Enter filename, or <Return> to exit:
```

In the second instance, MORE will ask for a file to view. In release 1.3 this command prompts with some help information.

When MORE is invoked in this way, MORE fills the current Shell window. However, a more interesting approach can be gained using RUN. This example opens the Startup-sequence:

```
1>RUN MORE S:Startup-sequence
```

You should notice how MORE opens its own window and does not interfere with the current Shell. Moreover, in release 2 and higher, calling the command in this way makes it prompt with a standard file requester:

```
1>RUN MORE ; AmigaDOS 2 and above only!
```

From a PIPE

MORE can take input from a pipe in a similar fashion. It can be useful to RUN MORE for this, because it will wait until a stream appears at the pipe. The following example simulates passing a message to MORE via a background pipe.

```
1>RUN MORE PIPE:A   ; open a blank more window
[CLI 2]
1>COPY S:SPAT TO PIPE:A
```

CBM suggest a redirection operator is used for this technique. However, the only difference is in the title bar, which does not carry the name of the pipe. Try this for yourself.

```
1>RUN MORE <PIPE:A  ; open a blank more window
[CLI 2]
1>COPY S:SPAT TO PIPE:A
```

Options:

MORE does not take command arguments in the truest sense, the following options are available as key presses when the command's window is open and active.

Text	Search. Look for the next occurrence of "Text". This is not case sensitive so "ABC" and "abc" are the same.
/Text	Search. Locate the next occurrence of "Text". This is case sensitive so "ABC" and "abc" are different.
Backspace	Less: Go back a page. This function is not available when input is being taken from a pipe because pipes aren't those sort of girls.
Ctrl+L	Refresh the window.
H	Help: Pull up a short help screen and list the commands available in the version being used. This is the only key press you need to remember – and even then, MORE usually prompts you when you use an undefined key.
n	Next: Repeat the last search.
Q	Quit: Close MORE and return to the calling process.
Return	Down: Move down 1 line.
Space	More: Go forward one page.

New – AmigaDOS 2:

%N	Absolute: Move to an absolute position N percent through the file.
<	First: Go to the first page of the file. This option is not available when viewing pipes because the output is uni-directional and does not support a seek function.
>	Last: Go to the last page of the file.
b	Back: Same as backspace in the original version.
E	Edit the file directly using the editor defined in global environmental variable, EDITOR.

MOUNT

Synopsis:

2.04: MOUNT <device>: [FROM <file>]

1.3: MOUNT <device>: [FROM <file>]

1.2: MOUNT <device>:

Templates:

2.04: DEVICE/A, FROM/K

1.3: DEVICE/A, FROM/K

1.2: DEVICE/A

Path:

C:

Use:

This command adds new devices to the Amiga system. It must not be confused with "[mounted]" disks. It is rarely necessary to use this command outside the Startup-sequence script; in any event, most users will never need it apart from one special instance.

Most physical (hardware) devices like disk drives and RAM expansions automount using a file in the SYS:Expansion directory, so there is no need to use this. The only case where it should be used is to mount certain software devices like SPEAK: and PIPE:. Every mountable device has an entry in the mountlist (DEVS:MountList) which is scanned for when the command runs. An error occurs if a mountlist entry (or an associated handler) cannot be found or there is an error in the mountlist itself.

The special case where you might want to specifically mount a device yourself is for the recoverable RAMdrive, RAD:. Since RAD: is not always required and can occupy large chunks of user memory, it can be explicitly mounted when required. Once mounted RAD: remains attached to the system until flushed with REMRAD. Example:

```
1>MOUNT RAD:
```

When you purchase a new piece of hardware (or software) any special files required for mounting and so on will usually be supplied with it.

New – AmigaDOS 1.3:

The new version of this command allows a device to be mounted using a customised mountlist. This is primarily for advanced usage but does allow for variable configurations of certain devices. For instance you may want to have different sized RAD: devices. Since the size of RAD: is fixed (among other things) by the HighCyl= keyword it can be varied with ease and many combinations created. Examples:

```
1>MOUNT RAD: FROM DEVS:SmallRad
1>MOUNT RAD: FROM DF1:devs/MegaRad
```

For the sake of this example the size is calculated thus:

11264 * (HighCyl + 1) = Size of RAD in bytes

For more information on RAD: refer to *Mastering AmigaDOS 2 Volume One* – The RAM Disks.

Options:

DEVICE/A The device name for the command to attach to the system. If a FROM keyword argument is not supplied (see below) this device must have an entry in the MOUNTLIST. All device names must have a colon (:) appended to them. For example:

```
1>MOUNT PIPE:
```

Options (>AmigaDOS 1.3):

FROM/K Specifies a file to read the mounting information from, if the information does not already exist in the default mountlist – DEVS:Mountlist. The keyword is path sensitive so the complete path and filename should be supplied.

```
1>MOUNT DF2: FROM=DF0:Devs/PC-Mount
```

See also: Appendix D – The Mountlist

NEWCLI

Synopsis:

2.04: NEWCLI [<window requirements>] [FROM <startup file>]

1.3: NEWCLI [<window requirements>] [FROM <startup file>]

1.2: NEWCLI [<window requirements>] [FROM <startup file>]

Templates:

2.04: WINDOW, FROM

1.3: Window, From

1.2: Window, From

Path:

C:

Internal >2.04

Use:

This command provides access to the Amiga's multi-tasking from AmigaDOS. In early versions of the system (up to 1.2) this starts a new CLI process independent of the CLI which started it. It may have its own stack (see STACK) and its own priority (see CHANGETASKPRI). These values will be passed to any programs started from this CLI directly or launched in the background with the RUN command. In 1.2 versions of Workbench the CLI must be activated from Preferences before use.

Up to 1.3 this command uses the old console device (CON:) to provide terminal facilities. It does not support aliases, residents, command line editing or history and has been left in for compatibility with older software.

New - AmigaDOS 2:

NEWCLI uses the revised CON: device which behaves in the same way as 1.3's NEWCON:. For all intents and purposes it is now just a synonym for NEWSHELL. Older software calling NEWCLI will, in effect, open a Shell with all the associated features. NEWCLI is now a resident feature of the Shell.

Options:

WINDOW The default for NEWCLI is to open a CON: window of fixed size and position. This option allows the advanced user to specify the window requirements before the opening. This can be as simple as a smaller or larger window - but must be correctly specified to fit the current screen or the command fails. Any interactive AmigaDOS device can be used. Take this simple case:

```
NEWCLI CON:0/0/600/400/My-CLI
```

The name of the window may contain spaces and quotes if the specification is surrounded in quotes. Literal quotes must be escaped, however.

```
NEWCLI "CON:0/0/200/50/*"Emergency*" CLI"
```

This technique can be extended to the serial port to act as a remote terminal. See *Mastering AmigaDOS 2 Volume One – Multi-user Machine* for more details. Example:

```
NEWCLI AUX:
```

Important: In AmigaDOS 2 only – this argument suppresses the *close* box on the console window. Add /CLOSE option to create a close box. See NEWSHELL.

FROM By default, NEWCLI looks for a Startup file in S: called CLI-Startup*. This script is automatically executed when the window opens *but* before the prompt returns you to command mode. A FROM file allows you to customise the CLI to your own specifications. If the FROM script fails in some way NEWCLI will abort – starting the new process regardless. The option is path sensitive so the path must be specified if the startup file is not in the current directory.

Note: FROM is a keyword and *must* be specified if the WINDOW argument is omitted. Examples:

```
NEWCLI FROM DF1:MyStartup
NEWCLI AUX: Serial-Startup
```

*S:Shell-startup in AmigaDOS 2

See also: NEWSHELL.

NEWSHELL

Synopsis:

2.04: NEWSHELL [<window requirements>]
[FROM <startup file>]

1.3: NEWSHELL [<window requirements>]
[FROM <startup file>]

1.2: na

Templates:

2.04: WINDOW, FROM

1.3: Window, From

1.2: na

Path:

C:

Internal >2.04

Use:

Introduced for AmigaDOS 1.3, NEWSHELL is used to start a new Shell process independent of the CLI or Shell which started it. It may have its own stack (see STACK) and its own priority (see CHANGETASKPRI). These values will be passed to any programs started from this Shell directly or launched in the background with the RUN command.

This command was introduced to replace the ailing (and ageing) CLI. The CLI was retained for downward compatibility with older software but the command should normally be used in preference*. In release 1.3, only the Shell requires a special program which controls the command line history and several other features – this is called Shell-Seg and lives in the L: assignment. It is made part of the system resident list in the Startup-sequence. If Shell-Seg is not resident, NEWSHELL opens a CLI window.

Unless a window is specified, NEWSHELL opens a window to the NEWCON: device. NEWCON: must be MOUNTed for this to work. This is normally done as part of the Startup-sequence.

Every shell has its own set of aliases – common ones should be defined in the Shell-startup script (see below) – but shares any resident commands and system resident processes. Shell's command line history (a 2K circular buffer) and editing features are covered in a separate chapter – here is a brief summary.

Up cursor: Retrieve 1 line of command history backwards.

Down cursor: Retrieve 1 line of command history forwards.

Left cursor: Cursor 1 position left.

Right cursor:	Cursor 1 position right.
Shift + Up cursor:	Search history up for partial string.
CTRL + X *or* Shift + Down cursor:	Clear current line.
CTRL + A *or* Shift + Left cursor:	Move to start of command line.
CTRL + Z *or* Shift + Right cursor:	Move to end of command line.
CTRL + K:	Delete everything from cursor to END of line.
CTRL + U:	Delete everything from cursor to START of line.

Note: Only 20 concurrent processes can be started by NEWCLI.

• The only time where the NEWCLI can be used is to start an "Emergency" CLI which lives in some out of the way place on the screen – it uses marginally less memory than a Shell and is useful to get out of trouble if a rogue program goes haywire, locking the rest of the machine. See NEWCLI.

New – AmigaDOS 2:

NEWSHELL now uses the greatly extended CON: device which replaces CON: and NEWCON:. Also the "Shell-Seg" control program has been incorporated into Kickstart and no longer appears in the System resident list. The new Shell features a considerable number of "Internal" commands making it easier and faster to use. NEWSHELL is itself internal. The list may change from release to release – the main ones are listed in the PATH above. See RESIDENT for more details.

The new console device allows cutting and pasting between windows, window history and a close box which removes the need to use ENDCLI. Window history allows you to see more of the window by opening it further. These options are only supported by the new character-mapped windows, however. The "Cut and Paste" function can have unexpected results when used between Shell's since the invisible Carriage returns (at the end of lines) are copied. This has the effect of causing the pasted text to be executed. Nevertheless, one man's bug is another man's feature. Briefly, cut and paste is achieved thus:

1: Highlight a block to copy with the mouse.

2: Activate the window to be copied to.†

3: Press Right Amiga + V.

4: Repeat step 3 as often as required.

†This is not necessary if you are copying to the current window.

Note: The 20 process limit has been removed.

Options:

WINDOW The default for NEWSHELL is to open a NEWCON: window* of fixed size and position. This option allows the advanced user to specify the window requirements before the opening. This can be as simple as a smaller or larger window – but must be correctly specified to fit the current screen or the command fails. Any interactive AmigaDOS device can be used. Take this simple case:

```
1>NEWSHELL CON:0/0/600/400/My-Shell
```

The name of the window may contain spaces and quotes if the specification is surrounded in quotes. Literal quotes must be escaped, however.

```
1>NEWSHELL "CON:0/0/600/400/My *"Shell*" Window"
```

It is even possible to start multiple Shells using the same console window. This may be useful if memory is tight, if you like to work with just one window, or just for the sake of curiosity:

```
1>NEWSHELL *
```

This technique can be extended (more usefully) to the serial port to act as a remote terminal. See *Mastering AmigaDOS 2 Volume One* for more details.

New for AmigaDOS 2: As a matter of course the window Close gadget is ommitted. However, if you need a Close gadget you add the /CLOSE argument thus:

```
1>NEWSHELL CON:0/0/600/400/My-Shell/CLOSE
```

* NEWCON: has been replaced by CON: in AmigaDOS 2.

The following options are also available. You can use all of them in any order:

AUTO The window does not open until the program using it requests input or causes output. It is not usual to use this option directly with NEWSHELL because a new shell process causes output in announcing itself.

BACKDROP The window is pushed behind all the others and cannot be depth-adjusted. This option works well when combined with the NOBORDER switch too.

FROM By default, NEWSHELL looks for a Startup file in S: called Shell-Startup. This script is automatically executed when the window opens *but* before the prompt returns you to command mode. A FROM script allows you to customise the Shell to your specifications. If the

FROM script fails in some way NEWCLI will abort – starting the new process regardless. The option is path sensitive so the path must be specified if the startup file is not in the current directory.

Note: Although FROM is not a keyword it *must* be specified if the WINDOW argument is omitted. Examples:

```
1>NEWSHELL FROM S:Extended-Startup
1>NEWSHELL AUX: Serial-Startup
```

NOBORDER No border is attached to the window (in theory). To see this effect at its best combine the NOSIZE option too.

NODRAG The window remains in a fixed position on the screen and cannot be moved by its title bar.

SIMPLE This option is default for Shell windows. so that when a window is zoomed the text it contains is re-drawn to fit – even expanded if necessary. Compare to SMART.

SMART This option reverses the effect of the SIMPLE flag. (In my opinion, SIMPLE and SMART are the wrong way round.) This option makes AmigaDOS 2 CON: windows work like those in 1.3 – hummm? Console cut and paste is not available when this option is selected.

WAIT The window can only be closed with the close gadget or by pressing CTRL+\.

See also: ENDSHELL, NEWCLI, STATUS, and *Mastering AmigaDOS 2 Volume One*.

NOCAPSLOCK

Synopsis:

2.04: NOCAPSLOCK [priority=<n>]

1.3: na

1.2: na

Templates:

2.04: CX_PRIORITY/K/N

1.3: na

1.2: na

Path:

SYS:Utilities

Use:

This command effectively disables the Caps Lock key on the keyboard. This can be useful when you're working in a Shell and occasionally catch the Caps Lock when reaching for an "a". Don't panic, we all do it sometimes – I do it quite often in fact. When NOCAPSLOCK is active, you can still enter upper case letters by holding down either Shift key.

This command can be started in the usual manner, passing one parameter if you feel the urge (it isn't really necessary) like this.

```
1>NOCAPSLOCK
```

Whereupon the Shell freezes and you can do nothing else. This is a poor situation to be in, but is easily rectified. Either type CTRL-E or, better still, just multi-task the command like this:

```
1>RUN NOCAPSLOCK
```

and surely as Bob's your uncle, you have control and you don't get those awkward changes of case mid-line.

This command is best called from User-startup and forgotten about:

```
1>RUN >NIL: NOCAPSLOCK
```

That bit about NIL: allows the initial CLI window to close when ENDCLI is executed. If it is omitted, NOCAPSLOCK gets a *lock* on the window and the window will not be able to close.

If NOCAPSLOCK is called twice, the second invocation removes the first and terminates immediately. It is not possible to have two copies running at once. Therefore, you should not call it in automatic Shell-startups unless you write some code to check for it first.

Options:

CX_PRIORITY

The priority passed to the program on startup. This is its priority over other CX programs – not the process priority shown by STATUS. By default all CX programs have a CX_PRIORITY of 0. Higher priority programs have the first grab at incoming messages – key presses and such like.

General Note — Commodities Exchange

The Commodities Exchange (CX) programs are normally stored on the Extras disk. However, to keep the examples simple, we'll assume you have already changed to the correct directory or set the correct path.

Important: the CX programs *do not* return error conditions when an incorrect command line is entered – be aware of this. You can check they have launched correctly in scripts using STATUS.

See also: AUTOPOINT, BLANKER, EXCHANGE, CLICKTOFRONT, FKEY, IHELP

NOFASTMEM

Synopsis:

2.04: NOFASTMEM

1.3: NOFASTMEM

1.2: NOFASTMEM

Templates:

2.04: ,

1.3: ,

1.2: ,

Path:

SYS:System

Use:

This command traps EXEC's AllocMem function and ensures all future requests for memory are allocated from the free CHIP pool.

Why?

Very early Amiga 1000s came with only 256K of RAM – even though the custom chips could access 512K. Later machines saw the introduction of newer custom chips capable of accessing a full 1Mb or even 2Mb of RAM. Any RAM mapped outside these limits is often referred to as FAST RAM. It's called "fast" because the custom chips cannot stop the CPU accessing it whenever they feel like it.

However, some programs, because they were never tested on a machine with extra memory do not expect to find any. When they request memory from the free pool asking for *any* type, they expect to get CHIP and get FAST instead. This is caused by lazy programming. When they attempt to set the custom chip's memory address pointers to the allocated RAM, which is actually FAST, the top bits of the address are truncated and the pointer ends up at a random position in CHIP!

The effect can be anything from a screenful of junk or weird sprites if graphics are involved, or garbled noise if the sound system is in use. If the program is writing to disks, the result can be – and often is – catastrophic!

New – AmigaDOS 1.3.2:

In addition to its normal function, NOFASTMEM diverts calls requesting FAST memory to Public memory. This will only be noticeable in multiuser systems when (*if*) they become available.

See also: FASTMEMFIRST

OVERSCAN

Synopsis:

2.04: OVERSCAN [[FROM=]<file>] [EDIT] [USE] [SAVE]

1.3: na

1.2: na

Templates:

2.04: FROM, EDIT/S, USE/S, SAVE/S

1.3: na

1.2: na

Creates:

Overscan.prefs

Use:

This command is one of the new Preferences suite. It opens the Overscan preferences tool, changes the current settings or directly alters the defaults from saved files.

Preferences files are stored as IFF of type FORM PREFS/OSCN. So you can examine them like this:

```
1>TYPE SYS:Prefs/Presets/OVERSCAN.PRE HEX
```

No readable (text) information is available in this file, the following is provided *as is* to get you started.

Offset	Meaning
$003A	Text X overscan size
$003C	Text Y overscan size

Options:

FROM The full path and filename of a file to use for the font preferences. If OVERSCAN is being executed from a startup-sequence this should be combined with USE – see below. The file should have been previously created by OVERSCAN using "Save As..." from the project menu. Example:

```
1>OVERSCAN FROM SYS:Prefs/Presets/BigScream USE
```

EDIT/S Open the editor screen when the command runs. This switch is implied in the current release (unless USE or SAVE is specified) but it should be retained in scripts for future compatibility. Example:

```
1>OVERSCAN FROM SYS:Prefs/Presets/Overscan.Pre EDIT USE
```

USE/S — Supply this switch to open a FROM file and use the preferences settings from that file immediately. OVERSCAN's editor window is not opened unless the EDIT switch is also supplied. This command should be used with care from Shell because IPREFS will need to reset the screen and that means closing all Workbench-launched programs.

```
1>OVERSCAN FROM SYS:Prefs/Presets/Overscan.Pre USE
```

SAVE/S — Specify this switch to save the settings defined in the FROM file to the correct file in ENVARC:Sys.

```
1>OVERSCAN FROM SYS:Prefs/Presets/IC.Settings SAVE
```

PALETTE

Synopsis:

2.04: PALETTE [[FROM=]<file>] [EDIT] [USE] [SAVE]

1.3: na

1.2: na

Templates:

2.04: FROM, EDIT/S, USE/S, SAVE/S

1.3: na

1.2: na

Creates:

Palette.ilbm

Use:

This command is one of the new Preferences suite. It opens the Palette preferences tool, changes the current settings or directly alters the defaults from saved files.

Preferences files are stored as IFF of type FORM ILBM/CMAP. So you can examine them like this:

```
1>TYPE SYS:Prefs/Presets/PALETTE.PRE HEX
```

This is an IFF brush or colour file in effect.

Options:

FROM The full path and filename of a file to use for the font preferences. If PALETTE is being executed from a Startup-sequence this should be combined with USE – see below. The file should have been previously created by PALETTE using "Save As..." from the project menu. Example:

```
1>PALETTE FROM SYS:Prefs/Presets/GawdyColours USE
```

EDIT/S Open the editor screen when the command runs. This switch is implied in the current release (unless USE or SAVE is specified) but it should be retained in scripts for future compatibility. Example:

```
1>PALETTE FROM SYS:Prefs/Presets/Palette.Pre EDIT USE
```

USE/S Supply this switch to open a FROM file and use the preferences settings from that file immediately. PALETTE's editor window is not opened unless the EDIT switch is also supplied.

```
1>PALETTE FROM SYS:Prefs/Presets/Palette.Pre USE
```

SAVE/S Specify this switch to save the settings defined in the FROM file to the correct file in ENVARC:Sys.

```
1>PALETTE FROM SYS:Prefs/Presets/NewColours SAVE
```

PARK

Synopsis:

2.04: PARK [partition] [partition]... [INHIBIT]

1.3: PARK [partition] [partition]... [INHIBIT]

1.2: PARK [partition] [partition]... [INHIBIT]

Templates:

2.04: [partition] [partition, partition...] [INHIBIT]

1.3: [partition] [partition, partition...] [INHIBIT]

1.2: [partition] [partition, partition...] [INHIBIT]

Path:

SYS:System (Hard disk systems only)

Use:

Where hard disks are concerned, protection of the magnetic media is vital since they can hold 20 – 300Mb (or more) of precious data. At the very least, a simple checksum error can be a nuisance – at worst damage to the disk's surface is very expensive to repair. The PARK command can avoid all this, and a lot of tears into the bargain.

Surprisingly perhaps, the most dangerous thing you can do to a hard disk unit, short of moving or dropping it, is to switch it on or off. If a hard disk is attached to your machine the park command should be the *very last* command executed when you finish a session: before you switch off – don't even close the CLI. This ensures the next time you switch on, the heads are placed conveniently over an unused portion of the disk. The syntax of this command is simply:

```
1>PARK
```

This assumes DH0: is the only partition on your hard drive and appears as such in the Units list of the INFO command. It may be the partition has been given another name, WORK:, SYSTEM: etc. This appears in the HD Toolbox program supplied by Commodore. If this is the case the partition name can be supplied instead.

```
1>PARK Work:
```

From Workbench (like CLI) the command defaults to partition DH0: and if this is missing it will complain. The Workbench PARK Icon's tooltypes should, for instance, read:

```
PARTITION=Work:
```

On larger systems the hard disk may have more than one partition. If this is the case you should check the HD Toolbox program to check all partitions park at the same cylinder. This is usually the highest available on the disk.

Options:

Partition... The partition (or list of partitions) to be affected by the command. More than one Partition may be supplied if the INHIBIT switch is being used. In all other cases PARK should only be used on the partition with a correctly configured PARKing cylinder. Default DH0: (may be JH0: on some systems). But will accept a partition name, ie, WORK:.

INHIBIT This switch is used to stop access to one or more partitions. Unlike LOCK which prevents write access, INHIBIT prevents both READs and WRITEs. In effect it removes the partition from the system. This may be useful to protect private data, client records etc. To switch off accidental read/write access to partition 2:

```
1>PARK DH2: INHIBIT
```

Multiple partitions (on larger systems) can be parked thus:

```
1>PARK DH1: DH2: Work: INHIBIT
```

It is vital to realise that this option does *not* physically park the heads. Also, the switch is *only* software based and can be reset by a warm boot. It cannot be cancelled any other way.

Note: Although it is quite possible to inhibit the boot or system partition. This is not generally advisable because AmigaDOS would have no access to its commands. Use LOCK instead.

• This command is only supplied with hard disk systems†. The INHIBIT switch may not be available with third-party systems. In this case use LOCK – at least this prevents AmigaDOS writing to the disk.

† Some drives are "self-parking" (they move the heads automatically when power is removed) and do not require software parking.

See also: LOCK, *Mastering AmigaDOS 2 Volume One* – Hard Disks.

PATH

Synopsis:

2.04: PATH [<dir>] [ADD] [SHOW] [RESET] [QUIET] [REMOVE]

1.3: PATH [<dir>] [ADD] [SHOW] [RESET] [QUIET]

1.2: PATH [<dir>].[ADD] [SHOW] [RESET]

Templates:

2.04: PATH/M, ADD/S, SHOW/S, RESET/S, QUIET/S, REMOVE/S

1.3: ,,,,,,,,,, ADD/S, SHOW/S, RESET/S, QUIET/S

1.2: ,,,,,,,,,, ADD/S, SHOW/S, RESET/S

Path:

Internal

C: <2.04

Use:

This command is used to define the search path for AmigaDOS to follow when searching for commands. Ordinarily, when no paths have been set, this defaults to just the current directory and the C: assignment; usually this will be the C directory of the boot disk.

In normal circumstances this search path is far from adequate and only of any real use to non-standard boot disks for applications that do not require much in the way of other directories. For instance, with the default settings it is not possible to access system commands like FORMAT, which because they are not strictly AmigaDOS, are stored in the System directory. For most purposes PATH is used once only in the Startup-sequence to set the search paths required by Workbench and AmigaDOS. Used on its own the command lists the current path. For example:

```
1>PATH
Current directory
RAM Disk
Workbench 1.3:Utilities
Workbench 1.3:System
Workbench 1.3:S
Workbench 1.3:Prefs
C:
```

This means every time you type a command at the command line, AmigaDOS looks in every directory listed for a command matching the one specified. If the command is not found, AmigaDOS moves to the next directory on the list or, if the list has expired, reports an error saying Unknown command: nnn. Note though, the list is always searched *top* to *bottom*. If you issued a FREDDY command, and FREDDY was found in the current directory, that version would be executed even if a different version of the same name existed elsewhere on the path.

By adding more directories to the path, you can ask AmigaDOS to search farther afield. It's important to realise here, the paths defined in this example are *inserted* between the ones already in existence and before C:.

```
1>PATH Utils:C Utils:s DF2:c DF2:s
```

Because the C: assignment is always searched last of all, if you use AmigaDOS a lot – and we hope you will – adding the following path can speed things up a little. This should be placed either as part of the PATH command in the Startup-sequence script *or* as a separate command before the main paths are set:

```
1>PATH RAM: SYS:c
```

This has some interesting implications. Not least, it is possible to ADD the same path two or more times! In this case, it ensures that the BOOT disk's Command directory is always searched first (after searching the current directory). On floppy disk machines this can speed command searches considerably; more so in scripts.

More important, when the command is issued the volume *must* be mounted; if a device name is specified, the drive *must* contain a disk. Curiously enough, if the volume is removed at a later stage, the search path will remain in force *but* AmigaDOS will not ask for it back, skipping any temporarily unmounted volumes. This can be viewed as a bug or a feature. In any case: be aware of it.

More On the Default PATH

The curious may ask, why is C: searched last? This does seem strange at first – but it is logical. AmigaDOS is giving everything else a chance to execute first, which as a far as Workbench is concerned is what's required.

If you happen to be using AmigaDOS you'll probably want to search RAM: (which is very fast anyway) then SYS:C which is normally the command directory. However, the relationship between PATH and ASSIGN allows you to assign a secondary command directory and change it at will. C: defaults to SYS:C but there is no reason why it couldn't be DF1:C or even a utilities disk.

Hard disk users with 1.2 Kickstart should beware changing the PATHs and ASSIGNments made by the system early in the startup, since they are often used to transfer control to the hard disk sub-system.

New – AmigaDOS 2:

PATH uses the multi-args command parser so the limit of ten directories per command has been removed. It is *not* possible to define paths to DEFERred or PATHed assignments without first inserting (auto-mounting) the disks.

Options:

ADD — This switch instructs AmigaDOS to add the specified directories to its search path. Its use is arbitrary (it's default anyway) unless you are using the RESET switch earlier in the command line. Example to add the System directory to the search path:

```
1>PATH SYS:System ADD
```

SHOW — Like ADD this command is pretty arbitrary since the command defaults to printing the entire path list if no arguments are supplied. It should be specified when other switches are in effect to show the current path list. Example:

```
1>PATH SYS:System add SHOW
```

Note: It is not possible to find the state of a single path.

RESET — This switch should be specified either on its own or as the first on the command line. It tells AmigaDOS to reset the path back to default. This example removes all previous paths then adds a single one:

```
1>PATH RESET SYS:System ADD
```

Options (>AmigaDOS 1.3):

QUIET — Once a path has been defined path command will always try to find it when showing (default) or the SHOW switch is specified. This can (sometimes) mean AmigaDOS throwing up requesters for volumes to be re-inserted. QUIET prevents unwanted requesters; just the volume name appears in the path list. This example shows the complete path but eliminates paths on unmounted volumes.

```
1>PATH QUIET
```

Options (>AmigaDOS 2):

REMOVE — It may be occasionally necessary to add and subtract a path (or paths) at will – without disturbing the rest of the system. This switch takes the specified paths and removes them without resetting the entire path which was the only option until this release. For instance, to remove DF2:C and Tools:C directories:

```
1>PATH DF2:C Tools:C REMOVE
```

Note: The path scheduled for removal should be the same as the one added! That is if you specify a DRIVE name and let AmigaDOS find the volume you should not change the disk, then try to remove the path.

The "Pathfinder" Script

We mentioned above it is not possible to inquire the state of one path using SHOW – which would have been the logical way. Here then, is a very short script to search out the paths you want...

```
.KEY P/a,opt1
PATH >"T: " <opt1>
SEARCH "T: " :<P>
```

To use it simply type:

```
1>EXECUTE PATHFINDER <Pathname> [QUIET]
```

Any paths matching the specified pattern are listed. Example:

```
1>EXECUTE PATHFINDER System
..
4    Workbench1.3:System
```

We have kept this script as simple as possible to avoid confusion. The two "dots" come from the SEARCH command where it is trying to list the filename; which in this case happens to be a space! The line numbering can be suppressed if desired by adding NONUM to the search command 1.3+. It is largely a matter of personal taste, but shows the priority of the searched path.

This version does not multi-task at all – because of the temporary filename clash but this is unlikely to be a problem. Purists can append a <$$> to the name if they wish.

Note: The QUIET option (1.3+) is passed directly to PATH and not checked for syntax. You have several options here: remove the option altogether; include it in the script directly; check the syntax. This last takes time on pre-2.0 machines unless IF, ENDIF etc. are resident. Here's how to implement it – with multi-tasking capability added too:

```
.KEY P/a,opt1
IF "<opt1>" NOT EQ ""
  IF "<opt1>" NOT EQ "QUIET"
       ECHO "Bad option: <opt1>"
       QUIT 20
  ENDIF
ENDIF
PATH >T:Path<$$> <opt1>
SEARCH T:Path<$$> :<P>
```

See also: ASSIGN, CD

PCD

Synopsis:

2.04: [<new directory>]

1.3: [<new directory>]

1.2: na

Templates:

2.04: pat

1.3: pat

1.2: na

Path:

S:

Use:

Like DPAT and SPAT, this is another one of Commodore's useful (although rarely used) script examples. It works just like CD with the addition of remembering the previous directory. For the history feature to work, however, you must use the command at least once to change directory. Failing to do this causes a Shell redirection error. In this case, all this means is the CD command (in PCD) could not locate the temporary file holding the last directory.

Using the command is as simple as using CD. This example uses CD to show the interaction between the two commands:

```
1>CD
Workbench1.3:System
1>PCD Devs:keymaps
1>CD
Workbench1.3:devs/keymaps
1>PCD
1>CD
Workbench1.3:System
```

There are some interesting hangovers from the way this command works. PCD is a multi-tasking script – at least, the temporary files it creates are unique to every invocation. This means you can PCD several different directories in each Shell and always be sure each will return to its own.

Better still perhaps, because of the relationship with CD, you can use PCD to change one directory level, use CD for the rest of the time but at any stage get back to where the first PCD was called from. The same is true if you want to "toggle" between two directories as in this example – we are using CD to clarify what is going on, in a way that you can try. Normally you wouldn't need this because the prompt could show you:

```
1>CD                          ; We are here
Workbench1.3:
1>PCD Devs:keymaps            ; move to devs/keymaps
1>CD                          ; Just confirm that
Workbench1.3:devs/keymaps
1>PCD                         ; back to where I was
1>CD                          ; confirm that
Workbench1.3:
1>PCD                         ; move back AGAIN
1>CD                          ; Just confirm that
Workbench1.3:devs/keymaps
```

New – AmigaDOS 2:

Since this command is based around CD, any changes made there apply here too.

See also: CD, PROMPT, *Mastering AmigaDOS 2 Volume One* – three chapters covering scripts.

POINTER

Synopsis:

2.04: POINTER [[FROM=]<file>] [EDIT] [USE] [SAVE]

1.3: na

1.2: na

Templates:

2.04: FROM, EDIT/S, USE/S, SAVE/S

1.3: na

1.2: na

Creates:

Pointer.ilbm

Use:

This command is one of the new Preferences suite. It opens the Pointer preferences tool, changes the current settings or directly alters the defaults from saved files.

Preferences files are stored as IFF of type FORM ILBM/GRAB. So you can examine them like this:

```
1>TYPE SYS:Prefs/Presets/POINTER.PRE HEX
```

This is a sprite file. A simple IFF brush should do the trick nicely!

Options:

FROM The full path and filename of a file to use for the font preferences. If POINTER is being executed from a Startup-sequence this should be combined with USE – see below. The file should have been previously created by POINTER using "Save As..." from the project menu. Example:

```
1>POINTER FROM SYS:Prefs/Presets/WakkoPoint USE
```

EDIT/S Open the editor screen when the command runs. This switch is implied in the current release (unless USE or SAVE is specified) but it should be retained in scripts for future compatibility. Example:

```
1>POINTER FROM SYS:Prefs/Presets/Shadowed.Point EDIT USE
```

USE/S Supply this switch to open a FROM file and use the preferences settings from that file immediately. POINTER's editor window is not opened unless the EDIT switch is also supplied.

```
1>POINTER FROM SYS:Prefs/Presets/Pointer.Pre USE
```

SAVE/S Specify this switch to save the settings defined in the FROM file to the correct file in ENVARC:Sys.

```
1>POINTER FROM SYS:Prefs/Presets/NewPointer SAVE
```

PREFERENCES

Synopsis:

2.04: na

1.3: PREFERENCES [POINTER | PRINTER | SERIAL]

1.2: ?

Templates:

2.04: na

1.3: POINTER/S, PRINTER/S, SERIAL/S

1.2: ?

Path:

SYS:Prefs

Use:

This command opens the 1.2 or 1.3 Preferences tool. It is not usually called from AmigaDOS, except in very special circumstances; in a script for example. The Preferences screens are covered in the sister book *Mastering Amiga Workbench.*

Options:

POINTER/S	Go directly to the Pointer preferences screen.
PRINTER/S	Go directly to the Printer preferences screen.
SERIAL/S	Go directly to the Serial preferences screen.

PRINTER

Synopsis:

2.04: PRINTER [[FROM=]<file>] [EDIT] [USE] [SAVE]

1.3: na

1.2: na

Templates:

2.04: FROM, EDIT/S, USE/S, SAVE/S

1.3: na

1.2: na

Creates:

Printer.prefs

Use:

This command is one of the new Preferences suite. It opens the Printer Preferences tool, changes the current settings or directly alters the defaults from saved files.

Preferences files are stored as IFF of type FORM PREFS/PTXT. So you can examine them like this:

```
1>TYPE SYS:Prefs/Presets/PRINTER.PRE HEX
```

The following information will only be of use to hackers and is provided *as is* to get you started.

Offset	Usage
$0032	The name of the current printer
$0050	Printer port (1 byte) 0=parallel; 1=serial
$0052	Paper type (1 word) 0=Fanfold; 1=sheet
$0054	Paper size (1 word)
$0056	Paper length in lines (1 word)
$0058	Print pitch (1 word)
$005A	Print spacing (1 word)
$005C	Left margin in characters (1 word)
$005E	Right margin in characters (1 word)
$0060	Print quality (1 word) 0=draft; 1=NLQ

Options:

FROM The full path and filename of a file to use for the font preferences. If PRINTER is being executed from a Startup-sequence this should be combined with USE – see below. The file should have been previously created by PRINTER using "Save As..." from the project menu. Example:

```
1>PRINTER FROM SYS:Prefs/Presets/MainPrinter USE
```

EDIT/S Open the editor screen when the command runs. This switch is implied in the current release (unless USE or SAVE is specified) but it should be retained in scripts for future compatibility. Example:

```
1>PRINTER FROM SYS:Prefs/Presets/OtherPrint EDIT USE
```

USE/S Supply this switch to open a FROM file and use the preferences settings from that file immediately. PRINTER's editor window is not opened unless the EDIT switch is also supplied.

```
1>PRINTER FROM SYS:Prefs/Presets/EpsonQ USE
```

SAVE/S Specify this switch to save the settings defined in the FROM file to the correct file in ENVARC:Sys.

```
1>PRINTER FROM SYS:Prefs/Presets/EpsonX SAVE
```

PRINTERGFX

Synopsis:

2.04: PRINTERGFX [[FROM=]<file>] [EDIT] [USE] [SAVE]

1.3: na

1.2: na

Templates:

2.04: FROM, EDIT/S, USE/S, SAVE/S

1.3: na

1.2: na

Creates:

PrinterGfx.prefs

Use:

This command is one of the new Preferences suite. It opens the PrinterGfx Preferences tool, changes the current settings or directly alters the defaults from saved files.

Preferences files are stored as IFF of type FORM PREFS/PGFX. So you can examine them like this:

```
1>TYPE SYS:Prefs/Presets/PRINTERGFX.PRE HEX
```

No readable (text) information is available in this file. The following information will only be of use to hackers and is provided *as is* to get you started.

Offset	Meaning
$0033	Aspect (horizontal=0; vertical=1)
$0035	Shade
$0037	Image (positive=1; negative=0)
$0039	Threshold
$003A	Colour correct (3 bits where R=1, G=2, B=4)
$003B	Limits and limit type
$003C	Dithering type
$003F	Smoothing flag (bit 2, low nybble)
$003F	Scaling (bit 1, low nybble)
$003F	Centre picture flag (bit 0, low nybble)
$0040	Density
$0042	Width (1 word) divide by 10 for inches
$0044	Height (1 word) divide by 10 for inches
$0046	Left offset (1 byte)

Options:

FROM The full path and filename of a file to use for the font preferences. If PRINTERGFX is being executed from a Startup-sequence this should be combined with USE – see below. The file should have been previously created by PRINTERGFX using Save As... from the project menu. Example:

```
1>PRINTERGFX FROM SYS:Prefs/Presets/WW_Grafix USE
```

EDIT/S Open the editor screen when the command runs. This switch is implied in the current release (unless USE or SAVE is specified) but it should be retained in scripts for future compatibility. Example:

```
1>PRINTERGFX FROM SYS:Prefs/Presets/DPaint.set EDIT USE
```

USE/S Supply this switch to open a FROM file and use the preferences settings from that file immediately. PRINTERGFX's editor window is not opened unless the EDIT switch is also supplied. This command should be used with care from Shell because IPREFS will need to reset the screen and that means closing all Workbench-launched programs.

```
1>PRINTERGFX FROM SYS:Prefs/Presets/EpsonGrx.Pre USE
```

SAVE/S Specify this switch to save the settings defined in the FROM file to the correct file in ENVARC:Sys.

```
1>PRINTERGFX FROM SYS:Prefs/Presets/DPaint.set SAVE
```

PRINTFILES

Synopsis:

2.04: PRINTFILES <File> [<File>...] [F]

1.3: PRINTFILES <File> [<File>...] [F]

1.2: na

Templates:

2.04: [-F] file [file file...] [-F Formfeed]

1.3: [-F] file [file file...] [-F Formfeed]

1.2: na

Use:

This command is used to print text or graphics printed to a file. This is more powerful than simply copying a vanilla ASCII file to the printer thus:

```
1>COPY text to PRT:
```

In order to use this command you must first create a printfile – usually using CMD to redirect printing to a file. You might wish to do this in order to prepare several pages quickly and print them later – printing to RAM or disk is usually faster than printing direct to printer. Printfiles comes into its own when multi-tasked. For instance to print several chapters of a book, called chap1..4, you might use:

```
1>PRINTFILES -F Chap1 Chap2 Chap3 Chap4
```

Options:

-F This sends a CLS (ASCII 12) to the printer making it move to the top of form – assuming of course the paper has been set correctly.

See also: CMD

PROMPT

Synopsis:

2.04: PROMPT <new prompt string>

1.3: PROMPT <new prompt string>

1.2: PROMPT <new prompt string>

Templates:

2.04: ,

1.3: ,

1.2: ,

Path:

Internal

C: <2.04

Use:

The prompt is the AmigaDOS's way of telling you "I'm ready and waiting to take your command, O Master." And there's no reason why you couldn't have a prompt which said just that. Well, OK, you'd look a bit silly. The prompt command is used to customise the prompt which normally defaults to a simple >. The syntax just expects to find the new prompt string, but if you want to include spaces or special characters it should be delimited by quotes:

```
1>PROMPT A>

A>PROMPT "Next please...>"

Next please...>PROMPT

>
```

Even as far back as AmigaDOS 1.2, it is possible to include the current CLI number as part of the prompt. The variable %N expands to this anywhere in the prompt string. For instance, assuming you had set the standard prompt:

```
>

>PROMPT "%N.>"

1.>
```

Much more interesting, don't you think.

Really Interesting Prompts!

We've already mentioned that the variable can be expanded anywhere in the string – but why not in the middle?

```
1>PROMPT "(%N)>"
(1)>
```

Simple example. But since the string has no effect on the %N sequence–why not include ANSI escape sequences? There's nothing stopping you – here are a few to play with:

```
PROMPT "*e[33m%N.%S*e[31m>"
PROMPT "*ec%N>"
PROMPT "*e[4m%N.%S*e[0m>"
```

New – AmigaDOS 1.3:

As almost everyone should have realised if they have AmigaDOS 1.3 – the variable %S was added to show the current directory as well as the current CLI number as part of the prompt. So the new standard for Amiga prompts became:

```
>PROMPT "%N.%S>"
1.Workbench1.3>
```

Yippee! It is still not possible to include the date (as in MS-DOS, tut-tut) but at least the PROMPT can be expanded from an environmental variable. Why? Since the prompt is set in a Shell-startup script, it can be expanded from a variable. Change the variable and the next Shell to start gets the new prompt. In the Shell-Startup, the new PROMPT command appears thus:

```
PROMPT <ENV:pmt >NIL: ?
```

To set or change *new* prompts only:

```
SETENV <new prompt string>
```

Note: The %S variable takes its input from the CD command, so if CD has not been used, the %S part of the prompt may not expand. The way around this is to use CD <directory> *after* setting the prompt string.

New – AmigaDOS 2:

If no prompt string is supplied AmigaDOS now sets the prompt to the equivalent of:

```
PROMPT "%N.%S>"
```

This has the effect of always showing the current CLI number followed by the current directory. It is also possible to include the date and time as part of the prompt, but this freezes from when the prompt was set so it is of little use. Quotes *must* be used for this or the ">" character can get confused with the redirection symbol. For posterity here's how:

```
1>PROMPT "`DATE` .%N>"
29-Aug-90 20-07-05 .1>
```

A similar effect can be gained using CD. This freezes the directory prompt at whatever the current directory *was* when the command was issued.

Important: you *must* use the ALT key to access the apostrophe symbols on UK keyboards or this command expansion feature does not work.

Prompt can be expanded from an environmental variable (like 1.3) with the shortened form:

```
PROMPT $PMT
```

Options:

PROMPT The new prompt string. If a null string is supplied to prompt that's exactly what you get!

New for AmigaDOS 2: A null string resets the prompt back to the default of "%N.%S>"

%R Inserts the last RC return code. See SET and IF for more information.

Options (>AmigaDOS 2):

PROMPT As before but a null string resets the prompt back to the default of "%N.%S>"

See also: CD

PROTECT

Synopsis:

2.04: PROTECT [FILE] <file|pattern> [+|- <HSPARWED>] [ADD|SUB <HSPARWED>] [ALL] [QUIET]

1.3: PROTECT [FILE] <file> [+|- <HSPARWED>] [ADD|SUB <HSPARWED>]

1.2: PROTECT [FILE] <file> [<RWED>]

Templates:

2.04: FILE/A, FLAGS, ADD/S, SUB/S, ALL/S, QUIET/S

1.3: FILE/A, FLAGS, ADD/S, SUB/S

1.2: FILE/A, FLAGS

Path:

C:

Use:

Associated with every AmigaDOS file there are a set of five "protection" bits or flags. These are (in order of appearance) as follows:

A Archive: If *set* this indicates the file has been saved in an archive – copied. This flag is not supported by AmigaDOS, it is supplied instead for user and thirdparty software.

R Readable. When *set* the file may be READ by a program or displayed as text. Not used by AmigaDOS 1.2.

W Writable. When *set* the file can be *written* to by other software. It may *not* be possible to delete the file completely. It could be written 0 bytes long however. Not used by AmigaDOS 1.2.

E Executable. If *set* this file can be run by AmigaDOS or launched as a process by RUN. Not used by AmigaDOS 1.2.

D Deletable. If *set* this file can be deleted from the system completely. When *reset* it may still be possible to write to the file however.

As shown with release 1.2 just the "deletable" flag is recognised by AmigaDOS. Nevertheless, third party programs can access the flags and use them independently of AmigaDOS.

Note: If you use protect on a logical assignment which is assigned to a directory, the protection flag is changed on the directory name only – not the contents. This example clears the delete flag of the directory currently assigned to C:

```
1>PROTECT C: RWE
```

It is neither possible nor logical to protect non-directory assignments.

New – AmigaDOS 1.3:

The command has been changed so that a selection of flags can be reset or set at once *without* affecting the status of the others. Previously it was only possible to set or reset the whole lot in one fell swoop. Also, more than one flag can be altered at a time. For example to set the archive flag on a file, and protect it against alteration:

```
1>PROTECT MyFile +A
1>PROTECT MyFile -DW
```

Note that it is not possible to specify both SET (+) and RESET (-) on the same line.

Also new for this release are three more flags:

P The pure flag. Indicates a program which can be made resident. See RESIDENT for more details.

S The script (or sequence) flag. This allows scripts to be executed automatically just like a real command. AmigaDOS locates and loads EXECUTE for you. See EXECUTE for more details.

H The hidden flag. This is not used by AmigaDOS.

The E (execute) flag is now read correctly by AmigaDOS. Even if a command is executable, this flag must be set or the program will not run.

New – AmigaDOS 2:

The hidden (H) flag *may* be supported by AmigaDOS 2. Use it with caution, however, the results may not necessarily be reversible.

Options:

FILE/A This specifies the name of the file to be worked on. Note: Pattern matching is not allowed.

1.3: Use SPAT if you need pattern matching.

2+: Pattern matching is supported.

FLAGS The new set of flag bits to use. Any combination of HARWED.

1.3+: The set of flags to change and what action to take + or -. Also works in the same way as the 1.2 version. Any combination of HSPARWED.

Options (>AmigaDOS 1.3):

ADD/S This switch is another (perhaps clearer) way of saying +. This example uses each method to achieve the same effect – it adds the script flag.

```
1>PROTECT S:Shell-Startup +S
1>PROTECT S:Shell-Startup ADD S
```

SUB/S This switch works the opposite way to ADD or -, in that it resets the flags. This example uses each method to achieve the same effect – it clears the delete flag.

```
1>PROTECT C:type -D
1>PROTECT C:type SUB D
```

Options (>AmigaDOS 2):

ALL/S If this switch is specified, PROTECT protects everything on the disk from the current directory moving downwards through the hierarchy. This example protects all the files on the boot disk from accidental deletion:

```
1>PROTECT SYS:#? -D ALL
```

Note: Pattern matching only works on files and directories in the first searched directory. Also, you will not be able to update the Preferences settings if you protect them against deletion.

QUIET/S This switch suppresses all output from the command. It is equivalent to sending all output to the NIL: device. These two examples perform virtually the same function:

```
1>PROTECT SYS:#? -D ALL QUIET
1>PROTECT >NIL: SYS:#? -D ALL
```

The difference being, in the second case errors and warnings are not displayed. This has uses though; in scripts for example.

See also: LIST

QUIT

Synopsis:

2.04: QUIT [<error code>]

1.3: QUIT [<error code>]

1.2: QUIT [<error code>]

Templates:

2.04: RC/N

1.3: RC

1.2: RC

Path:

Internal

C: <2.04

Use:

This command can be used anywhere but only has any meaning within script files. It allows you to trap for errors and return a condition code (if applicable) indicating the severity of the error. Basically, QUIT could be used as in this simple fragment:

```
IF "{drive}" EQ "SYS:"
ECHO "Can"t format the system disk!"
QUIT    ; Leave the script NOW
ELSE
...
```

QUIT cannot be stopped and cleans up after itself. Any pending IFs are ignored and the script stops there and then. However, it is sometimes necessary to run a script from within a script. The behaviour of QUIT in these circumstances may be unexpected. Take this example of two simple scripts – the first executes the second:

Script #1:

```
; MAIN: This calls SUBSCRIPT
ECHO "This is script #1"
EXECUTE subscript
ECHO "Now I've finished"
```

Script #2:

```
; SUBSCRIPT: This is called by MAIN
ECHO "This is script #2"
ECHO "Now I'm about to QUIT..."
QUIT
```

You can try this example for yourself. See what happens? QUIT in the script #2 stops script #1 too; at the point where script #1 calls script #2. Now you see why we urge you to try it for yourself!

To speculate (we didn't write AmigaDOS remember) what seems to be happening is this: When QUIT runs, it signals (through AmigaDOS) to stop the current EXECUTE command. EXECUTE does some clever tricksand one is, that it doesn't spawn sub-CLI to run the script from. It also means messages to the current CLI – from QUIT for example go to the "wrong" EXECUTE – always the one run from process (CLI) level as it turns out.

No matter how deep the nesting is, QUIT will always return you back to CLI level. This is fine – unless you only want to go back to the calling script. To get around this, RUN each successive EXECUTE in the background. Because RUN spawns a sub-process, when QUIT runs, the message gets to the right EXECUTE and execution continues at the next nesting level up – or exits back to the calling CLI if at the top level. This sounds a lot more complex than it is – to see it in action modify script #1 above thus:

```
ECHO "This is script #1"
RUN EXECUTE subscript
```

Now the expected action takes place. This is useful, but wouldn't it be better if the subscript could return a result to the caller? QUIT's command line gives it away: QUIT RC. The RC bit means Result (or return) Code.

```
QUIT 5  ; Send a WARN condition to caller
```

This can be checked for by the caller using IF. However, if you want to send results of 10 and above you *must* set the failure limit higher than the highest possible result. If not, the caller may continue to execute and *only* return the fail condition after the script returns to the CLI!

Sadly it is not possible to set Result2 from QUIT. This is used internally by AmigaDOS to indicate the type of error – it's passed to FAULT. For most users this will not pose any problems since ECHO can (and should) report any errors – in *plain English*. Even if a script is for your own use, never use cryptic messages.

Note: QUIT must not be used to exit from ICONX scripts. If you need to leave one of these use SKIP..LAB to jump past the last line of the script. If ICONX encounters QUIT, the script stops and returns the user to a CLI and, because it's meant for Workbench users, this is not very satisfactory. At best they will have to type ENDCLI to get control back to Workbench where they feel safe.

Options:

RC The result code to return to the calling script. Almost any NUMERIC value is possible but adherence to the accepted limits is strongly advised:

0=SUCCESS

5=WARN

10=ERROR

20=FAIL

This example sends an ERROR condition to the caller.

```
QUIT 10
```

See also: FAILAT, IF, *Mastering AmigaDOS 2 Volume One* – three chapters covering scripts.

RELABEL

Synopsis:

2.04: RELABEL [DRIVE] <drive|volume>: [NAME] <new name>

1.3: RELABEL [DRIVE] <drive|volume>: [NAME] <new name>

1.2: RELABEL [DRIVE] <drive|volume>: [NAME] <new name>

Templates:

2.04: DRIVE/A, NAME/A

1.3: DRIVE/A, NAME/A

1.2: DRIVE/A, NAME/A

Path:

C:

Use:

This command changes the volume names of disks, that's all it does, and that should be the end of the discussion – but it has a hidden feature. As you might have noticed, the command template notes DRIVE/A but our synopsis notes drive *or* volume. This is an important feature which should not be overlooked.

The basic use of this command follows; in this example, the *disk* in drive 0 is having its volume name (title) changed to Backups. Note: the DRIVE and NAME keywords are optional but they are required arguments – both must be specified or the command will fail.

```
1>RELABEL DRIVE DF0: NAME Backups
```

Simple enough – but this affects any disk inserted into drive 0. If you put the wrong disk in it gets the new name instead. To overcome this you can RELABEL a disk by specifying its volume name instead. If the disk is not currently mounted, AmigaDOS will ask for it. In this example the volume called, C_FILES, is being renamed to C-BACKUPS. You *must* use a colon after the *original* volume name to tell AmigaDOS to search for a volume of that name:

```
1>RELABEL C_FILES: C-BACKUPS
```

A couple of other points are worth mentioning. If you want to include spaces and/or quotes in the old or new name the complete name must be enclosed in quotes – and quotes *must* be escaped using *. This example shows the disk in drive 1 having its name changed to "Why Me?":

```
1>RELABEL DF1: "*"Why Me?*""
```

Incidentally, although RELABEL does tell AmigaDOS about the change, it does not tell Workbench about it! If you try to access a RELABELled disk from Workbench, Workbench will ask for the disk to be inserted. You can't do this, of course, because the volume does not exist with that name any more! To get around this either remove and re-insert the disk, or better still use DISKCHANGE.

Note: Wait at least one second after issuing this command for the change to take effect on the disk. If the disk is removed (or the machine reset) during this wait period the change will *not* take effect on the disk.

Options:

DRIVE/A — The drive or volume to receive the new name. Volume names are treated like devices so must have a colon (:) appended to them

NAME/A — The new volume name for the specified drive. A quoted string may contain escaped quotes and spaces but *must not* contain ANSI escape sequences – these will not display correctly. Spaces are not recommended.

See also: DISKCHANGE, FORMAT.

REMRAD

Synopsis:

2.04: REMRAD [<drive>:] [FORCE <drive>:]

1.3: REMRAD

1.2: na

Templates:

2.04: DRIVE, FORCE

1.3: ,

1.2: na

Path:

C:

Use:

The recoverable ramdrive (RAD:) was introduced with Workbench 1.3 as a means of fast data storage like RAM:. Unlike RAM: however, the contents of RAD: are safe even if the Amiga is reset by the user or (heaven forbid) disappears up a Guru meditation. Also unlike RAM: which has dynamic RAM allocation, RAD: uses a fixed amount of storage. This is not a problem most of the time because RAD: has to be explicitly mounted. Once it is mounted, however, the RAM it uses cannot be accessed by the rest of the system – this is true even after a soft reset.

If you mount RAD: either in the Startup-sequence, or from the CLI and then find you need more memory, it has to be removed and this is what REMRAD (REMove Recoverable rAmdrive Device) does. The syntax is simply:

```
1>REMRAD
```

This makes RAD: give as much memory as it can back to the system free pool. A very small amount has to be retained due to the mounting. After the next soft-reset, RAD: vanishes completely.

This command fails if another process is already using RAD:. For instance, you might have ASSIGNed a logical directory to RAD: in which case it would be "illegal" to remove the drive. Poor programming can also give rise to this – in particular where a program launched from RAD: (or which has accessed it) has left a "lock" on a file stored there when it exited. Under AmigaDOS 1.3 nothing can be done about this short of a power off (hard) reset.

*Note: In some versions of the operating system, REMRAD does not recognise RAD: until the machine has been rebooted at least once.

Options (>AmigaDOS 2):

DRIVE — Defines the drive to remove. With AmigaDOS 2+ it should be possible to mount several RAD: ramdrives and this allows you to remove just one. This example removes the default drive:

```
1>REMRAD RAMBO:
```

FORCE/S — Forces REMRAD to remove the drive from the system list even if the drive is currently being used by something! This option *must* be used with care. In early versions of AmigaDOS 2 this option behaved like a keyword! These examples show both versions.

```
1>REMRAD FORCE=RAD:     ;Known version
1>REMRAD RAD: FORCE     ; Later version?
```

At the time of writing, Issue 1 of the system software (supplied with the first Amiga 3000s) behaved as in the first example.

See also: MOUNT, *Mastering AmigaDOS 2 Volume One.*

RENAME

Synopsis:

2.04: RENAME [FROM] {<file | pattern>} [TO | AS] <name or directory> [QUIET]

1.3: RENAME [FROM] <filename> [TO|AS] <new name>

1.2: RENAME [FROM] <filename> [TO|AS] <new name>

Templates:

2.04: FROM/A/M, TO=AS/A, QUIET/S

1.3: FROM/A, TO=AS/A

1.2: FROM/A, TO=AS/A

Path:

C:

Use:

This is a simple command for renaming files and directories. And that, in a nutshell, is it! These examples rename a file and a directory:

```
1>RENAME MyFile.C Editor-Main.C   ; Renaming a file
1>RENAME C-Files MoreC-Files ; Renaming a directory
```

Note that there is no difference in this function – AmigaDOS treats directory names just like filenames.

Because of the way the directory structure is formed, RENAME has another unexpected function – it can be used to *move* files from one directory to another directory on the same disk! It does this by changing the pointers in the file header block – so RENAMEing across disks is not possible (see below for a solution). This example moves the file called "Sleepy.S" from the root directory of the current disk to the Devpac/Source directory:

```
1>RENAME :Sleepy.S TO Devpac/Source
```

New – AmigaDOS 2:

RENAME can accept pattern matching. However, this only works for moving files since the destination name *must* be a directory. For example, to move all the "C" files in the RAM: disk (root) to the T directory.

```
1>RENAME #?.C RAM:T
```

Options:

FROM/A — Defines the source file which will be renamed. FROM itself can be omitted but the argument is required. Example:

```
1>RENAME FROM "Hello" "Goodbye"
```

FROM/A/M — RENAME in AmigaDOS 2 can take multiple source files and move them to another directory, which must exist. It is not possible to rename several files as one big one. Use JOIN to do that. For example:

```
1>RENAME file1 file2 file3 TO Detritus
```

TO/A — Defines the name which will be given to the FROM file. TO is optional and can be omitted but the argument is required for the command to work.

```
1>RENAME "Goodbye" TO "Hello"
```

Note: You may wish to use TO in a script to indicate the use of RENAME as a move.

AS/A — A pseudonym for TO.

```
1>RENAME FROM "Goodbye" AS "Hello"
```

Note: You may wish to use AS in a script to indicate the use of RENAME as a renaming function.

New - AmigaDOS 2:

QUIET/S — Suppress progress messages when multiple file option is selected through patterns etc.

The Eclectic MOVE script

We've already said, RENAME cannot be used to move files or directories across disks – but COPY can. However, using copy it is necessary to remove the source file after copying, so RENAME is better used on the same disk. This script solves the problems of remembering which command(s) to use by doing it all for you automatically!

```
.key from/a,to/a
.bra {
.ket }
echo "Moving from {from} to {to}"
failat 21
rename {from} TO {to}
if fail
failat 10
copy >NIL: "{from}" "{to}"
protect >NIL: {from} +d  ; This is optional
delete >NIL: "{from}"
endif
```

You use MOVE as you might use COPY/DELETE or RENAME. However the script does the hard work of deciding which to use for you. In fact, what it does is it attempts to use RENAME first, then if that doesn't work goes on to use the more longwinded version for moving between devices. The PROTECT part is optional in this script, it just makes doubly sure the source file is removed.

This example moves a file in RAM:C to DF0:C-Backups

```
1>EXECUTE MOVE RAM:C/Myfile.C DF0:C-Backups
```

Under AmigaDOS 1.3+ you can use pattern matching for this function – the S bit must be set in the MOVE script for this to work:

```
1>SPAT MOVE RAM:#? DF0:RAM-Backups
```

In AmigaDOS 2 there is no need to use SPAT since all the functions can use pattern matching anyway. The example above becomes:

```
1>MOVE RAM:#? DF0:RAM-Backups
```

RESIDENT

Synopsis:

2.04: RESIDENT [<resident name>] [<program name>] [REMOVE] [ADD] [REPLACE] [PURE] [SYSTEM]

1.3: RESIDENT [<resident name>] [<program name>] [REMOVE] [ADD] [REPLACE] [PURE] [SYSTEM]

1.2: na

Templates:

2.04: NAME, FILE, REMOVE/S, ADD/S, REPLACE/S, PURE/S, SYSTEM/S

1.3: NAME, FILE, REMOVE/S, ADD/S, REPLACE/S, PURE/S, SYSTEM/S

1.2: na

Path:

Internal

C: <2.04

Use:

RESIDENT was introduced as one of the new features in the Shell with the introduction of Workbench 1.3. In fact, this innocent looking command had very far reaching consequences for the whole of AmigaDOS! It also created a storm amongst the Amiga community (well, a small breeze at least). It suddenly became possible to hold copies of AmigaDOS commands in RAM.

But so what? This could be done just as easily by copying them to RAM:, couldn't it? In a way this is true, but resident commands are different: only one copy resides in RAM, no matter how many are running as processes. Commands copied to, and executed from RAM:, are copied into user RAM for every invocation. This is inefficient in two ways:

1) At least two copies are RAM resident while the command executes. For every concurrent invocation of the command, another copy is made – this uses RAM very quickly if a lot of processes are running.

2) The command has to be copied from RAM: to the RAM where it will be executed. Although this happens very quickly it still takes some time which could be better used; and during multitasking, time is crucial.

Resident commands avoid these problems because only one copy of the code sometimes called 'text' is in RAM and that copy is shared by all the processes running it. Commands must be specially designed to run resident – their code must be "pure". (This is discussed below). The pure flag indicates pure code – LIST can be used to discover if a command is pure. Here's a simple way to list all the pure commands:

```
1>LIST >RAM:pure C:
1>SEARCH RAM:pure -p
```

This example can be applied to any directory. It excludes scripts because they cannot be made resident.

Some commands are made resident in the Startup-sequence script. Resident can be used to discover which:

```
1>RESIDENT
Name     UseCount
CD             0
List           0
Dir            0
Resident       1
Execute        0
1>
```

As well as the name, this displays a curious variable UseCount. This is the number of processes currently *sharing* the resident copy of the command <Name>. Unless you happen to be multi-tasking one of the resident commands this will be 0. Resident will always display as at least 1 in this case – because you are using it to show the resident list.

Making a new command resident is simple:

```
1>RESIDENT C:ASSIGN
```

Note: even though you must supply the complete path for the command to be loaded, the resident name will be the basename of the path – that is the normal command name. This can be overridden using the name option:

```
1>RESIDENT NAME=RASSIGN FILE=C:ASSIGN
```

This allows you to use either the resident version of the command or the a different version from disk. A script for autoloading resident commands from anywhere in the path is provided under the description of WHICH.

New – AmigaDOS 2:

When executed without arguments RESIDENT lists all the commands on the internal list. It is possible (and very likely) that this list may change in later releases, so it is worthwhile checking the one on your machine. The commands noted in this volume as internal in this text are believed correct for release 2 at the time of going to press.

Options:

NAME — Specifies the name of the command as it will appear in the Resident list. This is an optional argument. A command's resident name defaults to the basename of the file made resident. If this option is used it must be placed before the filename to load. This example makes ED resident, giving it the resident name – RED:

```
1>RESIDENT RED C:ED
```

FILE — The name of the command to make resident. If the name option (above) is omitted, the basename of the path will become the command's resident name. Although this example makes SEARCH resident taking it from DF1:C – its resident name will still be SEARCH.

```
1>RESIDENT DF1:C/Search
```

REMOVE/S — This switch removes the named resident from the resident list. The name specified must be the command's name as it appears in the resident list. This removes FeFiFoFum:

```
1>RESIDENT FeFiFoFum REMOVE
```

Note: AmigaDOS 2 users must *not* remove internal commands as there is no way to get them back. This does not save RAM: anyway. If you need to replace an internal command, use ADD or even REPLACE instead. Internal commands removed are marked DISABLED.

ADD/S — Tells resident to add the specified command to the resident list. In this way a command can be *temporarily* added to the resident list (in a script for example) and removed later without affecting the user's own residents. This example adds LIST.

```
1>RESIDENT C:LIST ADD
```

REPLACE/S — This is the default switch – and is therefore rather arbitrary. RESIDENT always tries to replace an existing command of the same name if already resident; if not the command is added. Example:

```
1>RESIDENT C:CD REPLACE
```

This is best used in scripts to make the meaning of the command more clear to other users.

PURE/S — This switch *must* be used with care. It force loads a command onto the resident list regardless of the status of the pure bit. RESIDENT will issue a warning if this happens but will not fail (and stop a script). This example is from Workbench 1.3's startup-sequence. PURE is being used to force load the Shell-Seg program onto the system list:

```
RESIDENT L:Shell-Seg SYSTEM PURE ADD
```

SYSTEM/S Is context sensitive. That's to say, it has different meanings which are determined by the rest of the command line.

1) Used on its own, SYSTEM makes RESIDENT list the resident commands *plus* any programs resident on the system part of the RESIDENT list.

2) Used with a filename argument, this forces RESIDENT to add the specified program to the system part of the resident list. This usage is for developers only. Normal AmigaDOS programs *must* not be added to the system's resident list; it is for the private usage of the Amiga and AmigaDOS. See PURE for an example.

The Purity of Code

The complications do not end there though. If they did, RESIDENT would have probably been introduced long before it was. In order for a command to run resident it must have pure code – code that is both re-entrant *and* re-executable. It isn't difficult to design pure code tricky though it sounds – but it takes a little more thought. This is described for technoheads below.

Most third-party code is unlikely to be pure. If it is, the pure flag will have been set by the author. However, some usable software may be old enough to have preceded the pure flag. It is possible that a pure program (in the PD) has been downloaded from a BBS or even copied with the NOPRO switch in effect (see COPY). This would mark the program as "dirty" if you like – and incapable of being made resident. There are two tests for pure code each of which is listed below:

Testing for re-executable code

This is the first and most important test. Can the RAM *resident* copy of a program be executed more than once without the first invocation affecting the second.

1) Force load the test command into resident RAM using PURE.

2) Execute the command and use all of the possible options. * This may not be feasible with a CLI only program. In this case, use the minimum set of arguments to make the command work. Now leave the program.

3) Execute the command again. If the Amiga crashes, the program is not a suitable candidate. If everything seems to be working normally there is a chance the program is OK.

* CLI based programs should be tested first *without* arguments. If the command requires arguments and succeeds it is *not* suitable. If it fails, then proceed with a different set of arguments and make sure the expected result is achieved. Continue in this way until all the possible options have been tried – in every way you can think of!

Testing for re-entrant code

This test is also very important because it ensures the program can be run safely from more than one process at the same time. If a program passes the re-executable test, but fails this one – it can still be used, provided you never attempt to multi-task it.

1) Force load the test command into resident RAM using PURE.

2) Run the command simultaneously from two Shells at once. For CLI based commands, this isn't very easy, so we suggest one of the following methods:

   2a) Using a single shell use the "+" option to force AmigaDOS to wait until return is pressed before executing the first line.

```
1>RUN test+
test+
test
```

   2b) Write a simple script to run the command several times for you. Don't use SKIP..LAB! This will cause the command to run until the process list is full (or something falls over!).

3) Make sure that options used by the first program are not affecting options in the second. Menu items are a good bet; but large Intuition applications are rarely candidates for this kind of multi-tasking anyway. CLI based* programs and some smaller Intuition ones are good candidates *but* are less likely to be fully re-executable.

   * Programs which patch operating system functions like SETPATCH should not be made resident – primarily because most are intended to be run once only.

Designing Pure Code

Surprisingly perhaps, designing pure code is not a task which is as difficult as it first seems. As mentioned above, pure code must be both re-executable and re-entrant.

At the start of each run all the variables must be correctly initialised to their starting positions. That is, all internal variables must be set according to a user's CLI options and not contain what they did when the program ended.

One way around this is to reserve some part of the code as an uninitialised data segment. Assembly language programmers use the DS (Define Space) directives to do this. The main problem with this technique is that you have to copy a block of default values in there yourself. The other problem is that, while this does make re-executable code, it does *not* make it re-entrant.

A much better way is to use EXEC's Allocate function to obtain some RAM from the free pool. ALL variables used by the code *must* use this memory; which must be relinquished when the program exits.

"C" programmers note: this includes *all* structures and globals. Function local variables are usually stored on the task's stack so they automatically generate pure code.

Assembler programmers (for once) have an easier time of it. The first line of code should be a LINK instruction to reserve some stack for variable space. Since this saves the original stack pointer and initial value of the LINKed register, the code becomes pure by default. It is still possible to use Allocate (and associated calls) to grab blocks of RAM, provided the pointer to those blocks is stored locally. The program should have a single exit point which UNLKs (unlinks) the LINKed stack as the *very last* instruction before the RTS.

See also: PROTECT, WHICH

REXXMAST

Synopsis:

2.04: REXXMAST

1.3: na

1.2: na

Templates:

2.04: ,

1.3: na

1.2: na

Path:

SYS:System

Use:

This command is used to start the REXX resident process. REXXMAST must be running in order for REXX programs to work. Once the resident process has been started, it announces itself and control returns directly to AmigaDOS. For instance:

```
1>REXXMAST
ARexx version 1.14
Copyright c 1987 William S. Hawes
All rights reserved
```

Attempting to start the resident task more than once just results in an error, viz:

```
1>REXXMAST
ARexx version 1.14
Copyright c 1987 William S. Hawes
All rights reserved
REXX server already active
```

It doesn't hurt to check – and REXX programs won't run without this. The resident process doesn't take up much RAM, so, if you use REXX much, this command is best placed in the Startup-sequence script. Note: On some machines this may have already been done. If you really need to stop the resident task use the RXC (RexX Close) command.

RUN

Synopsis:

2.04: RUN <command> [+ <{command}>]

1.3: RUN <command> [+ <command>]

1.2: RUN <command> [+ <command>]

Templates:

2.04: COMMAND/F

1.3: ?

1.2: ?

Path:

C:

Use:

This command is used to start a command as a background process – that is: a process that does not take over the current console window. Commands launched in this way are often called asynchronous processes. In effect what happens is this: RUN starts a new CLI (like NEWCLI) but instead of opening a new window, it passes the input and output handles of the *current* window to the new process. The child process also adopts the current stack and priority settings. This is akin to NEWSHELL * but without the complication of multiple CLIs sharing the same console. You might like to try this for yourself.

RUN has some interesting side effects which will be discussed in a moment, but, here's how to use the command. Let's imagine you want to copy a large number of files from the floppy disk to RAM:. By normal means this is a time consuming task since you have to wait until the copying process finishes. Using RUN however, things are a lot simpler:

```
1>RUN COPY DFO:C/#? RAM: QUIET
[CLI 2]
```

The actual CLI number in "[ ]" will change, depending upon how many processes are being multi-tasked at the time the command is launched; it's there just for information. You might need this in case you wanted to send a break code. More important in this example is the use of QUIET. If this option was not specified, the output (from COPY in this instance) would be plastered all over the screen. Some commands don't have a QUIET switch. In this case just re-direct their output to NIL:. The example above could have read:

```
1>RUN >NIL: COPY DFO:C/#? RAM:
1>
```

The problem with this is, if errors are encountered you might not get to hear about them! The simple rule is this: if the command has a QUIET option use that instead. You should also note that RUNning a command with output redirection to NIL: suppresses the [CLI n] message. Advanced users may wish to specify NIL: in scripts and check for errors with IF. Under Workbench 2 serious errors cannot usually be hidden because output goes to a different handle.

Script files can be started much the same way. The AutoBack script (see WAIT) must be started in this way:

```
1>RUN EXECUTE AutoBack time=30 source=RAM:C dest=SYS:C
```

When used in this way, EXECUTE owns the subCLI so the whole script runs as if it was being run from a separate CLI.

Advanced Use of RUN

Because RUN spawns a sub-CLI, it provides a neat way of RUNning several commands in one go. All you do is place a plus (+) at the end of each line to send to the sub-CLI. The most commonly used example is not a very good one! Here is a version for posterity:

```
1>RUN COPY RAM:T/#? TO PRT: +
DELETE RAM:T/#? +
ECHO "All done."
[CLI 2]
```

It doesn't take a genius to spot the flaw in this. It works, *but* what if the first command had failed for some reason? Execution stops doesn't it... The example above is just like typing:

```
1>COPY RAM:T/.#? TO PRT:        ; Spot the ERROR!
1>DELETE RAM:T/#?
1>ECHO "All done."
```

We've deliberately introduced an error here to show you what could have happened. COPY can't find any files BUT doesn't fail as such. Next DELETE removes all the files in the RAM:T and echo says – "All done." Even though nothing has gone to the printer the files in RAM:T have been deleted! Very nasty. Here's a far better example – an alarm clock!:

```
1>RUN WAIT UNTIL 17:00 +
ECHO "Oi! Wake up – time to go! The time is:" NOLINE +
DATE
[CLI 2]
```

This uses WAIT to wait until a specified time then echo a message on the screen. This can be enhanced still further by typing CTRL+G inside the echoed quotes – it looks like a capital G in reverse video and makes the screen flash. WAIT isn't very accurate – it usually manages around 30-40 seconds late – and it relies on the real time clock to work! If you felt creative this example could just as easily display a picture and/or play a sampled sound too. The possibilities are almost endless!

Using RUN <command> + in Scripts

It is possible that you might want to use this feature of RUN in scripts. It works as if the command had been executed from the command line. However, this should only be used for very simple scripts. That is, ones that don't loop back on themselves or rely on the output from the asynchronous RUN created process. The example alarm above can be turned into a script like this. It doesn't have to be RUN itself and several alarm times can be set from the same CLI!

```
.key time/a,message
.def message "Hey, lazy bones – timer has finished!"
RUN WAIT UNTIL <time> +
ECHO "<message>"
```

Usage:

```
Alarm <time> [<message>]
```

See also: STATUS

SAY

Synopsis:

2.04: SAY [<text>] [m | f | r | n] [s=<n>] [p=<n>] [x=<file>]

1.3: SAY [<text>] [m | f | r | n] [s=<n>] [p=<n>] [x=<file>]

1.2: na

Templates:

2.04: [-m] [-f] [-r] [-n] [-s speed] [-p pitch] [-x filename]

1.3: [-m] [-f] [-r] [-n] [-s speed] [-p pitch] [-x filename]

1.2: na

Path:

SYS:Utilities

Use:

This command provides access to the Amiga's built-in text to speech facility. Called without options it works as if it had been called directly from the Workbench - which is ideal for experimenting with different values. Used from Shell or within batch files it can provide some entertaining – if not particularly useful – effects. For example:

```
1>SAY Hello Bruce -f-r
1>SAY -X S:Startup-sequence
```

Options:

m Use a male voice (default).

f Use a female voice (this requires some imagination).

r Robotic (?) No inflection. This option is a modifier for the female setting.

n Natural voice – human inflection. This is default.

s Speed. The rate at which the speaker attempts to read the text in words per minute. Range 40..400

p Pitch. The centre frequency used by the speak.device. Range 65..320

X Filename. When this option is used, say attempts to read and speak text from a file. This is the only option which requires the user to resort to Shell. For example:

```
1>SAY -X S:Startup-sequence
```

SCREENMODE

Synopsis:

2.04: SCREENMODE [[FROM=]<file>] [EDIT] [USE] [SAVE]

1.3: na

1.2: na

Templates:

2.04: FROM, EDIT/S, USE/S, SAVE/S

1.3: na

1.2: na

Creates:

Screenmode.prefs

Use:

This command is one of the new Preferences suite. It opens the SCREENMODE Preferences tool, changes the current settings or directly alters the defaults from saved files.

Preferences files are stored as IFF of type FORM PREFS/SCRM. So you can examine them like this:

```
1>TYPE SYS:Prefs/Presets/SCREENMODE.PRE HEX
```

Hackers and the curious might like to know that three bytes starting from offset $0033, determine the current screen mode. A list of current modes can be found under BINDMONITOR. For most mortals, nothing of interest can be viewed in this file.

Options:

FROM — The full path and filename of a file to use for the font preferences. If SCREENMODE is being executed from a Startup-sequence this should be combined with USE – see below. The file should have been previously created by SCREENMODE using Save As... from the project menu. Example:

```
1>SCREENMODE FROM SYS:Prefs/Presets/XtraHirRes USE
```

EDIT/S — Open the editor screen when the command runs. This switch is implied in the current release (unless USE or SAVE is specified) but it should be retained in scripts for future compatibility. Example:

```
1>SCREENMODE FROM SYS:Prefs/Presets/PalScreen.Pre EDIT USE
```

USE/S Supply this switch to open a FROM file and use the preferences settings from that file immediately. SCREENMODE's editor window is not opened unless the EDIT switch is also supplied. This command should be used with care from Shell because IPREFS will need to reset the screen and that means closing all Workbench-launched programs.

```
1>SCREENMODE FROM SYS:Prefs/Presets/Interlaced.Pre USE
```

SAVE/S Specify this switch to save the settings defined in the FROM file to the correct file in ENVARC:Sys. New settings will be used at the next re-boot.

```
1>SCREENMODE FROM SYS:Prefs/Presets/DfltPal.Set SAVE
```

SEARCH

Synopsis:

2.04: SEARCH [FROM]{files | pattern}[SEARCH]<string | pattern> [ALL] [NONUM] [QUIET] [QUICK] [FILE] [PATTERN]

1.3: SEARCH [FROM] <name|pattern> [SEARCH|NAME] <string> [ALL] [NONUM] [QUIET] [QUICK] [FILE]

1.2: SEARCH [FROM] <name|pattern> [SEARCH] <string> [ALL]

Templates:

2.04: FROM/M, SEARCH/A, ALL/S, NONUM/S, QUIET/S, QUICK/S, FILE/S, PATTERN/S

1.3: FROM, SEARCH, ALL/S, NONUM/S, QUIET/S, QUICK/S, FILE/S

1.2: FROM, SEARCH/A, ALL/S

Path:

C:

Use:

SEARCH is the AmigaDOS search utility. It allows you to find strings embedded within files. This must raise the question, why? One typical explanation is that this allows programmers to find out how well commented their code is. For instance a C programmer might use the following:

```
1>SEARCH FROM MyCode.C SEARCH /*
1 /* A really excellent program
2 /* All written in Lattice C
15 /* This is the start of the main code section */
2000 /* This is the end of main */
```

* The numbers at the start of each line indicate the line number where the text was found – relative to the start of the file.

The same is true of AmigaDOS. To search all the files in the scripts directory for comments you could use:

```
1>SEARCH S:#? ";"
dpat..
24 ; do wildcards for a double arg command
spat..
10 ; do wildcards for a single arg command
```

Note: FROM and SEARCH are optional and have been omitted from this example as has a large amount of would be output! Also the semi-colon

(;) delimits a comment so it must be enclosed in quotes or the command will not recognise it

Important: SEARCH is not very intelligent and can try to search binary (code) files. The results are unlikely to be catastrophic but the output is, to say the least, very messy. If you're using pattern matching or the ALL switch make sure SEARCH will not encounter any non-ASCII files.

SEARCH can generate a lot of output. And, as each file is searched its name appears in the list. The listing can be paused by pressing <space> and resumed by pressing the backspace key. To make it easier on yourself, it may be better to redirect output to a file and examine it with ED. Here's how:

```
1>SEARCH >RAM:search S:#? ";"

1>ED RAM:search
```

From AmigaDOS 1.3, its probably better to use MORE and a pipe. This may look a little odd – but its a very practical way to use SEARCH – when pattern matching is being used:

```
1>RUN MORE pipe:a

1>SEARCH >pipe:a S:#? ";"
```

New – AmigaDOS 1.3:

The 31 character restriction on the use of wildcards has been removed and several new command line options provided. Also, it returns a WARN condition for use in scripts if the string was not found. Here is an improved version of the AutoResident script (defined in the description of WHICH) using SEARCH to help trap for unexpected errors. A feature of SEARCH is used here to echo the error reported by WHICH.

```
.key command/a,opt1,name/k

.bra {

.ket }

WHICH >ram:Ares{$$} {command} NORES

SEARCH ram:Ares{$$} "not found" nonum

IF WARN

RESIDENT <ram:Ares{$$} >NIL: {name} {opt1} ?

ENDIF
```

This example uses some neat tricks to obtain the desired result. The problem with the basic version of this script is that, if the command cannot be found, WHICH reports the error to the file ARes{$$}. This is picked up by RESIDENT and causes a fatal error. This is not a problem, unless the user asks WHY the script failed, WHY would state: argument line invalid or too long. Using SEARCH we can kill two birds with one stone:

1) If WHICH fails: it reports an error "*command* not found". So we use SEARCH to look for: not found. If this is present, SEARCH

outputs the message (note QUIET is not being used). And because "not found" was there SEARCH does not generate a WARN so the RESIDENT is skipped.

2) If WHICH succeeds: it supplies the path description of the command. SEARCH cannot find *not*, so it does not output any message. Because "not found" wasn't present SEARCH generates a WARN so the RESIDENT is called.

Note: AmigaDOS 2 which returns WARN anyway – SEARCH wouldn't be required here. This is more efficient.

New – AmigaDOS 2:

Pattern matching has been added to the search string. This follows the standard patterns supported throughout the rest of AmigaDOS. Also, the output has changed slightly. Earlier versions of the command searching for file names just echo the name every time it is found. Now the command produces the complete path and name – which is more useful.

Options:

FROM — Specifies the directory or pattern to search. For instance to search for scripts which take arguments:

```
1>SEARCH S:#? ".key"
```

If this argument is not supplied AmigaDOS searches the current directory. In this case, the SEARCH argument must be treated as a keyword. See below.

AmigaDOS 2 also supports multiple file searches:

```
1>SEARCH File1 File2 These#? SEARCH "for something"
```

which is the same as this in 1.3:

```
1>SEARCH File1 SEARCH "for something"
1>SEARCH File2 SEARCH "for something"
1>SEARCH These#? SEARCH "for something"
```

SEARCH/A — This is a required argument which tells the command what string to search for. This is not a keyword but it must be supplied as such if a FROM argument is not supplied. These two examples show this:

```
1>SEARCH S:#? .key      ; Search S:
1>SEARCH SEARCH .key    ; Search THIS dir
```

Under release 2 this release pattern matching is available in the search string. See PATTERN/S.

ALL/S — This instructs SEARCH to search all files from the current or specified directory down through the hierarchy. This can be a source of confusion if the command attempts to search binary files (commands, artwork, sound samples and the like). Pattern matching only works on the first level of the search.

This example searches all the files and sub-directories in a logical directory SOURCE (as may be used by a C programmer) for C comments:

```
1>SEARCH SOURCE:#? /* ALL
```

Options (>AmigaDOS 1.3):

NONUM/S By default SEARCH outputs line numbers when it finds the string being searched for. This option suppresses the numbers. Example:

```
1>SEARCH S:#? ";"  NONUM
```

QUIET/S The switch is only for use in scripts. It suppresses all normal output from the command. If the search string is NOT found the command generates a WARN condition, otherwise it returns 0. This script fragment shows how this could be used:

```
SEARCH RAM:Test SEARCH "{command}" QUIET
IF WARN
ECHO "Not found"
```

QUICK/S This option changes the output format used by SEARCH slightly. Normally, SEARCH makes a list of all the files it is searching – as they are searched. This option stops each new filename occupying a newline. It may be useful if you are searching a lot of files for one special string:

```
1>SEARCH Haystacks: Needle ALL QUICK
```

FILE/S This switch has much the same effect as WHICH. It allows you to search a directory or even a complete disk for a filename. That is, as opposed to a string within a file. Probably best used with the ALL option since DIR can do the same job on single directories. This example finds out how many .info files are hiding on the disk in df0:. It does not show where they are!

```
1>SEARCH DF0: .info FILE ALL
```

In AmigaDOS 2 this option now lists the path where the file was found. Much more useful really.

Options (>AmigaDOS 2):

PATTERN/S Informs SEARCH that the string includes a pattern. This must be specified because otherwise wildcard characters will be taken as a literal string. This example finds all occurrences of .KEY and .KET!

```
SEARCH S: .k?? PATTERN
```

PATTERN can be combined with the FILE switch.

See also: WHICH

SERIAL

Synopsis:

2.04: SERIAL [[FROM=]<file>] [EDIT] [USE] [SAVE]

1.3: na

1.2: na

Templates:

2.04: FROM, EDIT/S, USE/S, SAVE/S

1.3: na

1.2: na

Creates:

Serial.prefs

Use:

This command is one of the new Preferences suite. It opens the Serial preferences tool, changes the current settings or directly alters the defaults from saved files.

Preferences files are stored as IFF of type FORM PREFS/SERL. So you can examine them like this:

```
1>TYPE SYS:Prefs/Presets/SERIAL.PRE HEX
```

The following information may be of use to serial hackers:

Offset	Usage
$0034	Baud rate (2 bytes)
$0038	Buffer size (2 bytes)
$003E	Handshake (1 byte)
$0040	Parity (1 byte)
$0041	Data bits (1 byte)
$0042	Stop bits (1 byte)

Options:

FROM The full path and filename of a file to use for the font preferences. If SERIAL is being executed from a Startup-sequence this should be combined with USE – see below. The file should have been previously created by SERIAL using Save As... from the project menu. Example:

```
1>SERIAL FROM SYS:Prefs/Presets/AuxSet USE
```

EDIT/S Open the editor screen when the command runs. This switch is implied in the current release (unless USE or SAVE is specified) but it should be retained in scripts for future compatibility. Example:

```
1>SERIAL FROM SYS:Prefs/Presets/JRComm.Set EDIT USE
```

USE/S Supply this switch to open a FROM file and use the preferences settings from that file immediately. SERIAL's editor window is not opened unless the EDIT switch is also supplied.

```
1>SERIAL FROM SYS:Prefs/Presets/Serial.Pre USE
```

SAVE/S Specify this switch to save the settings defined in the FROM file to the correct file in ENVARC:Sys. New settings will be used at the next re-boot.

```
1>SERIAL FROM SYS:Prefs/Presets/AuxSet.Pre SAVE
```

SET

Synopsis:

2.04: SET [Variable] [String]

1.3: na

1.2: na

Templates:

2.04: NAME, STRING/F

1.3: na

1.2: na

Path:

Internal

Use:

The SET command was introduced for AmigaDOS 2 and is used to define local environmental variables. For most purposes there is no difference between a local and global environment variable, but it is worth pointing out that a local variable always has priority over its global cousin. Local variables are local to the Shell that sets them and once closed, their contents are lost forever.

When you start a new Shell, any current local variables are passed to it automatically. However, other concurrent Shell processes (and sibling shells started by them) cannot share local variables. If you need to share a local variable with another process you should pass it via a global variable or use a pipe. Local environment variables are read by GET and cleared with UNSET – see the descriptions of those commands for more information.

Examples:

Once defined, a local variable can be used just like a global one – although it cannot be updated as easily.

```
1>SET Counter 1
2>EVAL $Counter + 1
2
```

Used without arguments, SET lists the current local environmental variables, thus:

```
1>SET
Kickstart     37.175
Process       1
RC            5
Result2       0
Workbench     37.67
```

Most of this is fairly straightforward stuff, but two variables are worth noting here:

RC — The result code returned by the last command where:

0 = Success

5 = Warn. (a general condition flag)

10 = Error. Something went wrong

20 = Fail. Something went badly wrong

You can also retrieve the value of this variable in the prompt by including %R in the prompt string. See PROMPT for more information.

Result2 — The secondary result code is usually returned when a command fails with RC =10 or higher. In this case Result2 contains the reason code returned by FAULT.

NAME — The name of the variable which is to be defined.

STRING/F — The string (contents of the variable). Note this argument allows /F parsing and extra white space will be included, so you do not need to use quotes.

See Also: GET, SETENV, UNSET, UNSETENV

SETCLOCK

Synopsis:

2.04: SETCLOCK <LOAD|SAVE|RESET>

1.3: SETCLOCK <LOAD|SAVE|RESET>

1.2:

Templates:

2.04: LOAD/S, SAVE/S, RESET/S

1.3: LOAD/S, SAVE/S, RESET/S

1.2: ?

Path:

C:

Use:

With the exception of base models all Amigas are supplied with a battery backed-up clock. This is powered by a ni-cad battery which recharges when the system is turned on and should never need replacing. The clock for the Amiga A500 is located on the A501 RAM expansion so expanded machines should have one. Some low-cost, third-party expansion units lack a clock however – these should be avoided; the extra outlay is well worth it.

Note: If you have an unexpanded Amiga A500 the SETCLOCK command should be removed from the Startup-sequence – it takes almost a second to discover that the clock is missing!

Options (All versions):

All the switches provided with SETCLOCK are mutually exclusive. This just means you can only use *one* on any command line.

LOAD/S — Retrieve the current time and date from the battery backed-up clock and set the system date and time accordingly. This command is usually used in the Startup-sequence, so unless something affects the clock, you never need to use it.

```
SETCLOCK LOAD
```

SAVE/S — Set the battery backed-up clock from the current system time and date as provided by DATE. This function is automatically provided by the save option in preferences.

```
1>SETCLOCK SAVE
```

RESET/S Provided just in case a rogue program (or a virus) hits the battery-backed clock and either stops it, sets a queer time and date – or stops the command from recognising it somehow!

```
1>SETCLOCK RESET
```

New – AmigaDOS 1.3.2: This option doesn't perform a validity check on the clock before the reset takes effect.

See also: DATE, SETDATE

SETDATE

Synopsis:

2.04: SETDATE <file|pattern> [<date> <time>]

1.3: SETDATE <file> [<date> <time>]

1.2: SETDATE <file> [<date> <time>]

Templates:

2.04: FILE/A, DATE, TIME

1.3: FILE/A, DATE, TIME

1.2: FILE/A, DATE/A, TIME

Path:

C:

Use:

This command is used to change the datestamp of a file (as seen during LIST). In early versions of the system, both the file and the new date are required arguments. However, like DATE it does understand weekday names, also "today" and "tomorrow". The general format in the UK and Canada is the same as DATE – your country's date format may change slightly:

```
DATES: DD-MMM-YY
TIMES: HH:MM:SS or HH:MM
```

Leading zeros must be supplied or the command will fail. Here are two examples – note the time (which is 24 hour clock) is optional:

```
1>SETDATE MyFile 03-Jun-90
1>SETDATE MyFile 07-Jan-89 17:18
```

New – AmigaDOS 1.3:

If a date and time is not supplied, SETDATE now performs a touch on the filename. This means it sets the file's datestamp to the current system time and date. The input restrictions command have been relaxed so that it is possible to pass the output from DATE indirectly via a re-direction operator. It is no longer necessary to supply leading zeros. Some examples are:

```
1>SETDATE S:uper 2-jun-90
1>DATE TO RAM:date
1>SETDATE <RAM:date >NIL: S:Spat ?
1>DATE TO PIPE:date
1>SETDATE <PIPE:date >NIL: S:PCD ?
```

Note: The "?" *must* be supplied or this command will appear to work but send the current date and time instead – a "touch." In these examples this is what should happen in any case.

Options:

FILE/A The name of the file to receive the new datestamp. The complete path must be supplied unless the file exists in the current directory. Example:

```
1>SETDATE S:Startup-Sequence 15-Jan-90
```

New – AmigaDOS 2: Pattern matching has been introduced so it is possible to date (or touch) any number of files in a directory. For instance, to update (no pun intended) all the files in the S: assignment:

```
1>SETDATE S:#?
```

Note: unlike some commands – the ALL (#?) pattern is not implied by using an assignment and must be supplied. It is usually better to supply a pattern if you are unsure.

DATE(/A) The new date to add to the datestamp. This is a required argument in AmigaDOS 1.2 only. It can be omitted if the current date and time are required in later releases. Note also that, if you only supply a date, the file receives the current system time. Example:

```
1>SETDATE S:illy Tomorrow
```

TIME The new time to add to the datestamp.Note also that, if you only supply a time, the file receives the current system date. Example:

```
1>SETDATE S:illier 13:13
```

See also: DATE, SETCLOCK

SETENV

Synopsis:

2.04: SETENV [<name>] [<new value>]

1.3: SETENV <name> <new value>

1.2: na

Templates:

2.04: NAME, STRING/F

1.3: NAME/A, STRING

1.2: na

Path:

Internal

C: <2.04

Use:

Environmental variables came into being with release 1.3. They're already quite common on other systems. Manx were probably the first to introduce them to the Amiga – closely followed by Microsmiths with the ARP DOS. Needless to say, neither was compatible with the other – although ARP did support a decent set of environmental variables rather than the limited set provided by Commodore. The environmental handler lives in RAM: under the ENV: assignment. Nevertheless, the only program to support it in 1.3 was MORE. The EDITOR variable sets the editor MORE can call up if required. In scripts, IF has limited access to variables using the $name syntax.

There is nothing to stop users from using environmental variables for their own requirements however – this is what SETENV is for. Quite simply to define a variable you just give it a name and a value. For this example we'll set MORE's editor to ED:

```
SETENV EDITOR C:ED
```

There's no reason why you shouldn't access the ENV: assignment directly; many of the examples in this manual do just that! In many cases, this is the only way to set an environmental variable under program control. Here's the above example expressed differently:

```
ECHO >ENV:EDITOR "C:ED"
```

Of course, it's more long winded this way, so you should use SETENV if you can.

In release 1.3 only: variables must be reset by specifying their name with a null argument. You can cheat by using DELETE to directly remove them! These two examples do the same thing. Note DELETE may fail if the variable is being accessed when you try to remove it – this is a handy way to stop a script that has gone out of control in a counter loop:

```
1>SETENV EDITOR
1>DELETE ENV:EDITOR
```

New – AmigaDOS 2:

If SETENV is executed without a variable string, it displays the names (only) of the current global environment variables:

```
1>SETENV
Counter
Kickstart
Prompt
Workbench
```

Options:

NAME/A The name of the variable to set. If no string is supplied, the variable is cleared. It still exists, in fact, but with a null value. For example to initialise a counter:

```
SETENV Count 0
```

Note: This is not a required argument in release 2. See main text.

STRING Environmental variables are always text values – some may be interpreted as numeric locally to a process or script. Text strings may contain spaces but they must be delimited with quotes.

```
1>SETENV EDITOR Extras:Tools/MEMACS
```

In release 2, this argument *must* be the last on the line – that is, it must *follow* any other switches. Spaces can be included without using quotes *but* literal quotes should be escaped. The following is legal:

```
1>SETENV Mary had a little lamb!
```

"Mary" is the variable name – the rest of the line is its value.

See Also: GET, SET, UNSET, UNSETENV

SETFONT

Synopsis:

2.04: SETFONT <NAME> <SIZE> [SCALE] [PROP] [ITALIC] [BOLD] [UNDERLINE]

1.3: na

1.2: na

Templates:

2.04: NAME/A, SIZE/A, SCALE/S, PROP/S, ITALIC/S, BOLD/S, UNDERLINE/S

1.3: na

1.2: na

Path:

C:

Use:

This command was introduced with release 2 to help cope with the scaleable fonts available in the latest version. It only affects text in the current window. Workbench fonts are set in preferences – but the Shell relies on Topaz. The command basically requires two arguments – the fontname* and the size. For instance, to change the font in the current window to Sapphire:

```
1>SETFONT sapphire 14
```

SETFONT expects to find the named font in the current FONTS: assignment so it's not normally necessary to define the complete path. You can override this either by temporarily re-ASSIGNing FONTS: to another disk or specifying the complete path. These examples show both methods. The second example re-ASSIGNs FONTS: but remembers where FONTS: were – normally SYS:Fonts. This is defined as a script:

```
1>SETFONT DF0:fonts/smallfont 5
```

```
.key font/a,size/a,drive/k,o1,o2,o3,o4,o5,o6,o7
.bra {
.ket }
assign >T:fn{$$} FONTS: exists
assign FONTS: {drive} fonts
setfont {font} {size} {o1} {o2} {o3} {o4} {o5} {o6} {o7}
echo >T:ft{$$} "e/ /:"
edit T:fn{$$} T:fe{$$} with T:ft{$$}
assign <T:fe{$$} >NIL: ?
delete T:f?{$$} quiet
```

Usage:

```
GetFont <fontname> <size> [drive=<drive>:] [options]
```

This script is compatible with both versions of AmigaDOS – the version for 2 only is very similar, and this can be used with the PD versions of SETFONT. The only thing you have to supply is the normal options to SETFONT plus the drive (or volume) to use. Note this is a keyword and the fonts directory is supplied by the script.

Note: This command only affects text in the current window. If you want to use a new font with ED, for instance, you should pass the current console handle as its window argument:

```
1>ED S:Startup-sequence WINDOW=*
```

• You should *not* use proportional fonts like Times and Helvetica in CLI windows – these are not supported by the CLI editing.

Options:

NAME/A — The name of the font to get from the current FONTS: assignment; OR the complete drive and pathname of the required directory to search. Must be supplied. Current versions of SETFONT do not return an error if the font is not found.

SIZE/A — The required size of the new font. Unless the scale option is being used, the correct sized font should be available; results are unpredictable if it isn't.

SCALE/S — If SETFONT manages to find the font you requested – but not in the correct size, you can use this switch to tell the command to autoscale the font to another size. Range 1-125pts (1 pt= 1/72 inch). Unless you're working in SuperHiRes Interlaced, sizes above about 20pt look quite ridiculous. Example:

```
1>SETFONT pearl 16 scale
```

Note: Many of the older Amiga fonts don't lend themselves well to scaling, if at all. Scaling is done algorithmically and multiples of two or three of a given font size work best.

PROP/S This command is not listed in the official documentation and PROP seems to have no effect.

ITALIC/S Algorithmically alters the font to give an italic (slanted) effect. Fine for outputting text to windows – but not much use for general editing.

```
1>SETFONT topaz 16 ITALIC scale
```

BOLD/S Algorithmically alters the font to give an emboldened (dark or heavy) effect.

```
1>SETFONT topaz 8 BOLD
```

UNDERLINE/S Algorithmically alters the font to give an underlined effect. Fine for outputting text to windows – but not much use for general editing.

```
1>SETFONT topaz 16 UNDERLINE scale
```

See also: ASSIGN, FIXFONTS

SETMAP

Synopsis:

2.04: SETMAP <keymap>

1.3: SETMAP <keymap file>

1.2: SETMAP <keymap file>

Templates:

2.04: KEYMAP/A

1.3: ?

1.2: ?

Path:

SYS:System

Use:

This command was introduced with AmigaDOS 1.2 to cope with the many varying keyboard layouts. It patches the system so that the keys you press generate the correct code, and therefore, the correct character on the screen! The keyboard settings default to the US layout – in the UK this means that keys like # and _ appear to be transposed. This command is usually called somewhere in the Startup-Sequence script – (User-startup on Workbench 2) because it's only needed once.

Keymap files normally live in the devs:keymaps directory. However, there isn't usually room to fit more than one in there on a Workbench disk – hard disk users don't have this problem. Also, the command is *not* path sensitive. That means if you asked it:

```
1>SETMAP df0:devs/keymaps/gb
```

it would complain that there's no such file as df0:devs/keymaps/gb! What you need to do therefore, is copy the keymap file that you require from the Extras Disk into devs:keymaps. Then you can issue the SETMAP with just the name of the keymap file you want to load*. The following commands assume you want the keymap file for the UK.

```
1>COPY EXTRAS1.3:devs/keymaps/gb DEVS:keymaps
1>SETMAP gb
```

• Advanced users often use this technique to generate new keymap files to assign ASCII strings to the function keys.

New – AmigaDOS 1.3.2:

A patch was added to stop keymap files spanning a 64K boundary. This only affects 1.2 and 1.3 Kickstarts.

Note: From AmigaDOS 2 onwards, the current keymap setting is stored in the KEYBOARD variable located in ENVARC:Sys.

SETPATCH

Synopsis:

2.04: SETPATCH [QUIET] [NOCACHE]

1.3: SETPATCH [R]

1.2: na

Templates:

2.04: QUIET/S, NOCACHE/S

1.3: ?

1.2: na

Path:

C:

Use:

No matter how careful the Amiga's designers are, it is inevitable that some bugs will creep into the system. After all, Kickstart 1.3 is no less than 256k long; Kickstart 2 is twice that! SETPATCH patches certain calls into the operating system so that they work correctly. As more bugs are discovered SETPATCH is modified to catch them. This should never be taken as a shortcoming – it's an advantage. How many companies can you name that either release new ROMs as an upgrade or just say "you'll have to live with the bugs!"

Kickstart 2 is very new – at the time of writing it has only been on general release for less than a month and hasn't even gone on ROM yet! Commodore hope to catch the bugs reported by developers and fix them before the new ROMs become available. At this point, therefore, SETPATCH may not be present on your disks if you're lucky enough to have version 2. Don't worry – if you need SETPATCH it will be released through the usual channels if and when it becomes necessary. This will probably be for free on a magazine cover-disk in the UK.

AmigaDOS 1.3:

The 1.3 version of setpatch patches the following:

exec.library Patched for the RAD: device

exec.library 020 and 881 exceptions patched to work correctly with the optional 68020 processor and 68881 maths coprocessor.

exec.library Alert: patches a bug in the old kickstart rom which causes "recoverable" alerts to Guru.

exec.library AllocEntry patched.

layers.library Patched.

AmigaDOS 1.3.2:

The 1.3.2 version of SETPATCH patches the following:

exec.library	Trackdisk GetUnit patch added.
exec.library	Alert fixed to work with 1Mb CHIP.
exec.library	Userstate() patched to work with 68010.
dos.library	Execute() patched to use resident RUN.

Options:

R Kickstart 1.2 and 1.3 were not designed for use with more than 512K of CHIP RAM. This option protects the RAD: device.

New — AmigaDOS 2

SETPATCH does not fail when the patches are already installed, however it does return a testable WARN condition. RC=5.

Options:

QUIET In AmigaDOS 2 only, this prevents the command from producing output.

NOCACHE In AmigaDOS 2 only, this turns off instruction caching on the 68030.

The version of SETPATCH distributed with AmigaDOS 2.04 patches the following:

SCSI.device:	Open() vector
Blitter:	Interrupts turned off

SKIP

Synopsis:

2.04: SKIP [<label>] [BACK]

1.3: SKIP [<label>] [BACK]

1.2: SKIP [<label>]

Templates:

2.04: LABEL, BACK/S

1.3: LABEL, BACK/S

1.2: LABEL

Path:

Internal

C: <2.04

Use:

This command is only for use in scripts. It is a form of the GOTO statement (unconditional branch) found in almost all high-level languages. Of course, since there are no line numbers in scripts, the command jumps to a label defined by LAB. Normally this will look like this – (the arrow just shows how control is transferred):

```
SKIP end

.

ECHO "This never appears"

.

LAB end
```

Control and execution resumes at the point immediately after the LAB skipped to. It is possible to have more than one LABel of the same name in a script – but this is poor programming. There is no reason why several skips can't jump to the same label though. This is a convenient way to jump out of a script and clean up in case of errors – it *must* be used with scripts meant for ICONX. If SKIP cannot find the label it requires, it will "fall off" the end of the script and report an error.

Surprisingly perhaps, you don't always have to supply a string! This is not good practice unless the jump is very small – say a couple of lines. Using too many blank labels in a script gets very confusing! Here's a typical example:

```
SKIP
ECHO "Look - no printing!"
LAB
```

• In AmigaDOS 1.3+ especially, SKIP should be controlled by IF..ENDIF constructs; otherwise there is a danger that a script could go out of control by continually looping back on itself.

** Early versions of AmigaDOS have to load this from disk every time it's used. In AmigaDOS 1.3 it is wise to make this command RESIDENT either in complex scripts where it can be removed on exit or, preferably RESIDENT all the time if you use scripts a lot. The command is already resident in AmigaDOS 2.

Options:

LABEL The name of the label to jump to (or null for short jumps). By default SKIP looks forward in the script. The name string may contain spaces if enclosed in quotes –but, like LAB it shouldn't contain any control characters no matter what you escape them with! Note: Labels are *not* case sensitive. For instance, to jump to the label FINI:

```
SKIP Fini
```

• In AmigaDOS 1.2 it is not possible to loop backwards without resorting to recursion – see ECHO for an example. Recursive scripts are explained in *Mastering AmigaDOS 2 Volume One.*

Options (>AmigaDOS 1.3):

BACK/S This forces SKIP to search backwards through the script for the required LABel. If the label is not located, SKIP "jumps off" the top of the script and complains. Example to create a loop:

```
SKIP Start BACK
```

See also: ENDSKIP, LAB, *Mastering AmigaDOS 2 Volume One* – three chapters covering scripts.

SORT

Synopsis:

2.04: SORT [FROM] <file|pattern> [TO] <file> [COLSTART <n>] [CASE] [NUMERIC]

1.3: SORT [FROM] <file|pattern> [TO] <file> [COLSTART <n>]

1.2: SORT [FROM] <file|pattern> [TO] <file> [COLSTART <n>]

Templates:

2.04: FROM/A, TO/A, COLSTART/K/N, CASE/S, NUMERIC/S

1.3: FROM/A, TO/A, COLSTART/K

1.2: from/a, to/a, colstart/k

Path:

C:

Use:

This is a simple routine for sorting text files. At first glance this seems a bit pointless. Why would you want to sort a script file for example? And no one in their right mind would ever want to sort a word processed document. Nevertheless, as the examples elsewhere in this manual illustrate, there are many cases where SORT is indispensable. Before proceeding to look at where you might use it let's just review the command. Two arguments specify the source (FROM)† and destination (TO) file. This gives rise to one possible example:

```
1>SORT FROM RAM:UnsortedFile TO RAM:Sorted
```

But what generated the unsorted file? The main source of unsorted files is LIST. Unlike DIR, LIST does not sort the files – displaying them as they are located instead. So this example could have read:

```
1>LIST #? TO RAM:ListOut
1>SORT RAM:ListOut TO RAM:SortedList
```

To view the sorted file list you would then have to use TYPE (or MORE). With a bit of imagination however, there is an easier way:

```
1>SORT RAM:ListOut TO *
```

This displays the sorted output to * – the current console window. With very little more effort this example can be made far more useful. Using pipes, and some trickery with RUN generates this example:

```
1>RUN MORE PIPE:B
[CLI 2]
1>LIST TO PIPE:A
1>SORT PIPE:A PIPE:B
```

MORE has to wait until PIPE:B becomes full. LIST generates output to PIPE:A. SORT sorts the listed output from PIPE:A to PIPE:B – which sends it to MORE. You may have to push MORE's window out of the way to see this in action – this works better in a script. Alternatively you could re-arrange it a little:

```
1>RUN LIST TO PIPE:A +
SORT PIPE:A PIPE:B +
MORE PIPE:B
```

Sorted Order

SORT can only sort ASCII files; and the file will be sorted line by line in ascending ASCII order. Each line must be delimited by a line feed – this is normal practice and you need not worry about it. However, it is worth pointing out the default SORT order: line feed is ASCII 10 so blank lines will appear first. Space is ASCII 32 and lines starting with that appear next. Next come the numbers starting with 0 (ASCII 48). Finally, are the letters A (a), B (b), C (c) and so on; case is ignored in AmigaDOS 1.3.

Options (All versions):

FROM/A The input file name. This will normally be a disk file but it can come from *any* AmigaDOS device capable of generating ASCII output and EOF – that includes pipes and even the console! This pointless example proves it:

```
1>SORT FROM * TO *
```

If you try this, you *must* close the file with CTRL+\.

TO/A Specifies the file that output from SORT will be sent to. Like FROM this is usually another file, but it can be any AmigaDOS device capable of accepting input. The examples above show that the use of *, (the current console) is quite common. This example opens its own window – TO has been used as a keyword for clarity.

```
1>SORT file TO CON:0/0/600/200/Sort
```

Note: this example closes the window immediately the the output (TO) file sends EOF (CTRL+\).

COLSTART/K

As we've already said, SORT sorts a file line by line. By default it starts at the first column of each line and works inward. There are cases (particularly produced by LIST) where this wouldn't sort the file in the required order. Say for example that you had a file of LISTed files and want to display them listed by size. Since the size of each file starts at column 28 this example fits the bill: output is directed to screen.

```
1>SORT RAM:Files * COLSTART=28
```

Note: COLSTART is a keyword and must be supplied if the option is required. The start number does not have to be exact if you expect to sort leading spaces. By default COLSTART=1.

If this option is used and two lines match exactly, SORT wraps round to the start of each line until it either finds a difference or the column immediately before the one specified is reached.

Options (>AmigaDOS 2):

CASE/S By default SORT is not case sensitive. If this switch is used, the SORT is made case sensitive and *capital* letters will be listed first. Example:

```
1>SORT file * CASE
```

Note: A buggette in early versions of release 2 make this option work the wrong way round! That is, by default the command is *case* sensitive and this switch turns it off!

NUMERIC/S By default numbers in the sorted output appear at the start of the list (order in ASCII priority). This option forces numbers to be listed last. The rest of the file is *not* sorted.

```
1>SORT numbers RAM:NumSort NUMERIC
```

† SORT is a fragile command. According to Commodore, if the input file contains more than about 200 lines** the Amiga will crash – caused by a stack overflow. It you are unsure – set a larger stack. One rule of thumb is to set a stack equal to 21 times the maximum number of lines in the input file. You can find this using TYPE file OPT N. The stack can always be set back to its default later on.

** The authors have sorted files containing over 550 lines with a stack of just 2500 bytes!

See also: STACK

SPAT

Synopsis:

2.04: SPAT <COMMAND> <PATTERN> [<opt1>] [<opt2>] [<opt3>] [<opt4>]

1.3: SPAT <COMMAND> <PATTERN> [<opt1>] [<opt2>] [<opt3>] [<opt4>]

1.2: na

Templates:

2.04: com/a, pat/a, opt1, opt2, opt3, opt4

1.3: com/a, pat/a, opt1, opt2, opt3, opt4

1.2: na

Path:

S:

Use:

Like DPAT, SPAT is a script. Using LIST, this adds the option of pattern matching to argument commands – that is, commands with FROM arguments like PROTECT. For example, to make all the commands in the S: assignment run like commands (by setting the S bit):

```
1>SPAT PROTECT S:#? +s
```

SPAT takes two arguments – the other options have been provided for the sake of any commands which may need them. In this example they are:

com=PROTECT ... PROTECT adding pattern matching.

pat=S:#? ... The pathname and pattern to use.

This may be useful for developers to discover the version numbers of all the libraries. This can be done thus:

```
1>SPAT VERSION LIBS:#?
```

* It should be noted that, since SPAT relies on EXECUTE, it is limited by the command parser supplied with that command. Therefore "" should not be used to refer to the current directory and * should not be used to refer to the console. (* can be used if you use "escape" it with **). The current directory may be referred to using its full path description however.

New – AmigaDOS 2:

Most of the commands have had pattern matching added in any case, so SPAT especially is starting to look a little redundant. However, it does not take up much room on a disk and should not be deleted; it may come in useful for some third-party and PD software. One possible use is to find out the version numbers of all the AmigaDOS commands – this is a new feature.

```
1>SPAT VERSION C:#?
```

Options:

COM/A — This is the command SPAT will execute for each file/directory matching the pattern specification. This argument *must* be supplied.

PAT/A — The pattern to match the files in the source directory. PAT may include a source path but pattern matching can only be used as the last part of the string. Note: This latter restriction has been lifted for release 2. This argument *must* be supplied.

opt1..4 — These four option strings are passed directly to the command (COM/A). In the unlikely event of a command requiring more than four options simply surround the *optional* parts of the command line with quotes (").

See also: DPAT

STACK

Synopsis:

2.04: STACK [<n>]

1.3: STACK [<n>]

1.2: STACK [<n>]

Templates:

2.04: SIZE/N

1.3: size

1.2: size

Path:

Internal >2.04

C:

Use:

Every AmigaDOS command requires a certain amount of stack to use as workspace while it operates. A more technical explanation is provided below. Most users only need to know that this command has two functions: it allows you to change or read the current stack value in bytes. It is very unlikely that you will ever need to change the default amount of stack (4000 bytes) unless:

1. You are trying to sort a large text file.
2. You are using an ALL switch in DIR (or LIST release 2+), for example, on a directory hierarchy deeper than six sub-directories.
3. Using BRU (see BRU).

By default this command returns just the current stack:

```
1>STACK
Current stack size is 4000 bytes
```

To change the stack simply set the new value – this sets a larger stack for deep directory searches:

```
1>STACK 6000
```

It should be noted that all processes launched from this CLI will adopt the current priority and stack size; that includes any new CLIs. So if you change the stack – don't forget to change it back if you need another CLI with a default stack.

WARNING: The only way the Amiga can tell you it has run out of stack is by crashing. Even with the improved error trapping of AmigaDOS 2, it is unlikely that you will get chance to save your work. Also setting too large a stack will not improve matters – only eat lots of memory.

Options:

Size/N Optionally set the new stacksize. This can be as low as 1600 bytes although very few commands can operate at this level. Most require at least 4000-5000 bytes – some even more.

What About the Stack?

When AmigaDOS starts a new process it creates a process node, just an extension of the task node. Located in the task node is a pointer to the task's stack. When EXEC gets round to executing the task, it loads this pointer into the 680x0's USER stack pointer. In other words, when you start messing with the STACK command you are tinkering at a very low level in the operating system. The process itself needs a small amount of stack – that's one reason why you can't set it too low.

If a recursive program runs out of stack space the processor doesn't mind – it just wraps the stack around on itself. This means the return address gets stomped on – and things go haywire! Some operating systems and compilers provide stack checking, the Amiga doesn't. Why? It slows things down – and who wants to lose speed for the sake of an occasional crash.

See also: STATUS

STATUS

Synopsis:

2.04: STATUS [<process>] [FULL] [TCB] [CLI|ALL] [COMMAND <command>]

1.3: STATUS [<process>] [FULL] [TCB] [CLI|ALL] [COMMAND <command>]

1.2: STATUS [<process>] [FULL] [TCB] [CLI|ALL]

Templates:

2.04: PROCESS/N, FULL/S, TCB/S, CLI=ALL/S, COM=COMMAND/K

1.3: PROCESS, FULL/S, TCB/S, CLI=ALL/S, COM=COMMAND/K

1.2: PROCESS, FULL/S, TCB/S, CLI=ALL/S

Path:

C:

Use:

This command lets you examine what AmigaDOS is up to. That is, how many processes are currently running and what they are doing. As explained elsewhere, an AmigaDOS process is an extended version of an EXEC task. EXEC level tasks cannot be listed with this command – very few users need to bother about them. It is important to make this distinction because commands loaded as processes are executed as tasks with special privileges – access to the dos.library for instance. It's also possible – and very common – for a process (or processes) to exist without actually running a command. These are often called empty CLIs because that's exactly what they are: CLIs or Shells which are just waiting to execute something.

If STATUS is executed without arguments it lists the processes current and running – together with any empty CLIs. Not all processes have a CLI window, and this is the only way of discovering what they are up to! This example came from an Amiga 3000.

```
1.SYS:>STATUS
Process 1: Loaded as command: STATUS
Process 2: Loaded as command: iprefs
Process 3: No command loaded
Process 4: No command loaded
Process 5: Loaded as command: WAIT
Process 6: No command loaded
Process 7: Loaded as command: WAIT
```

Explanation:

Process #1: This is the current process – so that must be STATUS.

Process #2: This is "iprefs" a background process started by the Amiga.

Process #4: This "empty Shell" appears to belong to Workbench 2.

Process #3 & #6: Just a couple of empty Shells.

Process #5 & #7: These are running as alarm clocks to tell the author when its time for dinner (4) and Star Trek (6)! The script responsible for this feat can be found in the section on WAIT.

There's more to STATUS that just that however. The FULL switch makes the command list a lot more useful information about the processes. In this example we have selected a process to look at.

```
1>STATUS 2 FULL
```

```
Process 2: stk 4096 gv 150 pri 0 loaded as command: iprefs
```

Most of these values should be self-explanatory:

pri: The task priority as set by CHANGETASKPRI.

stk: The task stack as set by STACK.

gv: The size of the global vector table.

Note: we've used the term task. That's because the priority and stack size belong mainly to the task started by the process. The sticky one is the mysterious "global vector table". In fact the value of this never changes – it's always 150 bytes long.

The global vector is an invention from the BCPL days of AmigaDOS and is just a list of jumps (vectors) shared and used by DOS programs internally. You need not worry about it – even programmers avoid it like the plague! So what's it doing in the output from STATUS? Probably because it's the only thing that a process can claim as its own – the rest of the info belongs to EXEC.

Options:

PROCESS/N The process number to display – the process must exist. This allows you to display just one of the many processes:

```
1>STATUS 3
```

```
Process 3: No command loaded
```

You may use this in conjunction with the FULL or TCB switches to tailor the output to your requirements.

FULL/S Changes the output of STATUS to display the TCB (see below) and the command name.

TCB/S — Changes the output of STATUS to display the Task Control Block (TCB). Example:

```
1>STATUS 2 TCB
Process 2: stk 4096 gv 150 pri 0
```

CLI=ALL/S — The default switch if no arguments are supplied. If you supply a process number as well, this switch is ignored.

Options (>AmigaDOS 1.3):

COM=COMMAND/K

Forces STATUS to return the CLI number running the command, or an error if no command of that name can be found. If more that one process of the same name exists this command only returns the process number of the first in the list. COM is a keyword and must be supplied if the option is required, for instance:

```
1>STATUS COM=WAIT          ; find "wait"
5
```

* This number can be used as an argument to BREAK – see BREAK's command description for more details.

See also: BREAK, CHANGETASKPRI, STACK

TIME

Synopsis:

2.04: TIME [EDIT]

1.3: na

1.2: na

Templates:

2.04: EDIT/S

1.3: na

1.2: na

Use:

This command is one of the new Preferences suite. It opens the Time Preferences tool and allows you to simply change the time and date. These features are well covered in AmigaDOS and this is just for weenies who can't remember what the commands are.

Options:

EDIT/S Open the editor screen when the command runs. This switch is implied in the current release but it should be retained in scripts for future compatibility. Example:

See also: DATE, SETDATE, SETCLOCK

TYPE

Synopsis:

2.04: TYPE <{file|pattern}> [TO <newfile>] [OPT H|N] [HEX] [NUMBER]

1.3: TYPE <file> [TO <newfile>] [OPT H|N] [HEX] [NUMBER]

1.2: TYPE <file> [TO <newfile>] [OPT H|N]

Templates:

2.04: FROM/A/M, TO/K, OPT/K, HEX/S, NUMBER/S

1.3: FROM/A, TO/S, OPT/K, HEX/S, NUMBER/S

1.2: FROM/A, TO, OPT/K

Path:

C:

Use:

TYPE is another one of the indispensable AmigaDOS utility programs. Like MORE, TYPE is a text viewer, unlike MORE, however, TYPE has a lot more options. It is not suitable for viewing long files because it is left up to you to pause the output. To get the command started all that's required is the name of a file to show:

```
1>TYPE S:Startup-Sequence
```

This types the file on the screen. Unlike MORE, TYPE will attempt to type binary files too. This means you could say:

```
1>TYPE C:type     ; NEVER DO THIS!
```

What you'll end up with is screens full of random looking junk. There is a way round this – don't try to type binary files. If you really must look at a binary file TYPE provides a special option to do just that:

```
1>TYPE C:type OPT H
```

New – AmigaDOS 2:

TYPE uses the multi-argument parser. This allows you to specify more than one file at a time. In fact, you can supply as many files as will fit on a line. Pattern matching is allowed too. For instance:

```
TYPE S:Start#? SPAT DPAT
```

Options:

FROM/A The file to type from. This required argument must be supplied. The filename usually refers to a disk based file but it could just as easily be any AmigaDOS device capable of generating output – including the current console. TYPE will keep typing until it receives an EOF marker (CTRL+\). This example types from a RAW:

window to the screen displaying the control codes:

```
1>TYPE RAW:0/0/400/100/RAW * OPT H
```

New – AmigaDOS 2: This option now allows multiple arguments as well as pattern matching. You can use a mixture of pattern matching and paths if necessary.

Note: Once a RAW: window has been opened it cannot be closed and TYPE cannot be stopped – even with CTRL+C.

TO

TYPE normally sends all its output to the current screen. This option allows you to redirect the output to a file or device without having to use redirection operators. It can also be used to copy pure text files, for instance:

```
1>TYPE S:SPAT TO RAM:SPAT
```

This is useful for AmigaDOS 1.3 since it can save resident space in a script or (RAM: in 1.2) where COPY might be used instead. This does *not* work with binary files because when TYPE reads an EOF character it will close the file. The nature of binary files means this could crop up almost anywhere.

For real memory misers, it can even replace ECHO to a very small degree – by TYPEing very small predefined messages.

New – AmigaDOS 2: This option is a keyword which must be supplied if required. This is to allow TYPE to distinguish between the keyword and the multiple arguments. If TO is being used with multi-args OR pattern matching the files are *joined*. This allows you to use TYPE in many places where JOIN would be used.

OPT/K

One option of the following:

N NUMBERS: Type the file with line numbers. Lines can wrap around on themselves – a new line number is generated when the line feed is reached.

H HEX: Type the file as a hexadecimal/ASCII dump. This is very useful for examining binary files – especially IFF screen dumps and sampled sounds.

The keyword must be supplied if the option is required. For instance to type the Startup-sequence with line numbers:

```
TYPE S:Startup-sequence OPT N
```

Options (>AmigaDOS 1.3):

HEX/S — This is a pseudonym for OPT H. The two must not be combined.

NUMBER/S — This is a pseudonym for OPT N. The two must not be combined.

See also: COPY, ECHO, JOIN

UNALIAS

Synopsis:

2.04: UNALIAS [<Alias>]

1.3: na

1.2: na

Templates:

2.04: NAME

1.3: na

1.2: na

Path:

C:

Use:

This command does exactly the opposite to ALIAS – that is it removes an alias definition from Shell's alias list. This command replaces the technique employed in AmigaDOS 1.3 where definitions were removed by using ALIAS with a null definition.

Executed without arguments, UNALIAS lists the current definitions. For example, to remove the alias definition of del:

```
1>UNALIAS del
```

Refer to ALIAS for more information on aliases.

Options:

NAME The name of the ALIAS to remove. It should have been defined first, but in the current release no error is generated

See also: ALIAS

UNSET

Synopsis:

2.04: UNSET [Variable]

1.3: na

1.2: na

Templates:

2.04: NAME

1.3: na

1.2: na

Path:

Internal

Use:

This command complements SET by removing a local environment variable. Executed without arguments this command lists the current local environment variables. Consult SET for more information.

Examples:

```
1>UNSET MyVar


1>UNSET
Kickstart      37.175
Process        1
RC             5
Result2        0
Workbench      37.67
```

Options:

NAME The name of the variable to remove.

See also: SET, GET, SETENV, UNSETENV, GETENV

UNSETENV

Synopsis:

2.04: UNSETENV [<Variable>]

1.3: na

1.2: na

Templates:

2.04: NAME

1.3: na

1.2: na

Path:

C:

Use:

This command does exactly the opposite to SETENV – that is it removes an environmental variable's definition from Shell's the ENV: handler. This command replaces the technique employed in AmigaDOS 1.3 where definitions were removed by using SETENV with a null definition. Executed without arguments, UNSETENV lists the current definitions. For example, to remove the enviromental definition of pmt:

```
1>UNSETENV pmt
```

Refer to SETENV for more information on enviromental variables.

Options:

NAME The name of the variable to remove from the environmental list. For example, to remove the EDITOR variable:

```
1>UNSETENV EDITOR
```

See also: SETENV

VERSION

Synopsis:

2.04: VERSION [NAME] [REVISION] [UNIT] [FILE] [INTERNAL | RES] [FULL]

1.3: VERSION [<library|device>] [<version #>] [<revision #>] [<unit #>]

1.2: na

Templates:

2.04: VERSION NAME, REVISION, UNIT, FILE/S, INTERNAL/S, RES/S, FULL/S

1.3: NAME, VERSION, REVISION, UNIT

1.2: na

Path:

C:

Use:

This command is normally used to retrieve the version number of the Workbench and Kickstart in use. In this sense it is not much use. However, it can be used to determine the current version number of a library or device. This is more useful – since users may upgrade parts of their systems but leave others. As a simple example the Workbench and Kickstart used during the compilation of this text were:

```
1>VERSION
Kickstart version 36.202. Workbench version 36.77
```

If you want the version number of a library or device the syntax is similar – all you do is specify the name of the library or device that you want to check. This checks for serial.device:

```
1>VERSION serial.device
```

Note: although this command can check for libraries in paths, it cannot check for devices; this is odd. To get the version numbers of all the libraries on an external disk you could use SPAT:

```
1>SPAT VERSION DFO:LIBS/#?
```

This does not work for devices. You can temporarily divert the DEVS: assignment though. See SETFONT for a script to solve a similar problem.

VERSION has one other little trick up its sleeve: if you supply a version number after the name of the library or device you want to check, VERSION will return RC=5 (WARN) if the version number requested is not high enough. Some caution is required here – version strings take the form: version.revision (39.1, 36.202 etc) *but* when you want to check for them the version # must be separated from the revision #. For example, let's say that you have some software which requires version 50, revision 2 of a fictional library called "branch". First we'll use VERSION to find out what the version really is:

```
1>VERSION branch.library

50.1
```

In the script you could check for version 50 of branch.library like this:

```
VERSION >NIL: branch.library VERSION 50

IF WARN

ECHO "Requires version 50 of branch.library!"

.

.          ; The rest of the script goes in here

.

However, to specifically check for revision 2 you
must specify that too! Like this:

VERSION >NIL: branch.library VERSION 50 2

IF WARN

ECHO "Requires version 50.2 of branch.library!"

.

.        ; The rest of the script goes in here

.
```

New – AmigaDOS 2:

All the commands in the C directory and most other executable programs have had a version string added. This is most useful for developers. Therefore, you should make it a standard practice to note the version number of a command if you think it's bugged. In this way the folk at Commodore can find out if you have the latest release – and possibly even fix the bug if it affects enough people. The following example uses SPAT (again) to list all the version numbers of your commands. If any show up lacking version numbers, they're probably just third party commands.

```
1>SPAT VERSION C:#?
```

Options:

NAME   The name of the library or device you want to inspect or test for. An error is returned if it is not found. Note: This command can only check for devices in the CURRENT DEVS: assignment. The complete name of the library or device is not implied by this command and must be supplied.

VERSION — Only for use in scripts, this defines the minimum version number to test for. A WARN condition is returned if the version requested is not available. The version number is the number left of the point. If version=36.202 then version number=36. Compare to REVISION.

REVISION — Only for use in scripts, this defines the minimum revision number to test for. A WARN condition is returned if the revision requested is not available. The revision number is the number right of the point. If version=36.202 – revision number=202. Compare to VERSION. This argument should *not* be used unless a VERSION number is also supplied.

UNIT — In very rare cases, devices support version strings for each of several device units. This allows you to test for the specific unit. When testing for unit this should be treated as a keyword unless VERSION and REVISION arguments have been supplied – for instance:

```
VERSION Multi.device UNIT 3
```

New – AmigaDOS 2:

A slight bug can occur when using VERSION with the 2.04 revision. You might like to prove this for yourself. The following should display "Wrong version..." (diskfont is revision 58 in the Workbench 2.04) but it doesn't:

```
VERSION LIBS:diskfont.library version=37 revision=57
IF WARN
 Echo "wrong version of diskfont library"
ENDIF
```

Note: Case is significant for some items. Library names are usually all lower case: "DOS.library" is not the same as "dos.library" and will produce an error.

Options — AmigaDOS 2>

FILE/S — This switch is normally implied but you can force it on.

INTERNAL/S — If the command or library is resident, you must specify INTERNAL or RES on the command line, viz:

```
1>VERSION LAB INTERNAL
Shell 37.69
```

Note in this case (as with all dot commands) you must specify just the command name. Shell resident commands are listed as Shell (version). If you have given a command a resident name, the real command name is displayed, ie:

```
1>VERSION X INTERNAL
Execute 37.11
```

RES/S An alternative to the internal switch. In later releases this might be used to differentiate between a RESIDENT command and a Shell command.

FULL/S Full causes VERSION to list extra version information about the specified library. In the current release, it includes the compilation date. For instance:

```
1>VERSION C:DIR FULL
dir 37.5 (4.6.91)
```

WAIT

Synopsis:

2.04: WAIT [<n>] [SEC|SECS] [MIN|MINS] [UNTIL <time>]

1.3: WAIT [<n>] [SEC|SECS] [MIN|MINS] [UNTIL <time>]

1.2: WAIT [<n>] [SEC|SECS] [MIN|MINS] [UNTIL <time>]

Templates:

2.04: /N, SEC=SECS/S, MIN=MINS/S, UNTIL/K

1.3: , SEC=SECS/S, MIN=MINS/S, UNTIL/K

1.2: , SEC=SECS/S, MIN=MINS/S, UNTIL/K

Path:

C:

Use:

WAIT is another one of those curious utility programs that seems to serve no useful purpose. Why would you want to hold up a process for a certain amount of time? As it turns out, there are dozens of uses for this command mainly in scripts. The trick with WAIT is that it allows a process to hang around – without holding up the rest of the machine.

One simple case is in a script where a RUN launched process involves a lot of disk access. The Charityware program Sleepy 3 is just such an example. It's launched from the startup-sequence and loads a series of short files to combine as an animation. While Sleepy 3 is loading, the rest of the script will try to execute. This has a very nasty effect as the machine tries to load part of an animation file and then part of a command and so on. The disk heads end up thrashing up and down the drive – slowing the script down considerably.

By making the script WAIT a few seconds while the RUN launched process completes, all this is avoided. The same is true of many programs. Here's an example using Sleepy:

```
RUN <NIL: >NIL: Sleepy Eg1 Eg2 Eg3 Eg4 Eg5 Eg6 Eg7 Eg8
WAIT 5 SECS
```

In the case of VirusX 4 (which has a variable length startup dependent on the number of mounted disks) a better way would be to make the main script wait until the program finishes. This can be done with a subscript like Commodore used in Workbench 1.3:

You could add the following to the Startup-sequence:

```
RUN EXECUTE VirusX4-loader
WAIT >NIL: 1 MIN ; It won't wait this long
Now VirusX4-loader...
VIRUSX
BREAK 1 C ; Signal to Startup-Sequence I'm all done.
```

It works like this: BREAK in the second script stops the action of WAIT in the first. The re-direction of WAIT to NIL: prevents the "***Break" message appearing. This technique only works with programs that either install tasks and exit *or* complete after a short while. This wouldn't work with Sleepy 3 for instance, because it *must* be launched as an asynchronous process.

The best way to describe WAIT is by example: the following are all scripts based on features of the command. They should be simple enough to follow – if you get stuck check back with the relevant command descriptions – and the chapters specific to script programming to be found in *Mastering AmigaDOS 2 Volume One.*

Example #1: AutoBack

Programmers of all flavours should find this example (written as a script) useful. It backs up the contents of a source disk after a specified time – every half hour by default:

```
.key time,source,dest
.def time 30
.def source RAM:#?
.def dest DF0:
LAB start
WAIT <time> MINS
COPY <source> <dest> QUIET
SKIP start BACK
```

Usage:

```
[RUN] AutoBack [<time>] [<file|pattern>]
[<directory>]
```

Note: you must supply the full path and pattern of the source directory and destination to override the internal defaults. This script must be RUN to get the best effect.

Example #2: TimePark

Here's another little script along the same lines. This one parks the hard disk after a set length of time. Note this is a simple script – it attempts to park the hard disk *every* 10 minutes by default.

```
.key time,partition,opt1
.def time 10
.def partition "DH0:"
LAB start
WAIT <time> MINS
PARK <partition> <opt1>
ECHO "Parked at:" NOLINE
DATE
SKIP start BACK
```

Usage:

```
[RUN] TimePark [<time>] [<partition] [INHIBIT]
```

Example #3: AtTimePark

This little goody is dedicated to those working in offices where someone might start fiddling after you go home at 5pm. This one is called AtTimePark – because it prevents access to the hard disk after a specified time. Placed in a startup-sequence this is effective enough to stop inexperienced meddlers.

```
.key time,partition
.def time 17:00
.def partition "DH0:"
RUN WAIT UNTIL <time> +
PARK <partition> INHIBIT
```

Usage:

```
AtTimePark [<time>] [<partition]
```

Options:

/N This is the number of seconds or minutes to wait if either the SECS or MINS switches are being used. Default=1 second, for example:

```
1>WAIT
```

SEC=SECS/S If this switch is used, the number preceding is taken as a number of seconds to wait. This switch is mutually exclusive to MINS so if you wanted to wait for say 1 minute 45 seconds use 105. (60 * seconds) + minutes.

MIN=MINS/S When this switch is used, the number preceding is interpreted as the number of minutes to wait. This switch is mutually exclusive to SECS. If you need to wait for several hours use: MINS = (60 * hours) + minutes.

UNTIL/K This switch precludes the use of the MINS and SECS switches. It tells WAIT to wait until a specified time (as read from the RTC). The time can only be expressed in hours and minutes. For example:

```
RUN WAIT UNTIL 12:05
```

Remember: The UNTIL keyword is not very accurate. WAIT exits some time *after* the time has been reached. Exactly how long after depends upon the priority of the process launching it. The lower the priority – the less accurate the exit time is likely to be.

See also: BREAK, RUN

WBPATTERN

Synopsis:

2.04: WBPATTERN [[FROM=]<file>] [EDIT] [USE] [SAVE] [WORKBENCH] [WINDOWS]

1.3: na

1.2: na

Templates:

2.04: FROM, EDIT/S, USE/S, SAVE/S, WORKBENCH/S, WINDOWS/S

1.3: na

1.2: na

Creates:

WB.pat; Win.pat

Use:

This command is one of the new Preferences suite. It opens the WBPattern preferences tool, changes the current settings or directly alters the defaults from saved files. WBPattern, unlike the rest of the preferences tools does not save IFFs. The two patterns are stored separately:

win.pat	The background pattern for drawer windows
wb.pat	The background used in the Workbench window.

Options:

FROM — The full path and filename of a file to use for the font preferences. If WBPATTERN is being executed from a Startup-sequence which should be combined with USE–see below. The file should have been previously created by WBPATTERN using Save As... from the project menu. Example:

```
1>WBPATTERN FROM SYS:Prefs/Presets/Moira USE
```

EDIT/S — Open the editor screen when the command runs. This switch is implied in the current release (unless USE or SAVE is specified) but it should be retained in scripts for future compatibility. Example:

```
1>WBPATTERN FROM SYS:Prefs/Presets/WBPattern.Pre EDIT USE
```

USE/S — Supply this switch to open a FROM file and use the preferences settings from that file immediately. WBPATTERN's editor window is not opened unless the EDIT switch is also supplied. This command should be used with care from Shell because IPREFS will need to reset the screen and that means closing all Workbench-launched programs.

```
1>WBPATTERN FROM SYS:Prefs/Presets/Bland.Pre USE
```

SAVE/S Specify this switch to save the settings defined in the FROM file to the correct file in ENVARC:Sys. New settings will be used at the next re-boot.

```
1>WBPATTERN FROM SYS:Prefs/Presets/MacBack.Set SAVE
```

WORKBENCH/S
Use the specified pattern file for the Workbench background. If this option is added to the SAVE switch, the file is copied to the defaults in ENVARC:Sys.

```
1>WBPATTERN SYS:Prefs/Presets/MacBack.Set SAVE WORKBENCH
```

WINDOWS/S Use the specified pattern file for the background of drawer windows. Use this with care, it can make things messy! If this option is specified with SAVE, the file is copied to the defaults in ENVARC:Sys.

```
1>WBPATTERN SYS:Prefs/Presets/Cute.Set SAVE WINDOWS
```

WHICH

Synopsis:

2.04: WHICH <command> [NORES] [RES] [ALL]

1.3: WHICH <command> [NORES] [RES]

1.2: na

Templates:

2.04: FILE/A, NORES/A, RES/A, ALL/S

1.3: FILE/A, NORES/S, RES/S

1.2: na

Path:

C:

Use:

WHICH is another one of those commands that seems a little useless at first glance. The idea is to locate a command anywhere on the current search path. A similar option is possible with SEARCH – but this is considerably slower. By default WHICH searches the resident list, then the current path until it either finds the file or runs out of places to look. And, its very fast. For instance to locate FORMAT in your setup:

```
1>WHICH FORMAT
Workbench1.3:System/Format
```

The description of WHICH in most texts implies that it can only look for commands – this is not true – WHICH can locate *any* file in the current path. This gives rise to example #2 below. The format is just the same as it would be for any normal file. Say you wanted to locate tools.info:

```
1>WHICH tools.info
tools.info
```

In this case tools.info, was in the current directory. But what if it wasn't?

```
1>WHICH tools.info
tools.info not found
```

Why? In fact the file "tools.info" was located in the root directory of the system disk. When WHICH was executed from root, it was found because the search path includes the current directory. This could be fixed with a PATH command:

```
1>PATH SYS: ADD   ; Put boot's root in the path. Ummm?
1>WHICH tools.info
System1.3:tools.info
```

Example #1: AutoResident

This is an interesting use of the command which can load any PURE command file and make it resident. The command to load must be in the current path of course:

```
.key command/a,opt1,name/k
.bra {
.ket }
WHICH >ram:Ares{$$} {command} NORES
RESIDENT <ram:Ares{$$} >NIL: {name} {opt1} ?
```

Usage:

```
AutoResident <Command> [NAME=<new name>] [<PURE>]
```

(See SEARCH for a better version)

Example #2: PathCopy

This example uses WHICH to copy a command or a file from anywhere in the search path to a destination directory. It does not work with Workbench 2 – see note below.

```
.key file/a,dest/a
.bra {
.ket }
WHICH >RAM:where{$$} {file} nores
SEARCH RAM:where{$$} "not found" nonum
IF WARN
COPY <ram:where{$$} >NIL: TO {dest} ?
ENDIF
```

Usage:

```
Pathcopy <source> <destination>
```

New – AmigaDOS 2:

In example #2 above "not found" is not returned! Instead WHICH returns the WARN condition. In effect all you need to do is remove the SEARCH command.

WHICH continues to search the path until all occurrences of the file have been found. For instance, you might be looking for ED and find that something has copied it into the RAM: disk:

```
1>WHICH ED
RAM DISK:ED
System2:ED
```

WHICH can also search for INTERNAL commands:

```
1>WHICH FAULT
INTERNAL FAULT
1>WHICH CD
DISABLED CD    ; Removed earlier using RESIDENT CD REMOVE
```

Options:

FILE/A — The name of the command or file being searched for. If this is a resident command - WHICH searches for its resident name - which can be different from the disk loaded name.

NORES/S — This switch tells WHICH to search only for the file or command through the current path settings. The resident list is ignored. For example to locate CMD:

```
1>WHICH CMD NORES
System1.3:Utilities/CMD
```

RES/S — This is exactly the opposite to NORES – it tells WHICH just to search the resident list for the named command. Note: The name searched for is the resident name – not the disk name (this is discarded by resident. It's pointless looking for a non-command file on the resident list. For instance to locate EDIT:

```
1>WHICH EDIT RES
RESIDENT EDIT
```

New - AmigaDOS 2: Internal commands are listed by WHICH if this switch is used. For instance:

```
1>WHICH CD RES
INTERNAL CD
```

Options (>AmigaDOS 2):

ALL/S — This switch tells WHICH to search and list all the places where it found the file. For instance you might want to check if the INTERNAL CD is overriding a CD somewhere else on the path. This example assumes that you have assigned a path to a disk called System1.3:

```
1>WHICH CD ALL
INTERNAL CD
RAM DISK CD
System1.3:C/CD
```

See also: PATH, RESIDENT

WHY

Synopsis:

2.04: WHY

1.3: WHY

1.2: WHY

Templates:

2.04: ,

1.3: ,

1.2: ,

Path:

Internal

C:

Use:

When a command fails to work what's the first thing that goes through your mind? OK, the second... WHY? That's exactly what this command does – it tells you more about WHY a command failed.

In practice, most commands tell you the reason they failed, which seems to make WHY a bit redundant. There are cases though when a command fails to work and you get either a message like "bad args", "<command> failed returncode XX" or worse still, no message at all. This last might happen if you had re-directed the command's output to NIL:. This is just asking for trouble if you are at all unsure about how a command works!

Using WHY is a doddle. All you do is wait until a command fails and then type WHY. This example simulates an error and sends it to NIL: – if this happened in a script, the script should stop, assuming that the fail level has not been altered. If output re-direction is being used, the error message will get channelled to the file:

```
1>SORT >NIL: RAM:
1>WHY
The last command failed because required argument missing
1>SORT >NIL: RAM: RAM:
1>WHY
The last command failed because object not of required type
```

WHY is not intelligent; it can only work with the information it receives from the last command executed – Result2 to be precise. If Result2 has not been set, WHY will throw up its hands and say: "The last command did not set a return code". In fact, all that WHY does is pass the error code straight over to FAULT! If FAULT is missing therefore, WHY is rendered useless. This is not true in AmigaDOS 2 – both commands are internal.

Wildcards

Pattern matching is fully explained in Mastering AmigaDOS Volume One. This sheet provides just a short reference.

#	Match any number of the following character.
?	Match any character.
#?	Match everything up to next character.
|	Combine patterns (logical OR) only works in groups.
()	Group patterns.

New in Release 2:

~	Reverse action of next wildcard or pattern group. (NOT wildcard). Parenthesis must enclose patterns when NOT is in effect.
%	Match an empty string (NULL). Compare this to "?" which must match at least one character.
[...]	Character class. Match just the characters enclosed in [] . So [atx] matches only A, T or X. This is not case sensitive.
#[...]	Zero or more character class. Match just the characters enclosed in []. See above.
[..-..]	Character range. Match characters [from-to]. So [A-Z] matches all the letters in the alphabet, but ignores numbers and special characters.
#[..-..]	Zero or more of Character range. Match characters [from-to]. See above.

General:

AmigaDOS has probably the most powerful set of pattern matching routines in any "small" computer system DOS this side of UNIX but is often criticised for lacking the ubiquitous "*.*" construct. This argument is fair - up to a point. It looks a bit weak when you consider the same effect is gained using #? which is one less keystroke. Also, AmigaDOS patterns can be delimited by any non-wildcard pattern. Take an example from PC-DOS/MS-DOS. You have a set of files CHAP1-6.DOC. To delete the lot in MS-DOS you just use *.*; similarly in AmigaDOS you would use #?. To delete selected files (starting with CHA) you could use CHA*.* or CHA#?. Altering the specification, in MS-DOS *HAP.* selects ALL files - whereas in AmigaDOS #?HAP.#? deletes only selected files. When the pattern matching meets "H" the pattern is switched OFF. This difference is the cause for much heartache among beginners with the PC – just be thankful the designers of AmigaDOS got around it.

Examples:

This -->	Matches.
#?	everything.
???	any file with three letters.
#a	a, aa, aaa, aaaa, etc.
#?.info	all dot-info files.
~(#?)	nothing!
?~(U)#?	Anything NOT containing U at the second position.
S#?T	SAT, SPAT, SEAT, and anything else similar!

For the following examples, let's assume a directory contains 20 files called "TestN" where N is the file number from 1 to 20 plus 20 files numbered Test2N, plus a master file "test".

This	Matches
Test#?	All files: Test1, Test2…Test220
Test(#?)	All files: Test1, Test2…Test220
Test(%|1)	Test or Test1 only
Test(%|#2)	Test, Test2, Test22 only
Test[1-3]	Test1, Test2, Test3 only
Test[134]	Test1, Test3, Test4 only
Test#[0-9]	All files. Test1, Test2…Test220
T#[e-s]T#?	All files. Test1, Test2…Test220

;

Synopsis:

All versions: ; Comment string

Path:

None

Use:

The ";" (semicolon) operator is provided to place remarks in script files – something that should be done at any convenient point. It is good practice to start a script with some introductory comments to remind yourself just what it does. The rest of the script should then be punctuated with comments at other points – especially where the script does something cryptic. AmigaDOS ignores everything from the ; to the end of the line. This is akin to BASIC's REM (remark).

Example:

```
.KEY From/A,To/A,opt1,opt2,opt3
; This is a file copy script
; From    =   source
; To      =   destination
; opt#    =   The optional extras

SETPATCH >NIL:   ; Patch system functions
```

?

Synopsis:

AmigaDOS Command ?

Path:

None

Use:

The purpose of ? (query) is to ask AmigaDOS commands to produce their format templates. These are repeated here for the sake of clarity. In case this book is not to hand (heaven forbid) this should give some extra, if limited, help. This also places most AmigaDOS commands into interactive mode. That is, whatever you should have typed at the command line can also be entered here. This gives rise to some interesting possibilities which we shall see.

Example:

```
BREAK ?

PROCESS/A, ALL/S, C/S, D/S, E/S, F/S:
```

Synopsis:

Command >device:

Command <device:

Path:

Internal

Use:

These operators – sometimes referred to as chevrons or angle brackets – are used to redirect console input and output to and from devices. The same symbols also crop up under a different guise in the script language which is the crux of the problem. As a rule of thumb: always use .BRA and .KET to change the brackets for the script or you'll be in trouble when bugs crawl in. But, getting back to the redirection operators:

> Is the most common – and the easiest to use. It sends all console output from a command to a named file or device. If the file already exists it is overwritten. Example:

```
DIR >RAM:listing ; get directory to file
```

< This operator is the weird one since it takes output from a file and feeds it to a command. Technically speaking, it changes the console handle of the window to the handle of the named device. This is useful for RUNning commands in the background and preventing them locking the console input handle. The technique should be used with care however. Example:

```
RUN Sleepy <NIL: >NIL:  ; No lock CLI senor!
```

When direction I/O is ro a console window, the order of operator *is* specific. If you need an input window then specify < last!

New – AmigaDOS 1.3:

>> This is the least common. It is very similar to the > operator but instead of creating a new file with the same name, it appends output to the end of the existing one. The file must exist or an error will occur. The easiest way to do this is to use ECHO to create an empty file:

```
ECHO >T:empty "" NOLINE
DIR >>T:empty opt a
```

New – AmigaDOS 2:

If the specified file does not exist it is created.

(Command pronounced 'Star')

Use:

* is used to refer to the current console window: for input or output. Star can only be used with commands which have FROM and TO arguments. Note that it can also be used as an Escape character and this action is detailed after the next page.

Example:

COPY is the most common example:

```
COPY FROM file TO *      ; Like TYPE file!
```

Taking input from the console is a little more complex. The syntax is:

```
COPY FROM * TO file
```

However, AmigaDOS does not know where the file ends. This command will go on ad infinitum; until you send an EOF with CTRL+\.

""

(Command is pronounced 'double quotes')

Use:

"" Refers to the current directory: for input or output. Can only be used with commands which have FROM and TO arguments.

Example:

COPY is the most common example:

```
COPY FROM file TO ""    ; Copy to here
COPY FROM "" TO RAM:
```

When "" is used as a source, it refers to the whole directory. This is directly equivalent to #?.

(This command is pronounced ‘star’. This is confusing since “*” is also used to refer to the console window – even as a wildcard by other systems. This section describes * as it affects quoted strings. That is, a set of printable characters enclosed in quotes, ie, “This is a quoted string”).

Use:

*N Newline: Can be used wherever a new line is required to print text, in ECHOed strings for instance:

```
1>ECHO “First line*nNext line”
```

*E Escape: Used where the escape code (0x1B) is required in a quoted string. This is only usually necessary in scripts to start an ANSI escape sequence. This has the same effect as pressing the escape key in a console window.

```
1>ECHO “*e[32mHello!*e31m”
```

*" Quote: Insert a literal quote in a quoted string where the quote would otherwise confuse the command line processor. For example:

```
1>ECHO “My name is *”Fred*”!”
```

** *: Insert a literal star in a quoted string. For instance:

```
1>ECHO “2 ** 2 = 4”
```

*** ***: Insert two stars in a quoted string. May be required if a command quoted string creates another quoted string which in turn requires “escaped” characters. Rare.

'

(Pronounced 'tick' – Escape wildcard)

Use:

Tick is used to insert characters like # and ? which will normally be used as pattern matching wildcards. This is primarily supplied for filename compatibility with other systems. Imagine you have a file called: HELP#? (ok, so that's unlikely) which you want to delete. This could delete anything starting with the string HELP. Every pattern matching character must be deleted using a tick so:

```
DELETE HELP'#'?
```

Note: Tick can be used while creating files but this is discouraged since it gives rise to confusion. Imagine creating a file called #?; it's possible. Now imagine some poor user trying to delete it!

CTRL+\

(Pronounced 'End of file' (EOF))

Use:

To send the end of file (EOF) sequence to terminate input from the console to a file. For instance, when copying from * to a file:

```
1>COPY * RAM:test
```

Hold CTRL then press \. This closes the file and, stops COPY and returns you to the CLI prompt.

New - AmigaDOS 2:

EOF can be used to close console windows. Simply type the sequence at the CLI prompt and the window closes. This is akin to hitting the close gadget.

ALT+'

(Pronounced 'tick'. In version 2+ Insert command. Note that this only applies to UK keyboards. US keyboards may have a separate key for this character.)

Use:

One of those curious sequences you always wondered about. Although this just looks like an apostrophe (tick) on the screen AmigaDOS sees it rather differently. What happens is this: it removes the word surrounded by ticks; tries to execute it; then replaces the input string with the output of the command. Remember to use ALT+' if you try this:

```
1>ECHO "The date is 'DATE'"
1>COPY "'WHICH SEARCH NORES'" TO RAM:
```

The second example uses WHICH to locate the command SEARCH on the current path setting. The resulting line appears to AmigaDOS like this:

```
COPY "Workbench 2.0:C/SEARCH" TO RAM:
```

A: AmigaDOS Error Codes

It has been said AmigaDOS is a powerful disk operating system; but power implies complexity, and complexity is Mr Error's best friend. Hence the saying: "My program didn't work because I Mr Error." Missed the error, get it? Still, to 'err?' is human, to "Stupid machine!" is to operate a computer and to æ*#@#$!' is to be a programmer. We all make mistakes – after all, that's how we learn to do it right (or at least differently) the next time.

This process of making errors generally follows what mathematicians call a relaxed sine wave. As experience increases so the number of errors decreases, but the increase in knowledge tends to generate either a blaze attitude or experimentation with new ideas. This causes the number of errors to increase and the cycle repeats. After a while however, the user becomes experienced enough to make less mistakes so the frequency reduces.

That, however was academic. This isn't: Errors are a pain, errors are a nuisance; and just to compound the problem, error messages are usually about as clear as freshly baked mud.

AmigaDOS has a three tier error reporting system operating at command level. The first level often passes unnoticed because it is handled by the script language. When errors become more serious however, AmigaDOS goes to the level two – numerical messages, displayed by Workbench prior to Release 2. A third level (provided by FAULT) takes the error number and converts it into an English string for most level two errors.

Even the advanced features of the Amiga do not make FAULT very clear – even we had to refer back to the manual time after time. FAULT keeps the output brief, so for those times when it can't provide the answer you require here are some more verbose descriptions of what makes the Amiga complain so bitterly.

In this section all the known error codes generated by FAULT have been listed – sorted on error number. Each error is then detailed both in terms of the normal error message and where appropriate, some suggestions as to what caused it. Some of the messages new in Release 2 are not documented so we have taken an educated guess...

103 Insufficient free store

Memory is short (or too fragmented) for the command to run. This should never happen from the CLI or Shell. If it does, either something is wrong (a rogue program may not have returned memory to the free pool) or you need more memory.

- Are you running too many SHELLs or other processes? See STATUS
- Have you set the stack too high? See STACK
- Fragmentation can be cured by a reset
- Are you using a large RAD: device? See REMRAD.

105 Task table full

You have exceeded the upper limit of running processes. The maximum number of processes spawned by AmigaDOS (before release 2) is 20. However, there is no limit to the number of tasks maintained by EXEC – so this error should read Process table full.

- On AmigaDOS 2 the number of processes seems to be limited by the amount of memory. This feature is not documented officially yet so cannot be guaranteed.
- Reduce the number of unused Shells (CLIs) if possible. See STATUS.

114 Bad template

Programmer's error. The command parser has been supplied with a incorrectly formed template.

- Revise template definition

115 Bad number

You have supplied a non-numerical argument (ie a letter) to an argument or keyword which requires a number. Usually caused by a typo.

- Edit command line

116 Required argument missing

You have not entered a required argument. Some commands require arguments to work others not so.

- If you're unsure which one is missing use ? to recall the command line template and re-enter.

117 Argument after '=' missing

You have used a keyword or other argument and specified the optional = but have not supplied something to go with it!

• The reason for this error should be obvious. Edit the command line.

118 Too many arguments

You have supplied too many options or arguments.

• This error is often caused when paths are called for and the "/" symbol is missed out. The same error will occur if you use, say ECHO, to echo two or more words and forget to surround the string in quotes.

119 Unmatched quotes

Also known as too many or too few quotes.

• An easy one to make and a tricky one to spot, this error is commonly found when using quotes in LFORMAT strings and not escaping them with *.

120 Argument line invalid or too long

There is an error on the command line passed.

• Check the Reference section of this manual for the correct syntax.

121 File is not an object module

The program you have attempted to run is not valid AmigaDOS code.

• If the file causing the error is a script make sure the 'S' bit is SET or use EXECUTE. See PROTECT v1.3+

122 Invalid resident library

A resident library is not valid. This new error means about as much to us at this point as it means to you now!

202 Object in use

You have attempted to delete a file or directory which either belongs to (or has been assigned to) the system or a running process. See ASSIGN.

• This error can usually be ignored if it happens during a wildcard delete. Try deleting files by name.
• Sometimes caused by rogue software.

203 Object already exists

You have attempted to rename a file or directory with a name which already exists in the same directory. This is not possible since every file within a directory *must* have a unique name.

204 Directory not found

AmigaDOS could not find the directory requested by a function like DIR.

- Probably caused by a spelling mistake.

205 Object not found

The file requested could not be located on the specified path.

- Like error 204, this is most often caused by a spelling error.

206 Invalid window description

The window request passed to CON:, NEWCON: or RAW: devices could not be fulfilled.

- Are the X and Y co-ordinates correct?
- Does the window description have a negative size?
- Is the machine running in PAL mode? (Bug in some Fat Angus chips)

207 Object too large

We have not been able to duplicate this new error and can only assume it appertains to the proposed multi-user system.

209 Packet request type unknown

This is a programming blob (AmigaDOS's internal messaging system has got confused).

- This should never occur in release versions of the software.

210 Invalid stream component name

Part of the command line passed to an AmigaDOS command was a control character.

- Best to re-type the line. Don't use the history feature of the Shell unless you can see the offending letter.

211 Invalid object lock

A program has tried to grab a lock (ownership) on an AmigaDOS object that either:

(a) does not exist
(b) does not support locks.

- This should not occur in release software.

212 Object is not of required type

You are attempting to do something with a file/disk or directory etc. that it doesn't support.

- It may be possible to get this from the command line but it's more likely programmers will be the only people to see it.

213 Disk not validated

The most likely cause for this error is a corrupted disk. It can be caused by the overzealous attempting to read or write a disk while it is being validated after insertion. This can sometime happen on a hard disk in which case you should keep re-trying until either AmigaDOS gives up or you get bored.

• This sort of error can be disconcerting when it happens during startup. This is caused when AmigaDOS tries to write a temporary file to the T: assignment. Unless you can re-assign T: to RAM: (as the first line in the startup) sit tight and keep retrying.
• Try again a couple of times. If a requester appears complaining the disk cannot be validated try using DISKDOCTOR (covered in the Command Reference Section).
• Wait for the disk to finish validating – this takes about a second.

214 Disk write protected

The Amiga's hardware cannot write to a disk which is write-protected – which is a useful way to stop viruses running riot through a system. It is possible that you are attempting to write to the wrong diskette – possibly an commercial software disk. If in doubt, use a different disk.

• 3.5" diskettes: write-enable with the tab.
• 5.25" diskettes: remove the write-protect tab.

215 Rename across devices attempted

You have tried to RENAME a file on two different devices. This is impossible.

• Use COPY if that's what you wanted to do. See COPY.

216 Directory not empty

You have attempted to delete a directory which still contains files.

• Delete the files in the directory first.
• Use the ALL switch with care.

217 Too many levels

218 Device not mounted

You have tried to access a device (or volume) which AmigaDOS does not know about.

• Have you spelt the device name correctly?
• Is the disk being accessed formatted?
• Does the drive exist (external drives on 2000 and 3000 machines are DF2:!
• Does your Startup-Sequence MOUNT the device? See MOUNT.

219 Seek failure

The device handler reported that it does not support the seek function or the track requested is not available.

• This would be caused by programming error and should not occur in release software.

220 Comment too big

The maximum size of a file comment is 79 characters.

• Reduce the length of the comment string. See FILENOTE.

221 Disk full

The disk being written to has been filled. During "wildcard" copying it is possible that some smaller files will fit, however.

• Use more specific wildcards in the search. See COPY.

222 File is protected from deletion

You cannot delete (remove) a file which has been specifically marked against deletion.

• See PROTECT, DELETE FORCE.

223 File is protected from reading

You cannot have read access to this file, although it could be deleted or written. The flag is ignored prior to release 2.0.

• See PROTECT.

224 File is protected from writing

This file cannot be written to. It may be possible to read it, however. The flag is ignored prior to release 2.

• See PROTECT.

225 Not a DOS disk

The disk is recognised by the Amiga but has not been initialised by AmigaDOS. This may occur if the boot sectors fail for some reason. Perhaps the disk was only partly copied by a diskcopy operation. See DISKCOPY.

226 No disk in drive

Is a disk inserted in the drive specified?

232 No more entries in directory

This error is usually non-fatal and is returned by AmigaDOS to programs performing a directory scan. It may be generated by DIR if a wildcard pattern fails to match any entries.

233 Object is soft link

You have attempted some operation on an AmigaDOS object that only exists as a link to some other object. Some operations will not be possible on links and must be performed on the objects they refer to.

234 Object is linked

This is the same as 233 (above) but the object is a hard link.

240 Record not locked

241 Record lock collision

242 Record lock timeout

243 Record unlock error

303 Buffer overflow

304 ***Break

Guess what! This error is generated by user action – ie, pressing CTRL-C or running the BREAK program. The error code is now generated by FAULT rather than being private to each command.

305 File not executable

You have tried to run a file which is not a legal AmigaDOS program. It may just be a script. This option appears to supersede the old "file is not an object module error".

• If the file is a script either use EXECUTE or better still set the S protection bit. See PROTECT.

B: The Virus Menace

Beyond Goldilocks

Let us tell you a story: Once upon a time, on a computer far away there lived a bear; a great big bear with black eyes, yellowing hungry teeth – and breath so foul it could knock out a charging Rhino at fifty paces. The bear lived in the great RAM cavern, between port Eye-Oh and the city of See-Pea-You. Every so often it would enter the great forest of Disks in search of easy prey.

The Files (who lived in Disk forest) existed in such fear of the bear that they posted a guard on Mount VeeDeeYoo. When the guard set eyes on the bear, he would cry out to the great god, Operator:

"Please, feed the bear!"

But sometimes, Operator was angered with the files and he ignored their pleas. Thus the bear would see its hunger fulfilled and the guard would vociferate. "The bear was hungry, and now it's eaten one of your files!"

This is, in truth, something of an apocryphal tale – but describes in prosaic form, one particular virus rumoured to have "infected" an early computer system. In this language, it sounds childish enough to be a harmless prank. Childish certainly, but dangerous enough none-the-less to wipe a computer system clean before the culprit is eliminated! In this example The Bear could be satiated by entering a keyword at the "Feed the Bear" prompt. If the keyword (or phrase) was known, the menace went away – for a while. All this may seem light years away from the Amiga but, as many have discovered to their dismay, viruses crop up everywhere. Usually on pirate disks (serves them right?) and in the Public Domain. Until recently, the only software guaranteed clear of the problem were commercial offerings, but now even this last line of defence has come under attack.

What Is a Virus?

The word virus derives from the 16th Century Latin for slime or a poisonous liquid. In modern terms, it belongs to any of a vast group of sub-microscopic DNA nuclei dressed in a protein coat. These simple organisms are one of the most basic forms of life, only capable of living and reproducing within the cells of other animals and plants. Many are pathogenic – creating symptoms ranging from mild discomfort to death. Computer viruses ape their protein-coated namesakes very closely. So closely in fact, some pundits have speculated they constitute a simple form of life. However, that is a philosophical avenue best explored during a late night discussion over several glasses of an intoxicating substance.

Going back to the real world: in a nutshell, a computer virus is a (usually small) program capable of duplicating itself. The effects of the virus on the system depend on the actions of the program; precluding bugs in the code, effects designed by a person or persons unknown. This chapter describes the effects of known viruses but avoids the technical information needed to create them. This may be of interest, but it is not the authors' intention to aid would-be virus writers.

When Is a Virus Not a Virus?

Simply when it's a bootblock loader. Long time virus-hunter Steve Tibbet, released several versions of his VirusX utility with protection against some of the bootblock loaded virus killers. His rationale was that some of these well-meaning programs wrote their own code to the bootblock when they found signs of a known virus. Bugs in these simple programs caused them to write over some legitimate bootblocks, believing them to be Limpet viruses like SCA, Byte Bandit and so on. However, the same was true of Steve's own VirusX utility – it too identified several genuine bootblocks as the SCA Limpet.

This is one of the hazards of virus hunter programs. Users unsure of the problem, and in fear of letting a virus run riot through their system, destroy a legitimate bootblock! The trick lies in determining what is a Limpet virus and what isn't. There are no hard and fast rules for this. The best way is to copy the suspected disk, trash the suspect bootblock and reboot the new copy. If the disk still works, then a virus was responsible, if it does not then one of two things has happened:

- The virus killer has destroyed a genuine bootblock. So the original disk was OK. Remember, if a Limpet attaches to a disk with a legitimate bootblock loader, the disk will stop working anyway.

- The software protection (if present) has worked correctly – defeating the copier.

This second point raises some interesting moral and legal issues. Under UK law, it is not legal to duplicate a disk *without* the copyright owner's permission – for any reason, even for archiving purposes†. This is more an act of severely bending the law, not breaking it. It is, however, wiser to check first, and get an answer in writing before proceeding. State that the intention is to use the copy as a "Canary" for a suspected virus. Chances are, the software company concerned will check the disk for you – *if* the suspect virus came from them – or more likely – confirm that the bootblock loader is correct.

Interestingly too, although recent legislation does not go far enough, steps are being taken to punish virus authors with large fines and even jail sentences. This comes under the new hacking laws under the heading of "Altering Data". The real trial though, is likely to be catching the person responsible!

Who Writes Viruses?

Any computer virus is a computer program; and programs do not write themselves. Even though there are "virus creation kits" there is no getting away from the fact: behind a program there must be some pathetic individual – with nothing better to do – somewhere along the line. They would probably regard themselves as programmers but programmers produce something productive – not destructive. Despite what some may think, viruses are *very* easy to write – just about any fool with an assembler or even a BASIC compiler could do it. So who are the culprits?

The common name for these people is "pirates", or sometimes "hackers". The latter being a perversion of the erstwhile term used for sensible computer experts – stolen by the pirates in sick tradition. Pirates remember are the people responsible for producing disks of copied software, for removing the protection and distributing copies all over the world. Put another way, threatening the very livelihood of thousands of people.

At the risk of sounding too much like a FAST advert, think about this: Pirates only serve their own needs. Sick little viruses endanger the computing at every level. If the software houses can't make a living, they will stop producing games – leaving the pirates on a sticky wicket with nothing left to copy. The computer companies will go out of business because no one will buy a product with little or no support: remember the MTX512, MSX, Oric, Enterprise, etc.? Eventually, even the magazines will have nothing to write about... and the whole house of cards will come tumbling down.

Count on Dracula

There are several distinct "strains" of computer virus – variants of the way the infection (replication) code is written and each has a name. As can be seen from this, viruses are ostensibly simple to write – which is why there are so many around:

Limpet

Often called the bootblock or boot sector virus. The term Limpet derives from the way the virus "adheres" to the bootblock of infected disks. These are the simplest viruses of them all – and usually the easiest to catch; also the first viruses to appear on the Amiga.

The very first Amiga Limpet came courtesy of Swiss Crackers Association or SCA – no prizes for guessing, Pirates. Bootblock viruses consist of a small section of code which loads a disk's boot sectors when the computer is booted from an infected disk. Every time a new (write-enabled) disk is inserted, the virus writes itself back to the new disk thus infecting it. Depending on the type of Limpet, some write themselves back during soft resets – others to every uninfected disk inserted.

Doppleganger

These work by replacing the code of an original program completely with its own. Next it moves the code of the original program somewhere else on the same disk and gives it a blank name. When the original program is called, the virus runs (doing its dirty work) then exits by launching the *real* program. Sound complex? Not at all – three simple AmigaDOS calls can be used to do this. BSG9 was an early example of this type and can be identified by the tell-tale "blank" file it leaves in the DEVS directory of the infected disk. The AmigaDOS's LIST command shows it up – DIR does not. If found, BSG9 is usually the first command in S:Startup-sequence and has a bytesize of 2608 when listed.

Trojan Horse

Sometimes just called a Trojan, this type has yet to crop up on the Amiga in large numbers for reasons which will shortly be revealed. Trojans get their name from the Greek fable of the Trojan (or wooden) horse.

As the story goes, the Greeks bluffed the Trojans by leaving a wooden horse outside the gates of Troy. The Trojans dragged the horse inside, and at nightfall the Greeks hidden inside the beast crept in under cover of darkness and murdered the Trojans in their beds.

In the same way, a Trojan virus is a computer program usually placed in the Public Domain not by Greeks, but still with a very sharp sting in its belly. The reason why real Trojans are rare is because they take some skill to implement. The only way they will spread is if the program hiding the stinger is useful enough for lots of people to use. And once the Trojan is uncovered – everyone stops using it. For this reason Trojans use a time-bomb technique whereby they only activate after they have been used a set number of times or, sometimes, on a certain date. Most Amiga Trojans are genuine programs infected by a Parasite – see below.

Parasite or Linkvirus

Also called Worm, Zombie, Lycanthrope, and Vampire. These bloodsuckers are the scourge of utility software and generally a real pain in the Startup-sequence. Like "real" vampires they duplicate by attaching themselves to other programs. The problem with parasites is they turn genuine software into "Trojans" by locking onto their code and transferring across onto all and sundry. Like Trojans, parasites are tricky to implement so there are less around. Unlike the Limpets, they multiply between disks *and* across directories at an alarming rate. Also they're very tricky to catch without software specifically designed for the purpose – Peter Cushing never had it this tough.

Signs of Infection

There are two mainstream effects of virus infection: destructive and nuisance. Neither are very pleasant – some viruses exhibit both.

Nuisance Effects

Silly messages "Software piracy is theft...", "AmigaDOS presents: The IRQ Virus", "Something wonderful has happened" and so on. The only wonderful thing that could happen to the persons responsible for these gems would be the spontaneous combustion of their Amiga's.

Reversed keys The two Amiga keys, for example, suddenly become transposed.

Lock outs The whole machine stops accepting keyboard input – but everything else appears to be working normally.

Obscene mouse pointers
We kid you not – is nothing sacred?

Nasty Effects

Random trashing of files
Has the effect of causing programs to suddenly crash without warning, corrupts data in pictures, music and text. Lamer Exterminator is known to have this effect.

Random trashing of disk block checksums
Difficult one to pin to a virus because it can also happen through wear and tear, badly stored disks

and a whole host of other things. Likely sign of a virus if it starts suddenly.

Random guru meditations
As above, this can happen through poorly written software so might happen quite innocently. It is possible to guru AmigaDOS at a pinch.

Protecting Against Them

It only takes one slip to catch a virus because once the little beggars get onto a disk, they spread *very* quickly. This checklist covers the most important points.

- No known virus can get past the write protection notch on a floppy. *Never* insert a write enabled disk unless something has to write to it. Better still keep DATA disks separate from program disks. If a virus gets into memory it can only spread to disks which are either (a) never booted or (b) don't contain any executable files.
- Keep a "Canary disk". This is a freshly formatted disk with a couple of commands and a Startup-sequence. If a Limpet tries to attach itself this disk will suddenly become bootable. A suit of programs to make Canary disks (and a lot more) is included with Mastering AmigaDOS 2 Volume One.
- Get a disk of Virus killers from your friendly PD library and check every file and bootblock of every disk you get *before* attempting to boot them or run any of the programs contained therein.
- *Never, ever,* use pirated software. This includes games, utilities and applications – it's a sure-fire way to catch a virus.

Virus Mythology

Myth *"Viruses can write to write protected floppy disks."*

Fact Only hard disks are at risk since they cannot be physically write protected.

Myth *"Viruses can hurt humans."*

Fact They can only inflict psychological damage by destroying files etc.

Myth *"Some viruses live in battery-backed clock memory."*

Fact There is not enough RAM, and even if there were the RAM is never executed. Some viruses key on the date or time however.

Myth *"Viruses can damage the machine."*

Fact — Virtually impossible. Damage is caused by inexperienced humans fiddling the hardware thinking that it's at fault when a virus is the real culprit.

Myth — *"All viruses come from BBSs."*

Fact — Only Trojans and Parasites can do this in other programs – this is unlikely since the *human* culprit would be too easy to catch.

Myth — *"I only ever boot from hard disk – I must be safe!"*

Fact — Trojans, and Parasites, and Dopplegangers only need to be executed (from CLI or Workbench) to start spreading to a hard disk.

Myth — *"I will never catch a virus."*

Fact — You might. Take that attitude and you probably will too.

Conclusion

Computer viruses are here, they have been for a long time and are showing no signs of going away. Even though the law is moving ponderously toward outlawing the perpetrators of these crimes, the problem of tracing the culprit still remains. The virus is seen by many as the perfect crime. In the end though, the only protection anyone has against viruses is common sense. They are becoming like the common cold: cliched and easy to catch; but the remedies are out there for the taking – all it takes is vigilance.

Adapted from an article originally published in Amiga Format

†The authors do not condone the use of copying equipment without the *written* permission of the copyright holder.

C: The Interchange File Format

When the Amiga was first introduced it took the world by storm. For the first time a home microcomputer had graphics that average users could hardly dare to dream about. Yet this could have created a serious problem – with such a wealth of screen formats, it would be impossible for art packages to "talk" to each other (exchange data) without some form of standard. The problem already existed on the PC. Users would have to use conversion software to update their images when they wanted to use another package, or simply view an alien file; always assuming such software was available. This was totally unacceptable – so they, Commodore-Amiga Inc., teamed up with Electronic Arts and developed the *Interchange File Format* (IFF).

Why a Standard?

At first glance, the whole idea of standardisation seems a little eccentric, however, as EA point out this trick has been successfully employed by word processors for years. Every word processor has (or should have) some method to read and write raw ASCII files; remember ASCII is an acronym for American Standard Code for Information Interchange. Internally, the software can employ any methods the programmer sees fit to make the program do its job most efficiently, externally all the user sees is a series of bytes representing plain text. In this way, word processors and text editors can exchange data very easily.

As things have developed in the five years since its introduction, IFF covers more than just pictures

– it has addressed every possible common file structure from animated graphics to sampled sound and music.

Also an IFF file can conceivably contain any mixture of sound, graphics, animation and text, which is what make the standard so powerful and so outwardly complex. For the purposes of simplicity – and space allowed – this introduction to IFF will only skim the surface of the standard. It must be said, this chapter assumes a certain amount of knowledge of Amiga programming (sorry – that's unavoidable); beginners are directed to the tables giving brief explanations of some of the terminology used.

How IFF works

IFF is essentially a very simple standard: simple should not be taken as meaning lacking power. The idea was to develop a standard file format which was, for most purposes, completely self-sufficient. Each file is based on a series of data segments or blocks called chunks. Chunks consist of three distinct parts: the identity – four bytes of ASCII data, the size of the chunk in bytes, and the data itself. The second number is important because it is the number of bytes in the chunk, *not*, as may be expected, the relative offset to the start of the file to the next chunk. A theoretical C fragment representing a chunk could look like this:

```
typedef struct {
ID
ckID        /* chunk identity */
LONG
ckSize      /* sizeof ckdata */
UBYTE
ckData[/* ckSize /*]
} chunk;
```

In assembler:

```
dc.l "BMHD"             chunk identity
dc.l BmhdLen            size of this chunk bitmap
dc.w 320,200            X,Y resolution
ds.w 8                  and so on. . .
BmhdLen  equ *-bitmap   Calculate chunk size
even                    Insert pad byte if reqd.
```

Or in BASIC:

```
1000 DATA "B","M","H","D"    :REM chunk
                              identity=BMHD
1010 DATA 2,0                :REM chunk size
1020 DATA 1,64,0,200         :REM X,Y resolution
                              (320*200 as bytes)
1030 DATA 0,0,0...           :REM more data
```

These examples are meant as illustrations; they are not intended to represent each other, just the important parts of chunks. Table 1 (next page) has a complete list of the chunk IDs used by Amiga graphics programs. Typically, an IFF picture will consist of several chunks chained together and enclosed in an IFF "form". Think of the chunks as biscuits and the form being the wrapper that contains them; each IFF form is a complete package.

The introducer IDs may also appear in the form LISn, CATn or FORn where "n" is the version number of the standard in use (0-9) (INS1 is an example). All IFF reader software should be aware of these. LIST, CAT and the associated ID, PROP are advanced features of IFF beyond the scope of this book.

Note: This list is in constant flux and it is possible that new chunk types may have appeared since it was compiled. Very common formats rarely change much, but authors frequently design their own chunks. This is not generally encouraged unless the chunk type is registered first with CATS (Commodore Amiga Technical Support). Unregistered developers should avoid confusing the issue and stick to the defined standard.

How Chunk Data Is Arranged

When writing (or reading) an IFF chunk, the following points must be observed:

1) All 16 and 32 bit wide numbers (words and longwords) must be arranged high byte first. This is normal practice on the 680x0 series of CPUs so your assembler/compiler should perform the conversion automatically. BASIC programmers must ensure that data is written in the correct sequence. It is essential that the byte order is maintained for chunk size and chunk ID strings – but CPU ordering of chunk word and longword data is allowed. This last will only affect IFF file transfers to/from CPUs which store the low byte first – for example, the Intel range and the 65xx series.

2) Word and longword data *must* be aligned on an even address relative to the start of the file.

3) Every odd length chunk must be padded with an extra byte to ensure correct alignment of the next chunk. This pad byte must not be counted in the chunk's data length.

4) IDs are constructed of four bytes of ASCII data in the range " " (space) through to "~" (tilde). Leading spaces are not allowed. Also note, because IDs are matched using a longword (unsigned long int) comparison, case matters. This system is used primarily for speed.

IFF Form Introducers

Name	Function
CAT	a set of concatenated IFF forms
FORM	start of an IFF standard form wrapper
LIST	holds a set of PROPs and FORMs. Sometimes LISTs and CATs
PROP	a shared properties chunk, information common to all forms

IFF Form Types

Name	Function
ILBM	Interleaved Bit Map – a graphics file
FTXT	IFF Formatted Text File – not widely used
SMUS	Simple Musical Score
8SVX	8-bit Sampled Voice – a sound sample.

Miscellaneous Chunks

Name	Function
ABIT	Amiga BITplanes (non-interleaved bitmap from ACBM)
ACBM	Amiga Contiguous BitMap (form type used by Amiga BASIC)
ANIM	form type for animations developed by Aegis
ANMB	ANimated bitMap (form type used by Framer and Deluxe Video)
ANHD	ANimation HeaDer chunk for Aegis ANIM forms
AUTH	the AUTHor's name (Bruce Smith, Mark Smiddy etc.)
ANNO	any text added by the author of the file
ATAK	The ATtAcK envelope of a sound sample (see RLSE)
BMHD	BitMap HeaDer
BODY	the ILBM data for the image
CAMG	Amiga specific information on screen modes: EHB, HAM etc
CCRT	as CRNG used by CBM's Graphicraft software
CHRS	The character types – follow the ISO/ANSI standard (FTXT only)
CMAP	the Colour MAP information
CRNG	Colour Register RanGe info used by EA's Deluxe Paint
DEST	bitplane scatter information
DLTA	DeLTA mode data for Aegis ANIM forms
FONS	The font descriptor for FTXT files
FSQN	playback sequence information for ANMB forms
GRAB	the "hotspot" of a sprite or brush
INS1	optional INStrument chunk for FORM SMUS
INST	older form of INS1 – now obsolete.
NAME	the NAME of the artwork/sample/score in a form
RLSE	The ReLeaSE part of a sound sample (see ATAK)
SHDR	simple Score HeaDeR (must appear before the TRAK chunks)
SPRT	this image is a SPRiTe
TRAK	one parallel TRAcK in a SMUS score
(c)	this is the copright information for the form.
	four spaces! A filler chunk – contains nothing useful.

Table #1: IFF "chunk" types and their meanings.

The Form Wrapper

When the chunks have been set up, the whole file is enclosed in a wrapper which tells other programs that this file is a valid IFF structure. The letters FORM (CAT or LIST) denoting the wrapper are always present as the first four bytes of any IFF file. These must be present or the file will not be recognised by an IFF loader.

Example #1 is an assembly language fragment showing how a partly initialised wrapper could be defined. The code is for an eight colour, 320 x 200 raster constructed from five chunks. The first chunk forms the IFF picture wrapper. The next three contain data specific to the layout and colours of the picture, the last is an array of interleaved bitmaps for the picture itself. Some of this data has not been initialised, for that, the contents of the individual chunks must be considered.

Example #1:

Simple assembler include file for an IFF picture.

```
form      dc.l    "FORM"    Chunk #0 (The IFF wrapper)
          dc.l    FormLen
          dc.l    "ILBM"    of type ILBM (graphics)
          dc.l    "BMHD"    Chunk #1 the bitmap
          dc.l    BmhdLen
bitmap    dc.w    320,200   Raster size in pixels
          ds.w    0,0       start position of this image
          dc.b    3         # of bitplanes
          dc.b    0,0       no compression plus padding
byte
          dc.w    0         transparent colour
          dc.w    10,11     aspect ratio
          dc.w    320,200   size of source page in pixels
BmhdLen   equ     *-bitmap
          even
          dc.l    "CMAP"    Chunk #2
          dc.l    CmapLen
cmap      ds.b    21        Colour data 21 bytes
CmapLen   equ     *-cmap
          even
          dc.l    "CAMG"    Chunk #3
          dc.l    CamgLen
camg      dc.l 0  ViewModes
CamgLen   equ     *-camg
          even
          dc.l    "BODY"    Chunk #4
          dc.l    BodyLen
body      ds.b    24000     The picture ILBM (3 bitplanes)
BodyLen   equ     *-body
          even
FormLen   equ     *-form
```

Chunk #0 (FORM)

The start of any IFF form. This marks the start of all forms. See also: LIST and CAT. The structure of the FORM chunk is:

```
UBYTE[]
ID
Longword ASCII ID 'BMHD'
LONG
length
Number of bytes in this structure


UBYTE[]
formType
Longword ASCII type must be ILBM for graphics
```

Chunk #1 (BMHD)

The bitmap header tells the reader program what to expect from the BODY data. Its contents are as follows:

```
UBYTE[]
ID
Longword ASCII ID 'BMHD'
ULONG length      Number of bytes in this structure
UWORD w,h         The raster's width and height, 16 bits
                  each
WORD x,y          The pixel position for this image
                  (normally 0,0)
UBYTE nPlanes     Number of bitplanes in the BODY(source)
                  data
UBYTE mask
```

Type of masking used:

0 = no masking (normal opaque image)
1 = has a mask (interleaved with BODY data)
2 = mask has a transparent colour
3 = lasso

```
UBYTE compression
```

Type of compression used for BODY data

0 = no compression
1 = ByteRun1 (repetition) compression

```
UBYTE pad           Padding byte only - must be=0
UWORD transparent   This colour should be treated as
                    transparent
UBYTE Xasp,Yasp     Pixel aspect ratio. Width:Height
WORD pageW,pageH    Source page's width and height.
```

Chunk #2 (CMAP)

Colour map data (palette) has three 8 bit entries with possible values from 0 to 255 for each colour register used. The Amiga uses four bits per register (12 bits=4096 colours) which must be packed in the high order bits so: for writing, shift each register value four bits left; reading, shift four bits right. Expect to find up to 96 bytes (32 colours) in the colour map. To achieve correct alignment an extra byte may be added at the end of the data. Reader programs may ignore extra entries in the map.

The CMAP's structure is a follows:

```
UBYTE[]
ID
Longword ASCII ID 'CMAP'
ULONG length    Number of bytes in this structure
UBYTE red       Colour register n red value 0-255
UBYTE green     Colour register n green value 0-255
UBYTE blue      Colour register n blue value 0-255
..
Repeated for all colour registers
.
UBYTE pad  Optional padding byte for word alignment
```

Chunk #3 (CAMG)

This chunk is only required by the Amiga and must be supplied and read by all Amiga IFF software. As the standard holds at the moment, only 16 of the possible 32 bits of the CAMG flags are used. Some of the existing flags are not appropriate and must be masked out. Examples #2 and #3 show how this is performed in C and assembler, although similar code will be required for all languages. The data structure for the CAMG chunk is simply:

```
UBYTE[]
ID
Longword ASCII ID 'CAMG'
ULONG length    Number of bytes in this structure
                (currently 4)
ULONG camg      The Amiga display (viewmodes) flags
```

Example #2:

Setting CAMG flags in C.

```
#include <graphics/view.h>
#define BADFLAGS (V_SPRITES|VP_HIDE|GENLOCK_AUDIO|
                         GENLOCK_VIDEO)
#define MASK (~BADFLAGS)
#define CAMGFLAGS (MASK & 0x0000FFFFL)
.
.
.
camg.ViewModes= MASK & myScreen->ViewPort.Modes /* writing
*/
NewScreen.ViewModes= MASK & camg.ViewModes /* reading */
```

Example #3

Setting CAMG flags in assembler.

```
include graphics/view.i
* on entry a0 -> pointer to your screen's ViewPort!
write
move.l
vp_Modes(a0),d0
```

For writing the structure:

```
and.l
#CAMGFLAGS,d0
move.l
d0,camg
rts
read
move.l
camg,d0
```

For reading the structure:

```
and.l
#CAMGFLAGS,d0
move.l
d0,vp_Modes(a0),d0
rts
GENLOCK_AUDIO equ $200
VP_HIDE equu $2000
BADFLAGS equ (V_SPRITES!VP_HIDE!GENLOCK_
                         AUDIO!GENLOCK_VIDEO)
MASK equ (~BADFLAGS)
CAMGFLAGS equ (MASK & $FFFF)
```

Chunk #4 (BODY)

This is the simplest structure to define, since it is usually just a copy of the BitMap (image) from the screen. Sometimes, software may incorporate a mask or template interleaved with the body data. If this is present, reader programs may wish to remove it; masks are defined in the BMHD chunk. The body is defined thus:

```
UBYTE
ID
Longword ASCII ID 'BODY'
ULONG length     Number of bytes in this structure
UBYTE data[]     Array of data representing the image
```

The Big Squeeze

Getting a quart into a pint pot is not always possible, but ILBMs are, by their very nature, large files so they are sometimes compressed into smaller versions. In the IFF standard, just the BODY data is compressed, it would be nonsensical to code the complete file. The technique used is called ByteRun1 Encoding and relies on byte repetition, that is: if you find two or more sequential bytes are the same then count the number, and save the number found and the value. ByteRun1 compression is defined in the BMAP chunk. Pseudocode for the unpacker looks like this:

```
UnPacker:
LOOP until finished with the file
READ the next source byte into n
SELECT
IF n [1..127] THEN copy the next n bytes literally
IF n [-1..-127] THEN replicate the next byte n times
IF n [-128] THEN do nothing
ENDSELECT
ENDLOOP
```

The packer is similar with a couple of extra considerations. A two byte repeat run should be coded as a replicate run unless it is preceded and followed by a literal run. In this case the complete run should be merged, then coded as a literal run. Three byte runs should always be coded as replicate runs. Also, every scanline of a raster is coded separately.

Data Types and Their Meanings

BYTE	8 bit byte or signed integer. Range -128..+127
BYTE[]	byte array – a sequence of one or more bytes
UBYTE	unsigned BYTE. Range 0..255
WORD	16 bit signed integer. Range -32768..+32767
UWORD	unsigned WORD. Range 0..65535
SHORT	pseudonym for WORD

USHORT pseudonym for UWORD

LONG 32 bit signed. Range -2,147,483,268..+2,147,483,267

ULONG 32 bit unsigned integer. Range 0..4,294,967,295

The unsigned versions of these types are often used as bitwise flag variables: a BYTE has eight 1 bit flags. Assembly language programmers should make careful note of data typing when calculating addresses and offsets

Why ACBM for BASIC?

AmigaBASIC uses an unusual form of bitmap structure called an ACBM or Amiga Basic Contiguous BitMap. The main file is very similar to a standard picture file with one important difference: the bitplanes are stored in such a way only one AmigaDOS read/write is required per bitplane. This results in a substantial increase in speed for reading IFF files from BASIC. Converting to and from the two formats is a simple matter of using the utility files supplied with AmigaBASIC on the Extras disk.

Using ChkIFF

This chapter would be very difficult to understand without some examples so to ensure this situation is not exacerbated, "Mastering AmigaDOS – The Disk" free with Volume One includes a simple IFF structure viewer. Unlike the ubiquitous VILBM or ShowIFF, the software searches and displays all the chunks in an IFF file. To use the program simply type its name from the CLI and select the file to view from the file selector. Output can be redirected to the printer by typing ChkIFF >PRT:.

If ChkIFF encounters a chunk that it understands, like a bitmap header, it decodes any relevant information. Lastly, because all IFF files follow roughly the same pattern, ChkIFF can decode IFF sound, music, animation and brush files too. To keep things simple, the program loops continuously until you select Cancel gadget on the file request.

Caveats

ChkIFF makes extensive use of the ARP system so you must have the ARP.LIBRARY present in the LIBS: directory of your boot disk. The program is not very intelligent, and cannot decode LISTs, CATs or other special forms. These are rare anyway so this should not prove too much of a problem.

• *Adapted from an article originally published in Amiga Format.*

D: The Mountlist

Every time your Amiga tries to add a new device to the system it scans a special file in the DEVS: assignment (usually SYS:devs) called MountList. The contents of MountList may seem a little mysterious at first but most are just simple keywords – just like the rest of AmigaDOS. The MOUNT command is used to add new user devices – specific information regarding that command can be found in the Command Reference Section.

Almost every peripheral device (with the exception of 3.5" floppy disks) and all the software devices have entries in the MountList. This allows the device driver to locate its handler (if any) and read its configuration. Necessarily, some entries are more complex than others – everything depends on the requirements of the device.

Only a very small number of you will ever need to define a MountList entry yourselves. However, for those that do and those intent on experimenting with the supplied entries, there are a few constraints which *must* be followed:

- Every entry must *start* with the name of the device it represents.
- Every entry must *end* with a hash (#) character.
- Keywords must be followed by an equals (=) sign.
- Keywords must be terminated by either a semi–colon (;) or a line break.
- Comments must start with /* and end */ – a standard C convention. They may cross as many lines as required *but* must be terminated by a following */ and comment characters *must* pair up.

MOUNT understands quite a number of keywords and these are discussed below. We have ordered them alphabetically to help you find them faster. Practical examples adapted from the original disks appear at the end of the section with brief descriptions of each. You may like to refer to these for further clarification.

Baud=

AmigaDOS 1.3.2+: The baud rate used by a multi-serial device entry (we assume – very little information is available for this entry.) The hardware doesn't exist at the time of writing.

Control=

AmigaDOS 1.3.2+: Used by a multi-serial device entry (very little information is available for this entry.) The hardware doesn't exist at the time of writing.

BlocksPerTrack=

Disks (and disk emulations) only. This defines the number of blocks (sectors) on each *surface* of every track of the formatted media.

BootPri=

Defines the boot priority of any device which can be both mounted and booted. The actual value can range from –129 (not bootable) to 127 (boot this every time. Drives such as RAD: should be set to –129 unless you have a reason for booting them; an ultrafast boot disk for instance.

Buffers=

The number of 512k cache blocks to allocate. This can be changed after mounting using ADDBUFFERS. (Disks and disk emulations only.)

BufMemType=

The type of memory to allocate for cache buffers:

1 or 2 = Any (CHIP or FAST)

3 or 4 = CHIP only

5 or 6 = FAST only

(Disks and disk emulations only.) It can be spectulated that bit 0 probably controls Public or Private memory. This is not implemented fully yet since it aplies to multi-user systems.

Device=

The name of the .device driver in the DEVS: directory: *trackdisk.device* etc. This keyword is path sensitive so the driver may be grabbed from almost anywhere. This is not recommended.

DosType=

This is a HEX value to determine if the FFS is in operation for the device. It should be 0x444F5301 if the FFS is being used (this funny number value stands for 'hex' (0x) 'DOS<CTRL-1>' – CTRL-1 appears on screen as an inverse 1). The default (for OFS) is 0x444F5300 (ASCII for 'DOS<CTRL-0'). This *must* be set correctly for programs such as DISKDOCTOR to work. (Disks and disk emulations only.)

Flags=

The Flag settings sent to EXEC's OpenDevice call. This is usually 0.

GlobVec=

The mysterious global vector crops up once more. This is a hangover from the BCPL days and is gradually being eliminated. Most programs do not require it and the keyword can be omitted.

–1 = No global vector

0 = Private global vector

1 = Shared global vector

Handler=

The name of the device handler in the L: directory: AUX-Handler etc. This keyword is path sensitive so the handler can be retrieved from almost anywhere. This is not recommended.

HighCyl=

The maximum number of tracks on the device. (Disks and disk emulations only.)

3.5" floppies = 79

5.25" floppies = 39 or 79

Hard disks vary – consult manual.

RAD: determines memory usage.

Interleave=

The interleave factor to use during formatting. This is very device dependent and should be left alone. Has no effect on disk emulations. (Disks only.)

LowCyl=

The first track number available on the device or the first track available to the named partition on hard disks. (Disks only.)

Mask=

Memory mask used with the FFS to determine the addressing range for DMA transfers. *DO NOT ADJUST.* (Disks and disk emulations only.)

MaxTransfer=

The maximum number of blocks to transfer in any one DMA access. This is used with the FFS. (Disks and disk emulations only.)

Mount=

If a positive value is supplied here, MOUNT loads the device handler immediately. By default the system waits until a device is first accessed.

PreAlloc=

Defines the number of private blocks reserved on a hard drive for its own use. This does not apply to all hard disks and the value can usually be left at 0 – consult the manufacturers manual. (Hard disks only).

Priority=

The priority passed to the task driver when it is launched by EXEC. Handlers require a value of around 5; filing system drivers, 10. Do not tinker with this unless you understand the implications of multi-tasking at an EXEC level.

Reserved=

The number of blocks reserved for the boot blocks. This will usually be 2. (Disks and disk emulations only.)

Stacksize=

The amount of stack required by the device or handler sub-task. This value is used by EXEC and since there is no stack overflow checking, setting this too low can crash the system. *DO NOT CHANGE.*

Startup=

This is a string passed to the handler, device or filing system when it is launched as a BPTR to a BSTR. This is for ancient compatibility.

Surfaces=

The number of sides a device has (or simulates). Floppy disks and disk emulations use two. Hard disks may use seven or more. *DO NOT ADJUST.* (Disks and disk emulations only.)

Unit=

The unit number of the device this entry refers to if multiple entries are possible. (Disks only.) Only one RAD: unit is possible at once.

Examples

Here are some sample MountList entries for software devices which are already in the MountList of some system disks.

This is the AUX: device which provides support for unbuffered serial I/O such as may be required for a remote terminal:

```
AUX:
  Handler      =  L:AUX-Handler
  StackSize    =  1000
  Priority     =  5
#
```

Now the PIPE: device. This pseudo-disk device was written for the Amiga by Matt Dillon and provides buffered FIFO communication between processes. It was introduced for Workbench1.3:

```
PIPE:
  Handler      =  L:PIPE-Handler
  StackSize    =  6000
  Priority     =  5
  GlobVec      =  -1
#
```

This device entry is for the NEWCON: device – which supplies a host of new features including the command line history. NEWCON was introduced with Workbench 1.3 and promptly removed in 2.0 when the whole system was revamped. For this reason, this entry does not appear in the MountLists of later machines:

```
NEWCON:
  Handler      =  L:NEWCON-Handler
  StackSize    =  1000
  Priority     =  5
#
```

The SPEAK: device was also introduced in Workbench1.3. This is a simple "input only" device which reads a string of text from the console and outputs it to the Amiga's speech subsystem.

```
SPEAK:
  Handler      =  L:Speak-Handler
  Stacksize    =  6000
  Priority     =  5
  GlobVec      =  -1
#
```

This is an entry for the recoverable ramdrive RAD:. This behaves just like a real disk drive and its contents are not destroyed by a reset. However, memory allocation for RAD: is not dynamic and the size required must be set first by adjusting the values of HighCyl and BlocksPerTrack:

```
RAD:
 Device          =    ramdrive.device
 Unit            =    0
 Flags           =    1
 Surfaces        =    2
 BlocksPerTrack  =    11
 Reserved        =    2
 PreAlloc        =    11
 Interleave      =    0
 LowCyl          =    0  ;  HighCyl = 79
 Buffers         =    5
 BufMemType      =    1
#
```

MountList entries for physical devices tend to be more complex than their software cousins. This entry is a theoretical mount for a hard disk partition. The first partition (tracks 0-20) has been prepared to boot using the OFS (early hard disks could not boot with FFS). This partition can then be mounted in the startup and the rest of the boot sequence performed from there.

```
FAST:
 Device          =    hddisk.device
 FileSystem      =    l:FastFileSystem
 Unit            =    1
 Flags           =    0
 Surfaces        =    4
 BlocksPerTrack  =    17
 Reserved        =    2
 Interleave      =    0
 LowCyl          =    21  ;  HighCyl = 800
 Buffers         =    30
 GlobVec         =    -1
 BufMemType      =    1
 Mount           =    1
 DosType         =    0x444F5301
 StackSize       =    4000
#
```

Lastly, this example is for a 5 1/4" floppy disk drive which may used by the PC emulators. With this mountlist the same device could be pressed into service as an extra Amiga drive.

```
DF2:
 Device          =   trackdisk.device
 Unit            =   2
 Flags           =   1
 Surfaces        =   2
 BlocksPerTrack  =   11
 Reserved        =   2
 PreAlloc        =   11
 Interleave      =   0
 LowCyl          =   0  ;  HighCyl = 39
 Buffers         =   20
 BufMemType      =   3
#
```

E: Telling FIBs

Thought for the day:

"This must be a TV dinner – it keeps repeating on me..."

There are two mainstream DOSs for the Amiga – the official one now at version 2; and the ARP (AmigaDOS Replacement Project) DOS created by the MicroSmiths. Both of these have an INFO function, but return different and often confusing values for the amount of free space on a disk.

There are two camps: the 880K per disk bunch (by far the majority) and the 838K lot, continually arguing over who's figure is correct. More recently, even FFS has been dragged into the fray since its arrival on floppy disk was heralded with the Workbench 2 launch.

The 838K crowd are supported by MicroSmith's excellent ARP DOS, whose DOS INFO function reveals 838K free on a blank disk. Over in the other corner, the AmigaDOS people claim to have 879K (or thereabouts) usable.

Here then, to set the record straight are the facts.

FACT: Amiga floppy disks, formatted by the system have 512 bytes per sector usable by DOS. There is no denying this. It's a nice binary number FM and MFM formats have always used some multiple of 2^n bytes: 128, 256, 512 and so on.

FACT: There are 11 sectors per track, 80 tracks and two sides to every disk. 1760 possible sectors in all: 1760 * 512 =901120 bytes or approximately 880K on a disk.

FICTION: Every block on a disk contains 488 bytes of data. This implies the sector format is also 488 bytes which is ridiculous.

FICTION: The maximum data storage on a disk is 838K (from the 488 bytes per sector premise). Since the first premise is wrong any derivations made from it must therefore also be incorrect. The figure in contention is bytes per block. Some say 512, others, 488. Commodore have been known to quote 488 – although it depends who you talk to, and in what context. This is the crux of the argument.

The 488 byte figure is arrived at from the capacity of an AmigaDOS DATA block. Avoiding the technicalities for a moment, every data block contains six longwords – 24 bytes – reserved for DOS. (Even though a slight misprint in Bantam's 1.2 AmigaDOS manual sets this at six words or 12 bytes.) Subtract 24 from 512 and you get: 488 – the magic number.

More Bytes From the Cherry

This is further complicated because for every file created on an Amiga disk by AmigaDOS, *at least one complete block* is reserved for use by the system. It's called the file header or file info block (FIB) and occupies a complete sector – 512 bytes in effect.

Now let's say you create a file which is one byte long. How many blocks does it take?

> One sector for the file header block
>
> One sector the data block
>
> = two 512 byte sectors or 1024 bytes or 1K

Therefore, since there are 1760 possible blocks on the disk, the maximum number of one-byte files you could possibly ever store an 880K floppy is 880. Slightly less in real terms since DOS reserves a few blocks hither and thither for other functions – such as the boot block, root directory and bitmap.

It might seem fair from this argument to suppose that a single file could occupy the entire capacity of the disk. As we've already said, data blocks contain 488 bytes of user data plus 24 bytes of DOS information. Fromthis premise you could be forgiven for thinking 488 bytes per block is more accurate (1760 * 488 = 838K). Actually, no!

Even if you did have the full disk to yourselves, the file header block can only hold a fixed number of block references. If this number is exceeded, DOS creates another subsidiary block called a file list block – which takes up another 512 byte sector – and starts filling that. If that gets saturated, then another list block is created until the disk gets filled. In practice, the largest single file that can be stored under conventional DOS is just over 820K when an extra 18K is taken by DOS. FFS is better – around 860K in practice can be stored as a contiguous file.

Directories and So On

Where do directories fit into all this? Well every directory takes at least a single sector on a disk for its own use – 512 bytes a piece. Two hundred odd bytes are reserved in the middle of the directory structure for the hash table. This is what allows AmigaDOS to locate a file or sub-directory very quickly – by best guessing the name from a hash calculation and then locating it by nipping down a linked list.

Each directory takes exactly 1 x 512 byte sector which can be proven simply by formatting a disk, getting its info, creating a single directory and getting info again. In theory therefore, it should be possible to create 1756 user directories on a disk – 1760 sectors minus two for the bootblocks, minus one for the bitmap and one more for the root directory. 1756 * 512 bytes = 878K! Needless to say though, there wouldn't be any room for anything else.

What About FFS

In general terms FFS is exactly the same with the exception that DOS doesn't store any information in a data block, therefore the storage for one block is a complete sector. Note: the sector size on MFM floppies never changes with OFS or FFS, it's the amount of user data that is held within the sector that varies.

It can be demonstrated, although data blocks do indeed contain a full 512 bytes, that the file header block, root block and bitmap are still present. Once again, the maximum number of files is limited to the number ofunallocated sectors. This also suggests that fragmentation can occur under FFS, as it will with any DOS. Where does that leave the data? Sprawling all over the disk in fact. So although FFS is quite a bit quicker than OFS, it could suffer more from fragmentation.

Where does all this leave us? Well the amount of data which can readily be stored on a disk depends almost entirely on the data itself. But to generalise that a block contains just 488 bytes of information is rubbish. It depends entirely on the type of information stored in the block. The amount of free store can only be calculated very approximately, and 512 bytes per sector is by far the best, and simplest, method.

The Bitmap

This is an area of the disk where the sector allocation table is stored. For floppy disks only, the bitmap starts at block 881 but can be anywhere! There are 220 bytes in the bitmap – each sector has 1 bit: 220 bytes * 8=1760 sectors. If the bit is set, the sector is clear, if unset the sector is in use.

Disk Layout — Ready Reckoner

1760 sectors are divided as follows:

Two sectors for the boot block: side 0, track 0, sectors 0 and 1

One sector for root block: side 0, track 39, sector 0

One sector for the bitmap: starting at side 0, track 39, sector 1

1756 sectors for DOS and user information

To calculate any block reference from track, cylinder and sector information, you use the following formula. Note AmigaDOS numbers the first track one, not zero:

(track+1)*22+(side*1)+sector

F: Mastering Amiga Guides

Bruce Smith Books are dedicated to producing quality Amiga publications which are both comprehensive and easy to read. Our Amiga titles are being written by some of the best known names in the marvellous world of Amiga computing.

When you buy a Bruce Smith Books title you are investing for the future as all our books are fully compatible with current Amiga computers and systems, including Workbench 1.3 and Workbench 2. So if you have 1.3 and plan to upgrade to 2 your *Mastering Amiga* title will continue to provide you with a wealth of fascinating information, plus hints, tricks and tips.

Below you will find details of five books in the Mastering Amiga range that are currently available plus one other that is due for publication in mid 1992, with other titles to follow.

Titles

- Mastering AmigaDOS Volume 1
- Mastering Amiga Beginners
- Mastering Amiga C
- Mastering Amiga Printers
- Mastering Amiga System
- Mastering Amiga Workbench

Brief details of these guides along with review segments are given below. If you would like a free copy of our catalogue *Mastering Amiga News* and to be placed on our mailing list then phone or write to the address below.

Our mailing list is used exclusively to inform readers of forthcoming Bruce Smith Books publications along with special introductory offers which normally take the form of a free software disk when ordering the publication direct from us.

Compatibility

We endeavour to ensure that all Mastering Amiga books are fully compatible with all Amiga models and all releases of AmigaDOS and Workbench.

Ordering

Details on how to order can be found at the end of this chapter.

Mastering AmigaDOS 2 Volume One

Smith & Smiddy, 368 pages, £21.95, ISBN: 1-873308-00-0

The sister volume to this one and perhaps the most comprehensive introductory tutorial ever written about the Amiga's very powerful and at times complex operating system, AmigaDOS. If you want to learn how to use AmigaDOS – and every Amiga owner should – then this is the perfect tutorial to do it with. Whether you are a complete beginner or seasoned user alike if your follow the exercises it will turn you into an expert!. By learning to program in AmigaDOS you will learn how to control the Amiga more fully. More importantly you will be able to use it to do the things you wish to do rather than being restricted to a basic set of menu options. This book – like all our others – provides full coverage not only of AmigaDOS 1.3, 1.3.2 and 2.04 but AmigaDOS 1.2 also! For shere imagination no other tutorial on AmigaDOS can compete and this proves to be one of our most consistently high selling titles.

"If you're a complete beginner or unsure of a few areas, this book is an amazingly informative read." – Amiga Format

"...the inclusion of AmigaDOS 2 details means that the investment now will hold good probably for several years. A1 bedtime reading for Amiga enthusiasts!" – AUI

Mastering Amiga Beginners

Phil South, 320 pages, £19.95, ISBN: 1-873308-03-5

A must for those struggling with the manual! If you have recently purchased an Amiga of any type, or have had one for some time but feel you are still not getting to grips with what lies behind the keyboard then this is definitely the book for you. This beginner's guide is written with the sole aim of getting you through those soul-searching first months with your Amiga. It does so in a logical manner, introducing items as and when they are needed so as to become a powerful torchlight through the fog of computer jargon. It will not make you an expert in any one topic but will provide a solid grounding to allow you to investigate those areas which appeal to you most, either on your own or with another book from the growing *Mastering Amiga* series. Applicable to all Amigas and versions of Workbench and AmigaDOS, the book comes with a free disk of PD software when ordered direct from Bruce Smith Books. Choose from a Wordprocessor (including spell check) or Games Compendium disk when ordering.

CU Amiga described this book as a *"Beginners Bible"* and said *".....this book is both a highly readable and entertaining introduction to the Amiga..... the book gives useful hints and tips rather than detailed instruction, and this works very well..... An excellent introduction to the Amiga, and even at £20 it's an extremely worthwhile investment for the beginner..... The first book a new user should buy – essential!'*

Mastering Amiga C

Paul Overaa, 320 pages, £19.95, ISBN: 1-873308-04-6

This is the book if you wish to learn C on your Amiga. C is without doubt one of the most powerful programming languages ever created, and it has a very special relationship with the Commodore Amiga. Much of the Amiga's operating system software is written using C and almost all of the Amiga technical reference books assume some proficiency in the language. This book assumes no prior knowledge of C but will soon get you programming and covers all major compilers, including Lattice/SAS, Aztec and NorthC. The free disks that come with the book when ordered direct from Bruce Smith Books contain the PD NorthC Compiler (normally £1.50 if ordered seperately) and also programs listed in the book. So for under £20 you can have the complete start to C programming on your Amiga!

"This book has been written with the absolute novice in mind. It doesn't patronise, yet neither does it baffle with jargon and slang." – CU Amiga review

Mastering Amiga Printers

Robin Burton, 336 pages, £19.95, ISBN: 1-873308-05-1

From dot-matrix to daisywheel, with inkjet and laser in between, printers can be the most misunderstood addition to any Amiga setup. Next to the Amiga itself, your printer is the largest and most important purchase you're likely to make! Whether you are looking to buy a printer, upgrade to a bigger and better one or are just looking to get the very best out of what you already have – then *Mastering Amiga Printers* is the book for you.

In the opening chapters the pros and cons of the various printer technologies are explained and assessed, how to decide which is the best one for you, and which questions to ask when you buy one. It explains how you can set up the Amiga's Preferences system properly to get the best out of bit image printing for graphics and pulls apart the Amiga's own printer control software, explaining from all points of view the Workbench and the operating system routines. Individual printer drivers are assessed and screen dumping techniques explained. It also takes an in-depth look at commercial software, particularly *Delux Paint*, and uses this as a guide to solve many other software-printer problems with a comprehensive Trouble-shooting section covering the most common problems. So, if you need to learn how to get the best from your Amiga-printer combination or just want a thorough understanding of printer technologies then this is the difinitive reference to have at your fingertips! Available from April 1992 with a free disk of programs from the book and PD printer utilities when ordered from Bruce Smith Books.

Mastering Amiga System

Paul Overaa, 400 pages approx, £29.95, ISBN: 1-873308-06-X

If you want to take over your Amiga then you need to understand how to use and program the Amiga System itself to write leagle, portable and efficient programs. But it's not easy! This book is an introductory guide on how to do just that! It shows you how to communicate with the system , how to handle tasks and processes, work with libraries and how to incorporate IFF graphics into your own applications. Perhaps the most exciting aspects of the Amiga's hardware are the custom chips which make it the all time great graphical computer.Through programming examples and explanations of the functions, field and flags you can harness the power of Intuition, the routines behind the Amiga's classic graphical interface. Also programming both the Copper and Blitter are dealt with in some detail with example programs to get you started and for you to expand upon when you are confident. Author Paul Overaa assumes that you have a basic knowledge of C but have not used the System before. This title should be available from April 1992 with a free programs disk from Bruce Smith Books. Reserve your copy *immediately!*

Mastering Amiga Workbench

Bruce Smith, 320 pgs approx, £19.95, ISBN: 1-873308-08-6

The Workbench is one of the most important aspect of the Amiga and holds within its bounds a wealth of facilities that largely go unused. From it you can access virtually all of the Amiga's functions and determine how your computer will operate from the moment it is switched on. In this volume Bruce Smith explores each of them and outlines how best to use them using screen illustrations throughout for ease of reference. This book covers both Workbench 1.3 and 2 and assumes no prior knowledge of the Workbench, but by the end of it should have made you an expert user . An ideal book after our best selling *Mastering Amiga Beginners*, this book should be available in August with a free disk of PD utilities. Reserve your copy *right now!*

Disclaimer: Errors and omissions excepted. In the case of currently unpublished items, please note that prices and contents are subject to change without notice. If in doubt contact us for up-to-date information.

Ordering Information

It couldn't be easier to obtain any Mastering Amiga title. You can order by phone, post or fax – note that we do not charge for P&P on books sent within the UK including BFPO numbers and 95% of our books are dispatched same day by first class post. Alternatively you should be able to order our books from your local bookshop (if they don't already stock them) simply by giving the ISBN number and cover price.

If a book is currently not available but you wish to reserve a copy then simply order it in the normal fashion. You details will be held on file and the book or books will be dispatched to you as soon as they are available. No cheques or credit cards will be cashed until the order is ready for dispatch.

By Post

Simply write to use stating your requirements or fill out the tear-out form located between pages 352 and 353 and send it with your remittance to the address at the foot of the page. Make cheques or postal orders payable to Bruce Smith Books remembering to write clearly your name and address, indicating the name of the book you require.

Ordering by Phone – Credit Card (Visa, Access, Mastercard)

Our phones are manned during the day and there is an answerphone service out of office hours where you can leave your order. When you phone please speak clearly and leave the following details:

Your name	—	as stated on your credit card
Your card address	—	address where the card is registered, ie where statements are sent too
Delivery address	—	if different from card address
Card number		
Card expiry date		
Daytime contact telephone number		

Please spell out unusual names or addresses clearly.

Telephone your order on: **0923 894355.**

Ordering by Fax – Credit Card (Visa, Access, Mastercard)

Please supply the same details as listed for Ordering by Phone and fax them to us on: **0923 894366.**

International Orders

Please pay by credit card or by cheque drawn on UK bank in sterling. Fax or post us your order. Please note that there is a charge for postage for overseas orders as follows:

Europe: Add £3 per book.

Outside Europe: Add £6 per book.

Note that there is a 2kg weight limit when sending books as small packets through the post. This equates to about two books. Therefore, if you are ordering more than two books, it may be necessary to post them in multiple packets. Please remember this, should only part of an order arrive initially. The rest will be on it's way!

Dealer Orders

Our UK and Eire distributor is Computer Bookshops Limited. Please contact their customer services department on 021-706-1188 for details.

Index

Symbols

"" 303
#? 47, 60, 71
$ 115, 140, 147
' 305
* 61, 302
*" 94, 239
+ 29
, ... 16
... . 15
.BRA 121, 161
.DEF 121
.font files 131
.KET 121, 161
.KEY 121
/ 47
/A 16
/F 16
/K 16
/M 16
/N 16
/S 16
/T 16
24 hour clock 254
32-bit 64
68000 63
68010 63
68020 64
68030 64
68040 64
7-bit ASCII 54
; 299
< 109, 301
<$$> 116
<> 15
> 109
> 215, 301
>> 301
? 16, 300

A

A1000 194
A2000 65
A2024 22
A3000 .... 63, 181
A3500 63
A500 .... 67, 252
A501 .... 67, 252
ADD 202

ADDBUFFERS 19
ADDMONITOR 21
ALIAS 23, 280
AllocMem 194
alpha information 155
ALT 217
ALT-' 307
AmigaDOS Commands 17
Amiga's ROMs 13
angled brackets 301
ANSI 92,137, 225
ANSI escapes in prompt 216
appending output to file 301
archive bit 218
argument 16
ASCII 113, 157
ASCII file 214
ASCII file viewer 182
ASK 25
asl.library 127
ASSIGN 27, 46
ASSIGN, multiple arguments 29
asterisk 91
asynchronous processes 238
AUTOPOINT 33, 50
AUX: 97
AVAIL 35

B

background processes 238
backing up 174
backup, hard disk 44
bar character 59
battery backed clock 67, 252
BCPL 13
BINDDRIVERS 37
BINDMONITOR 38, 242
bit, S 120
bits, protection 218
BLANKER 40
blocks, merging memory 181
blue 56
boot disks 37
brackets 114, 301
branch, unconditional 264
BREAK 42, 70
BREAK 3 42
BRU 44
brush file 197

Book Order Form

Full details of current books can be found in Appendix F. Please rush me the following *Mastering Amiga* books:

Mastering Amiga Beginners @ £19.95 with PD WP/Games Disk* £..........·......

Mastering AmigaDOS Vol. One @ £21.95 with Scripts Disk £..........·......

Mastering Amiga Printers @ £19.95 with Utilities Disk £..........·......

Mastering Amiga C @ £19.95 with Scripts & PD NorthC Disk £..........·......

Mastering Amiga System @ £29.95 with Programs Disk £..........·......

Mastering Amiga Workbench @ £19.95 with PD Utilities Disk £..........·......

Mastering Amiga News – catalogue of all titles — *FREE* —

Postage (International Orders Only): £..........·......

Total: £..........·......

I enclose a Cheque/Postal Order* for £ · p.

I wish to pay by Access/Visa/Mastercard*

Card number

Expiry Date: ..../......./..........

Name. ....

Address. ....

....

.... Post Code ....

Contact phone number..

Signed...

*Delete as appropriate. Cheques payable to Bruce Smith Books Ltd.

Send your order to:

Bruce Smith Books Ltd, FREEPOST 242, PO Box 382,
St. Albans, Herts, AL2 3BR.
Telephone: (0923) 984355 – Fax: (0923) 894366

buffers, memory allocation 19
bug 262, 285
burn-in 40
burst 65

C

cache 19, 62, 65
calculator 114
caps lock key 193
CD 45
Change Directory 46
CHANGETASKPRI 48, 186
changing volume names 224
chevrons 301
CHIP memory 35, 126, 194
CHIP RAM 81
ChkIFF 331
chunk data 324
chunk types 325
CLI 13
CLI number 94
CLI number in prompt 215
CLICKTOFRONT 50
CLOCK 52
clocks 67
close box suppression 187
CMD 54
code purity 234
codes, error 127
COLORS 56
colour file 197
colours in ECHO 92
comma 16
command search path 201
command templates 15
commands, making resident 231
commands, multi lined 239
comments, in files 127
commodities 33, 40, 50, 118, 132, 150, 192
comms 55
CON: 42, 57, 59
CONCLIP 57
condition code 221
condition flag 112
console window, current 61, 302
COPY 54, 58, 79, 153
copying directories 60
copying multiple files 59

copying subdirectories 60
CPU 63
creator, script 162
CTRL-C 70, 137, 278
CTRL-E 50, 133, 150, 193
CTRL-P 87
CTRL-S 151
CTRL-Z 151
CTRL-\ 306
current console window 61
customising prompts 215
cut and paste 189
CX 34, 41, 51, 119, 133, 151, 193

D

DATE 67
debugger 66
DEFER 29
deletable bit 218
deletable flag 62
DELETE 70, 133
designing pure code 235
device, logical 27
device, real 27
devices 28, 29, 92
devices, adding new 184
DEVS: 60, 82, 283
DH0: 199
DIR 70, 73
directories 28, 29
directories, adding to path 202
directories, copying 60
directories, renaming 228
directory toggles 206
directory, making 175
directory, remembering previous 205
disk copy, track by track 79
disk drive types 77
disk initialising 135
disk loader 158
disk, physical 135
DISKCHANGE 77, 225
DISKCOPY 79, 137
DISKDOCTOR 70, 79, 82
DISKSALV 82
display 21
DISPLAY 87
dollar operator 139

Doppleganger virus 318
double quotes 303
DPAT 89
dumping screens 142
DUPLICATE 175
duplication, file 58

E

ECHO 91
eclectic MOVE script 229
ED 96
ED-Startup 96
EDIT 98
EDIT Commands 100
editor 96, 98, 179
ELSE 107, 111, 146
ENDCLI 108
ENDIF 107, 111, 146
ENDSHELL 108, 109
ENDSKIP 112
ENV: 139, 256
ENVARC 134
environmental handler 256
environmental variables 95, 140, 144, 250, 281, 282
ERROR 124
error codes 127, 308
escape characters, ECHO 91
escape wildcard 305
EVAL 113, 134
EXCHANGE 118
EXEC 48, 54, 77, 110, 126, 194, 235
EXEC task 273
executable bit 218
EXECUTE 114, 120, 146, 222
expansion drawer 37

F

F1 151
FAIL 124
FAILAT 124
failure condition 124
Fast Filing System 19
FAST memory 35, 126, 194
FAST RAM 81
Fastbench 28
FASTFONTS 127
FASTMEMFIRST 126

fatal errors 125
FAULT 127
FF 127
FFS 19, 82, 137, 158, 172
file comments 127
file duplication 58
file linking 177
file viewer 277
file viewer, ASCII 182
file, appending output 301
file, brush 197
file, colour 197
file, Keymap 261
file, sorting text 266
file, sprite 207
FILENOTE 127
files, .font 131
files, joining 159
files, Preferences 143
files, renaming 228
files, temporary for PCD 205
final 16
FIXFONTS 131
FKEY 132
FONT 134
font files 131
font, pearl 128
font size 134
fonts, scalable 258
fonts, topaz 127
FONTS: 131, 258
FORMAT 23, 70, 79, 135, 293
FROM 58

G

GET 139, 250
GETENV 139, 140
GFX modes 38
graphic files, displaying 87
GRAPHICDUMP 142
graphics, printing files 214
graphics.library 127
green 56, 124
Guru 131

H

hackers 143
hanging around 287
hard disk 199
hard disk backup 44
HD partition 31
helper, Intuition 150
hexadecimal number 113
hidden flag 219
hierarchical directories 46
HighCyl 185
HL 178
hotkey 118, 151

I

ICONTROL 143
ICONX 145
IF 25, 107, 111, 146
IFF 87, 134, 143, 155, 197, 322
IHELP 150
indirect file link 177
INFO 152
information, alpha 155
initialising disk 135
INITPRINTER 154
INPUT 155
input string 25
INSTALL 157
installing commands 231
internal variables 235
Intuition helper 150

J

JOIN 159

L

key, caps lock 193
Keymap files 261
KEYMAPS 60
keyword 16
Kickstart 77
LAB 161, 264
label 265
labels, in scripts 161
LEN 93

LFORMAT 163
Limpet virus 318
LINK 236
links, creating new directories 178
Linkvirus 319
LIST 127, 162
LOADWB 170
local environmental variable 139, 281
local variables 250
LOCK 172
logical device 27

M

macro 125
MAGTAPE 174
MAKEDIR 59, 175
MAKELINK 177
Manx 256
MEMACS 179
memory allocation, buffers 19
memory, CHIP 35
memory, FAST 35, 126
memory, public 194
MERGEMEM 181
merging memory blocks 181
monitor burn-in 40
monitors, GFX modes 38
monochrome screens 40
MORE 182
MOUNT 184
MOUNTLIST 185
MountList 82, 332
MS-DOS 77
multi line commands 239
multi-tasking 48, 186
multiple 16
multiple arguments, in ASSIGN 29
multiple files, copying 59
Multiscan 22

N

NAME, definition 14
nesting 107
NEWCLI 186
NEWCON: 42
NEWSHELL 57, 186, 189
NIL: 94, 109, 124, 239

NOCAPSLOCK 192
NOFASTMEM 194
NOT wildcard 163
NTSC 22
NULL 153
number 16
number, CLI 94
number, version 283

O

octal number 113
options 15
OR 59
OVERSCAN 195

P

PAL 22
PALETTE 197
parallel 54
Parasite virus 319
PARK 199
partition 199
PAT 162
PATH 29, 81, 137, 201
Pathfinder script 204
pattern matching 59, 70, 89, 127, 163, 246, 269, 228
PCD 205
PD program 44
pearl font 128
physical disks 135
PIPE 147, 153, 182, 267
POINTER 207
POPKEY 118, 133, 150
POPKEY extensions 41
PREFERENCES 209
Preference files 143
Preferences 134
PRINTER 210
printer port 55
printer, resetting 153
PRINTERGFX 212
PRINTERS 60
PRINTFILES 214
printing screens 142
process 57
Project icon 145
PROMPT 46, 215

PROTECT 218
protection bits 218
pseudonyms, for commands 23
public memory 194
PURE 234
pure code designing 235
pure flag 219

Q

Query 16, 300
QUIT 50, 221

R

RAD: 80, 137, 184
RAD: removing 226
RAM expansions 67
RAM, CHIP 81, 126, 194
RAM, FAST 194, 81
RAM: 59, 80, 147
RC 222, 223, 283
RCLIM 124
re-entrant code 234
Readable bit 218
real device 27
recursive script 94
red 56
redirection 94
redirection operator 183
RELABEL 77, 224
REM 299
remarks in scripts 299
REMOVE 29
removing PATHs 203
removing RAD: 226
REMRAD 226
RENAME 59, 89, 228
renaming directories 228
renaming files 228
re-executable code 234
reset printer 153
RESIDENT 107, 111, 231
return code 222
REXX 237
REXXMAST 237
RUN 186, 222, 238
RXC 237

S

S bit 120
S: 120
SAY 241
scalable fonts 258
screen printing 142
SCREENMODE 242
script creator 162
script errors 124
script flag 219
script labels 161
script recursive 94
script, Pathfinder 204
scripts, remarks in 299
SCSI 48, 174
SEARCH 244, 293
search order, PATH 202
search path 201
sector buffer 19
semicolon 299
SERIAL 248
serial 54
serial debugger 66
serial port 55, 66
SET 250
SETCLOCK 252
SETDATE 67, 254
SETENV 256
SETFONT 258
SETMAP 261
SETPATCH 262
Shell-startup 33, 170
size, font 134
SKIP 112, 264
SORT 89, 164, 266
SPAT 269, 283
speech 241
sprite file 207
stack 186
STACK 271
stack pointer 272
star 302
Startup-sequence 33, 37, 52, 57, 124, 202
STATUS 43, 49, 273
strings 244
sub-process 222
subdirectories, copying 60
Sun Workstation 33

switch 16
synopsis 14
SYS: 138
SYS:C 202
system disks 37

T

T: 93, 122, 153
t:qwe 116
tape streamers 174
task priority 186
template 14
templates, producing 300
temporary files, PCD 205
text files, sorting 266
text viewer 277
text, printing files 214
tick 305
TIME 276
TO 58
toggle 16
Tool Types 145
tool, Preferences 209
TOOLS 179
tools.info 293
topaz font 127
track by track disk copy 79
trackdisk 77
Trojan Horse virus 318
TYPE 182, 277

U

UNALIAS 280
unconditional branch 264
UNSET 250, 281
UNSETENV 282
use 15
User-startup 33, 40

V

variables, environmental 95, 114, 140, 250, 282
variable, local environmental 139
variables, internal 235
variables, local 250, 281
VERSION 283

viruses 315
VirusX 110
volume name changing 224
volumes 28

W

WAIT 287
WARN 25, 124
WBCONFIG 171
WBPATTERN 291
WHICH 293
WHY 296
wildcards 59, 163,
workspace 271
writable bit 218

Z

ZOO 44

Notes

Notes

Notes